The Age of Globalization

The Age of Globalization

Anarchists and the Anticolonial Imagination

BENEDICT ANDERSON

VERSO

London • New York

First published by Verso as *Under Three Flags* in 2005
© Benedict Anderson 2005
This edition published by Verso
© Benedict Anderson 2005, 2007, 2013
All rights reserved

The moral rights of the author have been asserted

1 3 5 7 9 10 8 6 4 2

Verso
UK: 6 Meard Street, London W1F 0EG
US: 20 Jay Street, Suite 1010, Brooklyn, NY 11201
www.versobooks.com

Verso is the imprint of New Left Books

ISBN 13: 978-1-78168-144-2

British Library Cataloguing in Publication Data
A catalogue record for this book is available from the British Library

Library of Congress Cataloging-in-Publication Data
A catalog record for this book is available from the Library of Congress

Typeset in Times by Hewer Text UK Ltd, Edinburgh
Printed in the US by Maple Press

It's a mutual, joint-stock world, in all meridians.
We cannibals must help these Christians

Queequeg

In homage to Herman Melville
In memory of Tsuchiya Kenji
For Kenichiro, Carol and Henry

Contents

Acknowledgments

Many people and institutions have given me indispensable help in preparing this book. Among the individuals, my biggest debt has been to my brother Perry for tirelessly hunting up materials to broaden and complicate my thinking and for characteristically meticulous and perspicacious criticisms. Second only to him have been Carol Hau and Ambeth Ocampo. Others whom I would like deeply to thank are Patricio Abinales, Ronald Baytan, Robin Blackburn, Karina Bolasco, Jonathan Culler, Evan Daniel, Neil Garcia, Benjamin Hawkes-Lewis, Carl Levy, Fouad Makki, Franco Moretti, Shiraishi Takashi, Megan Thomas, Tsuchiya Kenichiro, Umemori Naoyuki, Wang Chao-hua, Wang Hui, Susan Watkins, Joss Wibisono, and Tony Wood.

The four institutions which have kindly made rare materials available to me are the Internationaal Instituut voor Sociale Geschiedenis in Amsterdam, the National Library of the Philippines, the Library of the University of the Philippines, and the Library of Ateneo de Manila University, especially the staff of the Pardo de Tavera Collection. I owe them all a debt of gratitude.

Introduction

If one looks up at a moonless, dry-season, tropical night sky, one sees a glittering canopy of stationary stars, connected by nothing but darkness visible and the imagination. The serene beauty is so immense that it takes an effort of will to remind oneself that these stars are actually in perpetual, frantic motion, impelled hither and yon by the invisible power of the gravitational fields of which they are ineluctable, active parts. Such is the Chaldean elegance of the comparative method, which, for example, allowed me once to juxtapose "Japanese" nationalism with "Hungarian," "Venezuelan" with "American," and "Indonesian" with "Swiss." Each shining with its own separate, steady, unitary light.

When night fell in revolutionary Haiti, yellow-fevered Polish troops under General Charles Leclerc, sent by Napoléon to restore slavery, heard their adversaries in the near distance singing the "Marseillaise" and "Ça ira!" Responding to this reproach, they refused an order to massacre black prisoners.[1] The Scottish Enlightenment was decisive for framing the American anticolonial insurrection. The Spanish American nationalist independence movements are inseparable from the universalist currents of liberalism and republicanism. In their turn Romanticism, democracy, Idealism, Marxism, anarchism, even, late in the day, fascism were variously understood as globe-stretching and nation-linking. Nationalism, that element with the highest valency of all, combined with all these others in different ways and in different times.

This book is an experiment in what Melville might have called political

---

1. See the moving description in C.L.R. James, *The Black Jacobins*, rev. ed. (New York: Vintage, 1989), pp. 317–18.

astronomy. It attempts to map the gravitational force of anarchism between militant nationalisms on opposite sides of the planet. Following the collapse of the First International, and Marx's death in 1883, anarchism, in its characteristically variegated forms, was the dominant element in the self-consciously internationalist radical Left. It was not merely that in Kropotkin (born twenty-two years after Marx) and Malatesta (born thirty-three years after Engels) anarchism produced a persuasive philosopher and a colorful, charismatic activist–leader from a younger generation, not matched by mainstream Marxism. Notwithstanding the towering edifice of Marx's thought, from which anarchism often borrowed, the movement did not disdain peasants and agricultural laborers in an age when serious industrial proletariats were mainly confined to Northern Europe. It was open to "bourgeois" writers and artists—in the name of individual freedom—in a way that, in those days, institutional Marxism was not. Just as hostile to imperialism, it had no theoretical prejudices against "small" and "ahisto-rical" nationalisms, including those in the colonial world. Anarchists were also quicker to capitalize on the vast transoceanic migrations of the era. Malatesta spent four years in Buenos Aires—something inconceivable for Marx or Engels, who never left Western Europe. Mayday celebrates the memory of immigrant anarchists—not Marxists—executed in the United States in 1887.

This book's temporal focus on the final decades of the nineteenth century has still other justifications. The near-simultaneity of the last nationalist insurrection in the New World (Cuba, 1895) and the first in Asia (the Philippines, 1896) was no serendipity. Natives of the last important remnants of the fabled Spanish global empire, Cubans (as well as Puerto Ricans and Dominicans) and Filipinos did not merely read about each other, but had crucial personal connections and, up to a point, coordinated their actions—the first time in world history that such transglobal coordination became possible. Both were eventually crushed, within a few years of each other, by the same brutish would-be world hegemon. But the coordination did not take place directly between the broken hill-country of Oriente and Cavite, but was mediated through "representatives," above all in Paris, and secondarily in Hong Kong, London and New York. Newspaper-reading Chinese nation-alists eagerly followed events in Cuba and the Philippines—as well as the Boer nationalist struggle against Ukanian imperialism, which Filipinos also studied—to learn how to "do" revolution, anticolonialism, and anti-im-perialism. Both Filipinos and Cubans found, to different degrees, their most reliable allies among French, Spanish, Italian, Belgian and British anar-chists—each for their own, often non-nationalist reasons.

These coordinations were made possible because the last two decades of the nineteenth century witnessed the onset of what one could call "early globalization." The invention of the telegraph was rapidly followed by many improvements, and the laying of transoceanic submarine cables. The "wire" was soon taken for granted by city people all over the planet. In 1903, Theodore Roosevelt sent off a round-the-globe telegram to himself which reached him in nine minutes.[2] The inauguration of the Universal Postal Union in 1876 vastly accelerated the reliable movement of letters, magazines, newspapers, photographs, and books around the world. The steamship—safe, speedy, and cheap—made possible unprecedentedly massive migrations from state to state, empire to empire, and continent to continent. A thickening latticework of railways was moving millions of people and commodities within national and colonial borders, linking remote interiors to each other and to ports and capitals.

During the eight decades between 1815 and 1894 the world was largely at conservative peace. Almost all states outside the Americas were headed by monarchies, autocratic or constitutional. The three longest and bloodiest wars took place on the periphery of the world-system—civil wars in China and the United States, the Crimean War on the northern littoral of the Black Sea, and the horrifying struggle of the 1860s between Paraguay and its powerful neighbors. Bismarck's crushing defeats of Austro-Hungary and France were achieved with lightning speed and without any huge loss of life. Europe had such vast superiority in industrial, financial, scientific, and financial resources that imperialism in Asia, Africa, and Oceania forged ahead without much effective armed resistance, except in the case of the Mutiny in India. And capital itself moved quickly and pretty freely across existing national and imperial boundaries.

But beginning in the early 1880s the preliminary tremors were being felt of the earthquake that we remember variously as the Great War or the First World War. Tsar Alexander II's assassination in 1881 by bomb-throwing radicals calling themselves The People's Will was followed over the next twenty-five years by the killing of a French president, an Italian monarch, an Austrian empress and an heir-apparent, a Portuguese king and his heir, a Spanish prime minister, two American presidents, a king of Greece, a king of Serbia, and powerful conservative politicians in Russia, Ireland, and Japan. Of course, a much larger number of *attentats* failed. The earliest and most spectacular of these assassinations were carried out by anarchists, but nationalists soon followed in their wake. In most cases the immediate

---

2. Telegraphic transmission of photographs arrived just after the period covered by this book. In 1902, the German scientist Alfred Korn showed how it could be done, and by 1911 wirephoto circuits already connected London, Paris, and Berlin.

aftermath was a mass of draconian "anti-terrorist" legislation, summary executions, and a sharp rise in torture by police forces, public and secret, as well as militaries. But the assassins, some of whom could well be described as early suicide-bombers, understood themselves as acting for a world-audience of news agencies, newspapers, religious progressives, working-class and peasant organizations, and so on.

Imperialist competition, till 1880 still largely between the United Kingdom, France, and Russia, was beginning to be intensified by such newcomers as Germany (in Africa, Northeast Asia, and Oceania), the United States (across the Pacific and into the Caribbean), Italy (in Africa), and Japan (in East Asia). Resistance was also beginning to show a more modern and effective face. In the 1890s, Spain had to send the hitherto largest military force to cross the Atlantic in its attempt to smash Martí's insurrection in Cuba. In the Philippines, Spain held on against a nationalist uprising but could not defeat it. In South Africa, the Boers gave the British Empire the shock of its aging life.

Such is the general proscenium on which the main actors in this book played their various nomadic parts. One could put this point more vividly, perhaps, by saying that the reader will encounter Italians in Argentina, New Jersey, France, and the Basque homeland; Puerto Ricans and Cubans in Haiti, the United States, France, and the Philippines; Spaniards in Cuba, France, Brazil, and the Philippines; Russians in Paris; Filipinos in Belgium, Austria, Japan, France, Hong Kong, and Britain; Japanese in Mexico, San Francisco, and Manila; Germans in London and Oceania; Chinese in the Philippines and Japan; Frenchmen in Argentina, Spain, and Ethiopia. And so on.

In principle, one could open the study of this vast rhizomal network anywhere—Russia would take one eventually to Cuba, Belgium would lead one to Ethiopia, Puerto Rico would bring one to China. But this particular study embarks from the Philippines for two simple reasons. The first is that I am deeply attached to it, and have studied it, on and off, for twenty years. The second is that in the 1890s, though on the outer periphery of the world-system, it briefly played a world-role which has since eluded it. A subordinate reason is the material available to me. The three men whose lives anchor the study—born within three or four years of each other in the early 1860s—lived in the holy time before the advent of the photocopy, the fax, and the internet. They wrote copiously—letters, pamphlets, articles, academic studies, and novels—in undeletable pen and ink, on paper that was expected to have a near-infinite life. (The United States Archives today refuses to accept anything xeroxed—it will become illegible within twenty years—or in electronic form—it will be unreadable, or readable only at prohibitive cost, even sooner, thanks to the hurtling pace of technological innovation.)

Nonetheless, a study that, however superficially, takes one to Rio de Janeiro, Yokohama, Ghent, Barcelona, London, Harar, Paris, Hong Kong, Smolensk, Chicago, Cádiz, Port-au-Prince, Tampa, Naples, Manila, Leitmeritz, Cayo Hueso, and Singapore requires its own combinative narrative style. In this style there are two central elements: second (historically) is Eisenstein's montage, while the first is that of the *roman-feuilleton* pioneered by Charles Dickens and Eugène Sue. The reader is thus requested to imagine that she is reading a black-and-white film or a novel *manqué* of which the conclusion is over the tired novelist's horizon.

There is one further burden on the good reader. In the late nineteenth century there was as yet no ugly, commercially debased "international language." Filipinos wrote to Austrians in German, to Japanese in English, to each other in French, or Spanish, or Tagalog, with liberal interventions from the last beautiful international language, Latin. Some of them knew a bit of Russian, Greek, Italian, Japanese, and Chinese. A wire might be sent around the world in a matter of minutes, but real communication required the true, hard internationalism of the polyglot. Filipino leaders were peculiarly adapted to this Babelish world. The language of the political enemy was also their private language, though understood by less than 5 percent of the Philippine population. Tagalog, the native language used in Manila and its immediate periphery, was not understood by most Filipinos, and in any case was useless for international communication. Many native speakers of rival local languages, especially Cebuano and Ilocano, preferred Spanish, even though this language was, in the Philippines, a clear marker of elite, even collaborationist status. To give the reader the most vivid sense of a vanished polyglot world, this study quotes liberally from the different languages in which these people wrote to each other and to non-Filipinos. (All the translations in this book are my own, unless stated otherwise.)

The formal structure of the book is governed by its method and its objects. It has a clear-cut, if arbitrary, beginning in the quiet, remote Manila of the 1880s, and then gradually fans out across Europe, the Americas, and Asia towards an even more arbitrary *finis* for which no "conclusion" seems feasible. It is anchored, if that is the best word for it, in the young lives of three prominent Filipino patriots born in the early 1860s: novelist of genius José Rizal, pioneering anthropologist and polemical journalist Isabelo de los Reyes, and coordinating organizer Mariano Ponce.

Chapters 1 and 2 are contrasting studies of two remarkable books: Isabelo's *El folk-lore filipino* (Manila, 1887) and Rizal's enigmatic second novel *El Filibusterismo* (Ghent, 1891). They investigate the ways in which: (1) the anthropologist openly deployed the work of contemporary European ethnologists and folklorists, combined with his own local research, to undermine the intellectual credibility of the colonial authorities, both clerical and lay; (2) the novelist borrowed alchemically from key figures of the French, Dutch, and Spanish literary avant-gardes to write what is probably the first incendiary anticolonial novel written by a colonial subject outside Europe.

The following chapter begins the move away from amateur literary criticism to the field of politics. *El Filibusterismo* is still the main topic, but it is explicated through the filter of Rizal's reading and experiences in Europe between 1882 and 1891, as well the fallout from his brilliant first novel *Noli me tangere*, which made him the symbol of Philippine resistance to colonial rule, and won him the bitter enmity of many in high places. It also deals with the political conflicts that sharpened among the Filipino activists in Spain. *El Filibusterismo* is argued to be a kind of global novel by contrast with its predecessor. Its characters are no longer simply the Spanish and their native subjects, but include nomads from France, China, the United States, and even, some personages suspect, Cuba. The shadows of Bismarck in Europe and East Asia, Nobel's innovation in industrial explosives, Russian nihilism, and the anarchism of Barcelona and Andalusia are all apparent in its pages.

Chapter 4 covers the four years between Rizal's return home in 1891 and his execution at the very end of 1896. It discusses above all the transformations in Cuba, and in the *émigré* Cuban communities in Florida and New York, which made it possible for Martí to plan and launch an armed revolutionary insurrection in 1895 (and his successors' success in holding off at huge cost the gigantic expeditionary force sent to crush it). The opening of this attack occurred within a week of the signing of the Treaty of Shimonoseki (following Japan's victory in the Sino-Japanese War of 1895), which, by turning Taiwan over to Tokyo, brought the first Asian power within a day's sail from the northern shore of Luzon. Substantial sections are devoted to Rizal's abortive plan to create a Filipino colony in northeastern Borneo (interpreted in some important quarters as taking a leaf from Martí's Tampa book), and to his fraught relations with the clandestine Katipunan which launched an armed uprising against Spanish rule in 1896.

Chapter 5 is the most complicated. Two months before the outbreak of the Katipunan uprising, the bloodiest of many anarchist bombings took place in wartime Barcelona. The conservative regime of prime minister Cánovas responded with martial law in the city itself, massive arrests of people on the Left, and the practice of the grimmest tortures in the gloomy fortress of Montjuich. Among those imprisoned was the remarkable creole Cuban anarchist Tarrida del Mármol. On his release he made his way to Paris, where he launched an extraordinary crusade against the Cánovas regime, mainly through the pages of *La Revue Blanche*, then the most important avant-garde journal in France, perhaps in the world. Tarrida's long series of articles, starting shortly before Rizal's execution, linked together the fierce repressions in Cuba, Puerto Rico, Barcelona, and the Philippines. Tarrida's crusade spread rapidly through the anarchist press in Europe and across the Atlantic, and soon developed powerful support from many other progressive organizations and journals. In Paris his key allies were Félix Fénéon and Georges Clémenceau: Fénéon, the driving intellectual force behind *La Revue Blanche*, was a brilliant art and drama critic, but also a committed anti-imperialist anarchist who did not hesitate to set off a bomb himself. Clémenceau, also a committed anti-imperialist, had been mayor of Montmartre under the Paris Commune, befriended many imprisoned anarchists, and worked hard, as journalist and politician, for the rights of workers. Both men played key roles in the Dreyfus affair which broke open in the autumn of 1897.

The chapter then turns to a consideration of the background to the assassination of Cánovas on August 9, 1897 by the young Italian anarchist Michele Angiolillo, which portended the collapse of the Spanish empire the following year. The key personality was Dr Ramón Betances, the legendary Puerto Rican conspirator for the independence of the Antillean colonies and enemy of both Spain and the voracious United States. The doctor was by no means an anarchist himself, but he found the most energetic European allies for his cause among Italian and French anarchists. The last two major sections pivot on the activities of Rizal's close friend Mariano Ponce, and on Isabelo de los Reyes. Ponce slipped out of Spain in the fall of 1896, and soon started to work as a key diplomatic and propaganda agent for the revolutionary Philippine government, first in Hong Kong, later in Yokohama. The book analyzes Ponce's remarkable correspondence with Filipinos and many kinds of foreigner—in Mexico City, New Orleans, New York, Barcelona, Paris, London, Amsterdam, Shanghai, Tokyo, and Singapore, and considers various indications of his impact, especially in Japan and the resident Chinese community there. Isabelo, on the other hand, was imprisoned shortly after the Katipunan uprising, and was eventually sent to Montjuich prison in Barcelona, where he got to know and was impressed by the Catalan anarchist inmates. It was he who, on returning to Manila to face the new American colonial regime, brought with him the first copies of works of Kropotkin, Marx and Malatesta to reach his country. He practiced what the anarchists had taught him in organizing the first serious and militant trade union central in the Philippines.

It remains only to say that if readers find in this text a number of parallels and resonances with our own time, they will not be mistaken. At the 2004 Republican convention in New York, which was guarded by many thousands of policemen and other "security" personnel, the metropolitan police chief told reporters that the danger came not from Communists, or even from fanatical Muslims, but rather from anarchists. At almost the same moment, a monument to the anarchist Haymarket Martyrs was erected in Chicago. The *New York Times* smugly remarked that "only now have the passions sufficiently subsided" for this inauguration to take place. It is true, America really is a continent.

1

Prologue: The Rooster's Egg

In 1887, at the Exposición Filipina in Madrid, a 23-year-old *indio* named Isabelo de los Reyes, living in colonial Manila, won a silver medal for a huge Spanish-language manuscript which he called *El folk-lore filipino*. He published this text in unwitting tandem with compatriot José Rizal (then aged twenty-five), who, after wandering around Northern Europe for some time, published his incendiary first novel, *Noli me tangere*, in Berlin that self-same year. This book helped earn him martyrdom in 1896 and, later, the permanent status of Father of His Country and First Filipino.

Who was Isabelo?[1]

He was born on July 7, 1864 in the still-attractive northern Luzon archiepiscopal coastal town of Vigan—which faces Vietnam across the South China Sea—to parents of the Ilocano ethnic group, the vast majority of whom were, in those days, illiterate. His mother Leona Florentino, however, was evidently a poet of some quality, so that at the Madrid and later expositions her poetry was displayed for Spaniards, Parisians, and people

---

1. Although Isabelo had a long and honorable career—aspects of which will be discussed in the final chapter of this book—no remotely adequate professional biography yet exists. The account of his youth that follows is drawn from the work of his eldest son, José de los Reyes y Sevilla, *Biografia del Senador Isabelo de los Reyes y Florentino, Padre de los Obreros y Proclamador de la Iglesia Filipina Independiente* (Manila: Nueva Era, 1947), pp. 1–6; José L. Llanes, *The Life of Senator Isabelo del los Reyes* (monograph reprinted from the Weekly Magazine of the *Manila Chronicle*, July 24 and 31, and August 7, 1949), pp. 1–6; and the entry under his name in National Historical Institute, *Filipinos in History*, vol. 2 (Manila: NHI, 1990), pp. 137–9.

DESPACHO DEL SR. OBISPO MÁXIMO

MONS. AGLÍPAY, P. H. POBLETE, ISABELO DE LOS REYES

Isabelo de los Reyes (seated, right).

in St Louis.[2] This accomplishment did not save her marriage, and the six-year-old Isabelo was entrusted to a rich relative, Mena Crisólogo, who later put him into the grammar school attached to the local seminary run by the Augustinians. It appears that abusive behavior by the Peninsular Spanish friars aroused in the boy a hatred of the Catholic religious Orders which persisted all his life and had serious consequences for his career. In 1880, aged sixteen, he escaped to Manila, where he quickly acquired a BA at the Colegio de San Juan de Letrán; after that, he studied law, history and palaeography at the ancient (Dominican) Pontifical University of Santo Tomás, then the only university in all of East and Southeast Asia.

---

2. According to Leona Florentino's semi-official minibiography, she was born into a rich Vigan family on April 19, 1849. Her parents had the same surname and were probably cousins of sorts. It seems that both were also close relatives of José Rizal's maternal grandfather. She was a precocious child, and started to compose verses at the age of ten, in Ilocano and in the Spanish her friar tutor taught her. She was married off at the age of fourteen, and gave birth to Isabelo at sixteen. Alas, she died at thirty-five, leaving five children behind. See the entry for her in National Historical Institute, *Filipinos in History*, vol. 5 (Manila: NHI, 1996), pp. 141–2.

Binondo Square in Manila, circa 1890.

Meanwhile, Isabelo's father had died, and the boy, obliged now to support himself, plunged into the burgeoning world of journalism, contributing to most of Manila's newspapers, and in 1889 even publishing his own, *El Ilocano*, said to be the first-ever solely in a Philippine vernacular. But while still a teenager, Isabelo read an appeal in Manila's Spanish-language newspaper *La Oceanía Española* (founded in 1877) asking readers to contribute articles to develop a new science, named *el folk-lore*, followed by a simple sketch of how this was to be done. He immediately contacted the Spanish editor, who gave him a collection of "folk-lore books" and asked him to write about the customs of his native Ilocos. Two months later Isabelo set to work, and soon thereafter started publishing—not merely on Ilocos, but also on his wife's township of Malabon, on the outskirts of Manila, on the Central Luzon province of Zambales, and in general terms, what he called *el folk-lore filipino*. It became one of the great passions of his life.

THE NEW SCIENCE

The question, naturally, is why? What was the meaning of *el folk-lore* for a clerically educated native youth in the 1880s? Much can be learned from the Introduction and first pages of his youthful masterwork.[3] There Isabelo described folk-lore, albeit with some hesitation, as a *ciencia nueva* (a new science), perhaps consciously echoing Giambattista Vico's *Scienza Nuova*, which, thanks to the efforts of Michelet and others, had burst on the trans-European scene in the mid-nineteenth century. Isabelo explained to his readers, in both the Philippines and Spain, that the word "folk-lore"—which he translated ingeniously as *el saber popular*—had only been invented in 1846 by the English antiquarian William Thoms, in an article published in the London *Athenaeum*. The first folk-lore society in the world had been organized in London as recently as 1878—a mere six years before he started his own research.[4] The French had followed suit nationally only in 1886—just as Isabelo was starting to write. The Spanish typically had been caught intellectually napping; when their turn came, they had no thought but to incorporate the Anglo-Saxon coinage into Castilian as *el folk-lore*. Isabelo was starting to position himself alongside pioneering Britain, above and ahead of the tag-along Peninsular metropole. He was like a fast surfer on the crest of the wave of world science's beetling progress, something never previously imaginable for any native of what he himself called this "remote Spanish colony on which the light of civilization only tenuously shines."[5] This position he reinforced in several instructive ways.

On the one hand, he was quick to mention in his Introduction that some of his research had already been translated into German—then *the* language of advanced scholarly thinking—and published in *Ausland* and *Globus*, which he claimed were the leading European organs in the field. *El folk-lore filipino* also judiciously discussed the opinions of leading Anglo-Saxon contemporaries on the status of the *ciencia nueva*, politely suggesting that they were more serious than those of Peninsular Spanish *folkloristas*. He must also have enjoyed commenting that "Sir George Fox" had been in conceptual error by confusing folklore with mythology, and

---

3. References hereafter will be mainly to the original text, published in Manila in 1889 by Tipo-Lithografia de Chofré y C. Where relevant, comparisons will be made with a recent reprint combined with an English translation by Salud C. Dizon and Maria Elinora P. Imson (Quezon City: University of the Philippines Press, 1994), to be referred to henceforth in abbreviated fashion as Dizon–Imson. This new version, a valuable endeavor in many ways, is nonetheless marred by hundreds of errors of translation, and some mistakes in the Spanish transcription.

4. *El folk-lore filipino* (henceforward *EFF*), p. 8.

5. *Ibid.*, p. 19.

some Castilian contemporaries had been in similar error by muddling mythology and theogony.[6]

On the other hand, the newness of this *ciencia* had a special colonial aspect to it, which he did not hesitate to underline. He dedicated his book to "Los folkloristas españoles de la Peninsula, que me han dispensado toda clase de atenciones" (the Spanish folklorists of the Peninsula, who have tendered me every manner of consideration). Isabelo's Introduction spoke warmly of "colleagues" in Spain—the boards of directors of the journals *El Folk-Lore Español* and the *Boletín de la Enseñanza Libre de Madrid* in the imperial capital, and the *Boletín Folklórico* in Seville—who had kept him abreast of research in the Peninsula that ran parallel to his own work.

The Peninsularity—so to speak—of these colleagues was regularly under-lined, as well as the Peninsularity of their research. Without explicitly saying so, Isabelo (rightly) insinuated that no colonial Spaniards or creoles were doing anything comparable in the Philippines. This suggestion, of course, permitted him to position himself as a far-ahead-of-the-colonial-masters pioneer of the new universal science. To explain this peculiar situation Isabelo resorted to an ingenious device—certainly made necessary by the violent, reactionary character of the clerically dominated colonial regime of the time. He described a series of courtly exchanges he had had in the Manila press with a liberal-minded (almost certainly Peninsular) medical doctor and amateur litterateur, who had contributed to local newspapers under the pen name Astoll.[7] This move allowed him to quote the Peninsular as admiring Isabelo's courage and imagination but feeling deeply pessimistic about his chances of success in the face of the overwhelming indifference, indolence, and mental stupor in the colony. "Here the only things that grow luxuriantly are cogon grass and molave—two tenacious local weeds."[8] And when Astoll finally broke off their exchange in despair, Isabelo, who had indirectly raised the question of why "certain corporations" (meaning the Orders) had contributed nothing, commented that in the circumstances "prudence war-rants no other course." Into the mental darkness of the colonial regime, then, Isabelo saw himself as bringing the light of modern Europe.

Newness came in still another guise in *El folk-lore filipino*, and this was related to the idea of *ciencia*. The Introduction contains a most interesting discussion of the larger debate on the scientific status of folklore studies. Isabelo had fun noting that one faction of the Peninsular *folkloristas* was so impatient to turn *el folk-lore* into a theoretical science that its members soon

---

6. Dizon–Imson, p. 30.

7. Isabelo identified him as José Lacalle y Sánchez, a professor of medicine at the University of Sto. Tomás. *EFF*, p. 13.

8. *EFF*, p. 14.

could no longer understand one another—opening the way for a much-needed international discussion, in which the Anglo-Saxons appeared both more modest and more practical. At the other extreme were those Spanish folklorists who were merely sentimental collectors of vanishing customs and conceptions for some future museum of the past. Isabelo made clear what he himself thought folklore was about, and how he saw its social value. In the first place, it offered an opportunity for a reconstruction of the indigenous past that was impossible in the Philippines by any other means, given the absence of pre-Spanish monuments or inscriptions, and, indeed, the near-absence of written records. (When Rizal tried to do the same thing later, he saw no other way to proceed than to read between the lines of the work of the best of the Spanish administrators of the early Conquest era.) Serious research on customs, beliefs, superstitions, adages, tongue-twisters, incantations and so on would throw light on what he referred to as the "primitive religion" of the pre-Spanish past. But—and here the young Ilocano sharply distinguished himself from amateur *costumbristas*—he also underlined the importance of comparisons. He confessed that before the completion of his research he had been sure that the neighboring Tagalogs and Ilocanos were *razas distintas* (distinct races) on account of their different languages, physiognomies, behavior and so on. But comparison had proved to him that he had been wrong and that the two ethnicities clearly derived from a single source. The implication of the title *El folk-lore filipino* was that further research would show that all the indigenous inhabitants of the archipelago had a common origin, no matter how many languages they now spoke or how different their present customs and religious affiliations. All this meant that, *contra* the colony's clerical historiographers, who began their narratives with the sixteenth-century Spanish conquest, the real history of the archipelago and its *pueblo/pueblos* (here he hesitated often) stretched far further back in time, and thus could not be framed by coloniality.

THE RICHES OF LOCAL KNOWLEDGE

On the other hand—and here Isabelo radically distanced himself from many of his Peninsular colleagues—the new science could not and should not be confined to sentimental excavations of the quaint. *El folk-lore filipino* is above all the study of the contemporary, in particular what he had termed *el saber popular*. (Today, we would use the term "local knowledge".) This *saber* was real knowledge, not "lore," with its musty, antiquarian connotations. He offered the hypothetical example of a *selvaje* (wild man, perhaps a savage) in the forests near his home region of South Ilocos who might any day (accidentally, Isabelo said) discover that a certain local fruit provided a

better antidote to the cholera bacillus than that currently manufactured at
the instance of the Spanish medical scientist Dr Ferran.[9] The framing for
such claims was the absence of serious scientific knowledge about almost
everything in the Philippines. For example, *Flora de Filipinas*, a new compilation by some Augustinian friars, was very far from complete.[10] The
indigenes had a much deeper knowledge of medicinal plants, of flora and
fauna, of soils and climatic variations than did the colonialists, and this huge
reservoir of knowledge, contained in the *saber popular*, was still unknown to
the world. The Philippines thus appeared not merely as a region containing a
mass of exotica unknown to Europeans, but also as the site for a significant
future contribution to mankind, springing from what the common people
knew, in their own languages, but of which Spanish had no conception. It
was exactly the "unknownness" of the Philippines that gave its folklore a
future-oriented character that was necessarily absent in the folklore of
Peninsular Spain. It was also, however, the living specificity of the Philippines that positioned it to offer something, parallel and equal to that of any
other *país*, to humanity. This is the logic that would much later make the
United Nations both possible and plausible. So far, so clear. Too clear,
probably. For Isabelo's text, under the bright lights of its major themes, is
not without its shadowy complications. We might provisionally think about
them under three rubrics.

First, what was Isabelo to himself? To begin with, it is necessary to
underline an ambiguity within the Spanish word *filipino* itself. During
Isabelo's youth this adjective had two distinct senses in common parlance:
(1) belonging to, located in, originating from, Las Islas Filipinas; (2) creole,
of the locally born but "pure Spanish" social stratum. What it did not mean
is what *filipino* means today, an indigenous nationality–ethnicity. One can
see how much things have changed over the past century if one compares
just one sentence in Isabelo's Introduction with its recent translation into
American by two Philippine scholars. Isabelo wrote: "Para recoger del saco
roto la organización del Folk-Lore regional filipino, juzgué oportuno
contestar al revistero del *Comercio* y, aprovechando su indirecta, aparenté
sostener que en Filipinas había personas ilustradas y estudiosas que
pudieran acometer la empresa".[11] This literally means: "To save the
organization of the Folklore of the region of the Philippines, I judged it
the right moment to rebut the view of *El Comercio*'s reviewer, and, taking
advantage of his insinuation, I pretended [presumed??] to maintain that

---

9. Dizon–Imson, p. 24.
10. *Ibid.*, p. 11. The editors say that the book, a compilation by various hands
and edited by Fr. Andrés Naves, was published in Manila in 1877 by Plana y C.
11. *EFF*, p. 13.

in the Philippines there exist enlightened [*ilustradas*] and studious persons capable of undertaking the task." The published translation—completely anachronistic—has: "I tried to defend the establishment of Filipino Folklore by answering the accusation of the columnist of *El Comercio*, by bravely stating that there are indeed Filipino scholars ready and capable of undertaking the task."[12] Where Isabelo was thinking of a sort of global folklore which included the regional portion of the Philippine Islands, and spoke of enlightened persons in the Philippines—no ethnicity specified—the translators have omitted "regional" to create a folklore of the Filipinos, and substituted for "enlightened persons" the novel "Filipino scholars."

FOREST BROTHERS

In *El folk-lore filipino*, Isabelo did not describe himself as "a Filipino," because the nationalist usage was not yet familiar in the colony. Besides, *un filipino* was then exactly what he was not: a creole. He did, however, describe himself in other ways: sometimes, for example, as an indigene (but never by the contemptuous Spanish term *indio*), and sometimes as an Ilocano. In a remarkable passage he argued: "Speaking of patriotism, has it not frequently been said in the newspapers that, for me, only Ilocos and Ilocanos are good? . . . Everyone serves his *pueblo* to his own manner of thinking. I believe I am here contributing to the illumination of the past of my own *pueblo*." Elsewhere, however, he insisted that so strict had been his objectivity that he had "sacrificed to science the affections of the Ilocanos, who complain that I have publicized their least attractive practices." Luckily, however, "I have received an enthusiastic response from various savants [*sabios*] in Europe, who say that, by setting aside a misguided patriotism, I have offered signal services to Ilocos, *mi patria adorada*, because I have provided scholars with abundant materials for studying its prehistory and other scientific topics relating to this . . . province [*sic*]."[13]

Rizal opened his enraged novel *Noli me tangere* with a celebrated Preface addressed to his motherland, which included these words: "Deseando tu salud que es la nuestra, y buscando el mejor tratamiento, haré contigo le que con sus enfermos los antiguos: exponíanlos en las gradas del templo, para que cada persona que viniese de invocar à la Divinidad les propusiese un remedio" (Desiring your well-being, which is our own, and searching for the best cure [for your disease], I will do with you as the ancients did with their

---

12. Dizon–Imson, p. 13.
13. *EFF*, pp. 18 and 17.

afflicted: exposed them on the steps of the temple so that each one who came to invoke the Divinity would propose a cure).[14] And in the last poem he wrote before his execution in 1896, he too spoke of his *patria adorada*. But was it Isabelo's?

There is a beautiful sentence in the Introduction to *El folk-lore filipino* in which Isabelo described himself as "hermano de los selváticos, aetas, igorrotes y tinguianes" (brother of the forest peoples, the Aeta, the Igorots and the Tinguians). These so-called primitive peoples, most of them pagan before the twentieth century dawned, and many never subjugated by the Spanish colonial regime, lived and live in the long cordillera that flanks the narrow coastal plain of Ilocos. In his boyhood, Isabelo would have seen them coming down from the forests in their "outlandish garb" to trade their forest products for lowland commodities. To this day, a form of Ilocano is the lingua franca of the Gran Cordillera. No one else in Isabelo's time, certainly no one who counted himself an *ilustrado*, would have spoken in such terms of these forest-dwellers who seemed, in their untamed fastnesses, utterly remote from any urban, Hispanicized, Catholicized milieu. (And in those days Isabelo did not speak of any other ethnic groups in Las Filipinas as his *hermanos*.) Here one begins to see how it was possible for him to think of his province as a big *pueblo* and a *patria adorada*, since in the most concrete way it linked as brothers the "wild" pagans of the mountains and a man who won prizes in Madrid. Here also one detects an underlying reason why, in his proto-nationalist strivings, Isabelo went to folklore rather than the novel or the broadsheet. Folklore—comparative folklore—enabled him to bridge the deepest chasm in colonial society, which lay not between colonized and colonizers—they all lived in the lowlands, they were all Catholics, and they dealt with one another all the time. It was the abyss between all of these people and those whom we would today call "tribal minorities": hill-people, nomadic swidden-farmers, "head-hunters," men, women and children facing a future of—possibly violent—assimilation, even extermination. Out of *el folk-lore*, child of William Thoms, there thus emerged a strange new brotherhood, and an adored father/motherland for the young Isabelo.

STRANGE BEAUTIES

What were the deeper purposes of the folklorist's work in Las Islas Filipinas? Apart from its potential contributions to the modern sciences, and to the reconstruction of the character of "primitive man," we can uncover three

---

14. José Rizal, *Noli me tangere* (Manila: Instituto Nacional de Historia, 1978), frontispiece.

which have a clear political character. First, there is the possibility—the hope—of local cultural renaissance. With a certain sly prudence, Isabelo allowed Astoll to speak on his behalf:

> Perhaps folklore will provide the fount for a Philippine poetry [*poesia filipina*], a poetry inspired by Philippine subjects, and born in the mind of Philippine bards [*vates*]. I can already hear the mocking laughter of those braggarts who have made such fun of you. But let them laugh, for they also laughed at other manifestations of the *pueblo*'s genius [*ingenio*], and then had to bow their heads in confusion before the laurels of [Juan] Luna and [Félix] Resurrección. And these traditions and superstitious practices which you are making known could one day inspire great poets, and enthusiastic lovers of the strange beauties of this rich garden.[15]

Elsewhere Isabelo quoted Astoll once again:

> If Sr de los Reyes's studies and investigations make connections to pueblos *como el filipino* [like the Philippine one? or is it perhaps even the Filipino one?] where the character of the indigenes [*naturales*] has been depicted solely by the brush strokes of dull-witted daubers, one can see how much potential value they have for the future.

Here Isabelo's work, printed in Manila, could open up the possibility of a great flowering of literary and poetic talent among the *naturales*, a talent before which boorish Peninsulars and creoles would have to hang their heads in confusion. This is the normal hope and strategy of anticolonial nationalists: to equalize themselves "up" with the imperialists.

The second of Isabelo's purposes would be to subvert the dominance of the reactionary Church in the colony, and is best shown in a wonderfully deadpan chapter entitled "Ilocano Superstitions that are Found in Europe." It opens in this vein:

> Taking advantage of the folkloric materials gathered by D. Alejandro Guichot and D. Luis Montoto in Andalusia, by D. Eugenio de Olavarría y Huarte in Madrid, by D. José Pérez Ballesteros in Catalonia, by D. Luis Giner Arivau in Asturias, by Consigliere Pedroso with his *Tradiçoes populares portuguezas* in Portugal, as well as others, I have drawn up the following list of superstitions which I believe were

---

15. *EFF*, p. 15. Juan Luna (1857–99), whom we shall meet again, was a fellow Ilocano who became the most famous native painter of the Spanish colonial era. His *The Death of Cleopatra* won the second medal at the 1881 Fine Arts Exposition in Madrid, his *Spoliarium* a gold medal at the same venue in 1884, and his *The Battle of Lepanto* a gold medal at the Barcelona Fine Arts Exhibition in 1888. Félix Resurrección Hidalgo y Padilla (1853–1913) was only slightly less successful. Hidalgo was a Tagalog, born in Manila and raised there like Luna.

introduced here by the Spaniards in past centuries. The list should not surprise anyone, given that in the early days of Spanish domination the most ridiculous beliefs [*las creencias más absurdas*] were in vogue on the Peninsula.[16]

Mischievously, the list begins thus:

> When roosters reach old age or have spent seven years in someone's house, they lay an egg from which hatches a certain green lizard that kills the master of that house; according to the Portuguese and French, however, what hatches is a snake. If it spots the master first, the latter will die, but that fate will strike the former if the master sees the snake first. The Italians and the English, as well as some Central Europeans, believe it is a basilisk that is hatched. Father Feijóo says: "It is true, the rooster, in old age, really does lay an egg." The Portuguese and the Ilocanos, however, agree that what is in the egg is a scorpion.[17]

Other irresistible examples are these: "To make sure visitors do not overstay, Ilocanos put salt on their guests' chairs. The Spaniards place a broom vertically behind a door, while the Portuguese put a shoe on a bench in the same spot, or throw salt on the fire." "In Castile, as in Ilocos, teeth that have fallen out are thrown onto the roof, so that new ones will grow." "According to the people of Galicia, if a cat washes its face, it means that rain is coming; the Ilocanos say it will rain if we give the animal a bath." "The people of Galicia say that a gale is coming when cats run about like mad; people in the Philippines substitute cockroaches for these cats." Finally: "Sleeping with the headboard facing the east is bad for Ilocanos. But for Peninsulars (Spaniards and Portuguese) it is good. All three agree that a headboard facing south is unlucky."

One can see why Isabelo felt a *singular placer* in dedicating his book to Peninsular folklorists, since they had offered him the scientific materials that would demonstrate the "ridiculous beliefs" of the conquistadors, and prove that, if the colonialists sneered at Ilocano superstitions, they should recognize many of them as importations of their own: any bizarreness in Ilocano folk

---

16. *Ibid.*, p. 74. In successive footnotes Isabelo gives the titles of these authors' works: *El Folk-Lore Andaluz*; *Costumbres populares andaluzas*; *El Folk-Lore de Madrid*; *Folk-Lore Gallego*; *Folk-Lore de Asturias*. He also casually mentions an earlier work of his own, described as a *largo juguete literario* (long literary skit), entitled *El Diablo en Filipinas, según rezan nuestras crónicas* (The Devil in the Philippines, as our chronicles tell it).

17. *Ibid.*, p. 75. Sources given are: Pedroso's above-cited work; Rolland's *Faune populaire de la France*; Castelli's *Credenze ed usi populari siciliani*; V. Gregor's *Notes on the Folk-Lore of the North-East Scotland (sic)*; and Larousse's *Grande dictionnaire encyclopédique du XIX siècle*. From Isabelo's footnotes, we can see that he was able to move out of Spanish to the other big Romance languages (French, Italian and Portuguese), and to English. German, which, as we shall see, was crucial for Rizal, seems to have been beyond his orbit.

beliefs had easy analogues in the bizarreries of Iberia, Italy, Central Europe, even England.

The third aim was political self-criticism. Isabelo wrote that he was trying to show, through his systematic display of *el saber popular*, those reforms in the ideas and everyday practices of the *pueblo* that must be undertaken in a self-critical spirit. He spoke of his work as being about "something much more serious than mocking my *paisanos*, who actually will learn to correct themselves once they see themselves described." In this light, folklore would be a mirror held up before a people, so that, in the future they could move steadily along the road toward human emancipation. It is clear, then, that Isabelo was writing for one and a half audiences: Spaniards, whose language he was using, and his own *pueblo*, whose language he was not using, and of whom only a tiny minority could read his work.

Where did Isabelo position himself in undertaking this task? At this juncture we finally come to perhaps the most interesting part of our enquiry. For most of the hundreds of pages of his book, Isabelo spoke as if he were not an Ilocano himself, or, at least, as if he were standing outside his people. The Ilocanos almost always appear as "they," not "we." For example: "There is a belief among *los Ilocanos* that fire produced by lightning can only be extinguished by vinegar, not by water." Better still:

> Los ilocanos no pueden darnos perfecta idea acerca de la naturaleza de los mangmangkík, y dicen que no son demonios, según la idea que los católicos tienen de los demonios.

> The Ilocanos cannot give us a complete idea about the nature of the mangmang-kík, and they say that they are not devils according to the Catholics' idea of what devils are.[18]

Isabelo here placed himself in the ranks of world folklore's savants, peering down at "the Ilocanos" from above, and dispassionately distinguishing their superstitions from the parallel credulities of "the Catholics."

At the same time, a number of passages have a rather different tonality. At the start of the exposition of his research results Isabelo wrote:

> The Ilocanos, especially those from Ilocos Norte [Northern Ilocos], before starting to cut down trees in the mountains, sing the following verse:

> > Barí, barí!
> > Dika agunget pári
> > Ta pumukan kamí
> > Iti pabakirda kamí

---

18. Dizon–Imson, p. 32.

Literally translated these lines mean: *barí-barí* (an Ilocano interjection for which there is no equivalent in Spanish), do not get upset, *compadre*, for we are only cutting because we have been ordered to do so.

Here Isabelo positions himself firmly within the Ilocano world. He knows what the Ilocano words mean, but his readers do not: to them (and by this he intends not only Spaniards, but also other Europeans, as well as non-Ilocano natives of the archipelago) this experience is closed. Isabelo is a kindly and scientific man, who wishes to tell the outsiders something of this world; but he does not proceed by smooth paraphrase. The reader is confronted by an eruption of the incomprehensible original Ilocano, before being tendered a translation. Better yet, something is still withheld, in the words *barí-barí*, for which Spanish has no equivalent. The untranslatable, no less; and beyond that, perhaps, the incommensurable.

Isabelo suspected, I am sure, that his Spanish was not perfect, and might be laughed at by "dull-witted daubers" and "braggarts." He probably was also aware that the particular folklore methodology he was using might be doubtful in its systematics, and perhaps was soon to be superseded as science continued its grand world progress into the future. But he had *barí-barí* in particular, and Ilocano in general, safely up his intellectual sleeve. On this ground he could not be contested. However, he needed to show, or half-show, his trumps. This is the satisfaction of the tease: Dear readers, here is Ilocano for you to view, but you can only see what I permit you to see; and there are some things that you are actually incapable of seeing.

There is still a third position, which complicates matters further. In a chapter on "Music, Songs and Dances," Isabelo wrote the following:

> The lyrics of the *dal-lot* are well worth knowing. The *dal-lot* is composed of eight-line stanzas, with a special Ilocano rhyming scheme which you can see from the following refrain:
>
> > Dal-lang ayá daldal-lut
> > Dal-lang ayá dumidinal-lot.
>
> I transcribe it for you, because I do not know how to translate it, and I do not even understand it, even though I am an Ilocano. It seems to me to have no meaning.[19]

But it remains "well worth knowing" because it is authentically Ilocano, perhaps even because it is inaccessible to the puzzled bilingual author himself. Isabelo leaves it at that. No speculations. But there is an intimation, nonetheless, of the vastness of the *saber popular*.

---

19. *Ibid.*, pp. 258–9.

Three ill-fitting situations therefore: Outside (they cannot give us a complete idea); Inside (there is no Spanish equivalent of *barí-barí*); and Outside Inside (even though I am an Ilocano myself, I do not understand this Ilocano-language refrain; but I am telling this to "you," not to "us").

COMPARATIVE REFLECTIONS

From the end of the eighteenth century down to our haggard own, folklore studies, even if not always selfconsciously defined as such, have proved a fundamental resource to nationalist movements. In Europe, they provided a powerful impulse for the development of vernacular cultures linking especially peasantries, artists and intellectuals, and bourgeoisies in their complicated struggles against the forces of legitimacy. Urban composers foraged for folk songs, urban poets captured and transformed the styles and themes of folk poetry, and novelists turned to the depiction of folk countrysides. As the newly imagined national community headed towards the magnetic future, nothing seemed more valuable than a useful and authentic past.

Printed vernaculars were almost always central. Norwegian folklorists would write in "New Norse" (against Danish and Swedish) to recuperate the Norwegian *saber popular*; Finns would write in Finnish, not Swedish or Russian; and the pattern would be reiterated in Bohemia, Hungary, Rumania, Serbia, and so on. Even where this was not entirely the case—a striking example is the Irish revivalist movement which operated both through Gaelic and through a colonially imposed English well understood by many Irish men and women—the ultimate object was national self-retrieval, "awakening" and liberation.

At first sight, Isabelo's endeavor strikes one as quite different, as he was writing as much as anything for non-nationals, and in an imperial language, which perhaps 3 percent of the *indios* of the Philippines understood, and maybe only 1 percent of his fellow Ilocanos could follow. If in Europe folklorists wrote mostly for their *paisanos*, to show them their common and authentic origins, Isabelo wrote mostly for the early globalizing world he found himself within—to show how Ilocanos and other *indios* were fully able and eager to enter that world, on a basis of equality and autonomous contribution.

Isabelo's study also marks his country off from the many neighboring colonies in the Southeast Asian region. In these other colonies, most of what we can informally classify as "folklore studies" was carried on by intelligent colonial officials with too much time on their hands in an age still innocent of radio and television; they were intended mainly to be of use to the colonial rulers, not to the studied populations themselves. After independence was achieved, these ex-colonies' folklore studies have led a marginal existence, while they have done significantly better in the postcolonial Philippines. Why should this have been so? One possible answer is that in all the other colonies there survived a substantial written record from precolonial times—royal chronicles, Buddhist cosmologies, monastic records, Sufi tracts, court literatures, etcetera—and it was these, more than folklore, that provided aboriginality and glorious authenticity when nationalist movements got under way. The remote Philippines had no tradition of powerful, centralized and literate states, and had been so thinly touched by Islam and Buddhism that most of the inhabitants were Christianized with remarkably little violence. Seen from this angle, folklore could substitute for ancient grandeur.

Another, maybe better, answer lies in the nature of nineteenth-century Iberian imperialism. Spain and Portugal, once the great imperial centers of the world, had been in decline since the mid-seventeenth century. With the loss of Latin America, the Spanish empire had been drastically reduced—to Cuba, Puerto Rico, the Philippines, and Rio de Oro. Throughout the nineteenth century, Spain was rent by the most violent internal conflicts as it struggled to make the transition from feudal past to industrial modernity. In the eyes of many of its own inhabitants, Spain was backward, superstitious, and barely industrializing. This understanding was widely shared not only in Europe generally, but also by the young intellectuals of the residual Spanish colonies. (This is why Isabelo was proud to have his writings published in Germany, while his later equivalents in other colonies tended to seek publication in their "own" imperial metropoles.) Progress was thus the flag of an Enlightenment (*Ilustración*) which had scarcely begun to prevail in Spain. Isabelo saw himself as an *ilustrado*, great-grandson of Denis Diderot; and thus naturally involved in a common struggle alongside substantial numbers of Spaniards in the Peninsula itself. This kind of transcontinental alliance was on the whole uncharacteristic of struggling nationalists in Europe itself. It thus seemed quite normal to the youthful Ilocano to dedicate his work to his colleagues in Spain.

At the same time, however, as we have seen, the "backward" Philippines was also the one colony in nineteenth-century Southeast Asia to have a real university—even if this was dominated by the *ultra* Dominican Order. Santo Tomás schooled Isabelo and many of his nationalist companions; here, ultimately, lay the reason why the Philippines became, at the century's end, the site of the first nationalist revolution in Asia.

Enlightment came to the Philippines through the unbackward language of "backward" Spain, and its prime agents, in every sense of the word, were therefore (at least) bilingual. (Many of the first generation of Philippine intellectuals also learned Latin, with some French, in Manila; if they went abroad, they might acquire some English and German as well.) Nowhere does one detect any marked aversion or distrust towards this Romance language so heavily marked by Arabic, the common vehicle of both reaction and enlightenment. Why this should have been so is a very interesting question. One answer is surely that, in complete contrast to almost all of Latin America, Spanish was never even close to being a majority language in the Philippines. Dozens of mainly oral local languages flourished then, as indeed they do today; nothing in Isabelo's writing suggests that he thought of Spanish as a deep menace to the future of Ilocano. Furthermore, Castilian appeared to him as the necessary linguistic vehicle for speaking not only to Spain but also, through Spain, to all the centers of modernity, science, and civilization. It was more an international language than it was a colonial one. It is striking that Isabelo never considered the possibility that, by writing in Spanish, he was somehow betraying his *pueblo* or had been sucked into a dominant culture. I think the reason for this seemingly innocent stance is that, in the 1880s, the future status of Las Islas Filipinas was visibly unstable, and some kind of political emancipation was looming on the horizon.

This instability had everything to do with local circumstances, but it was ultimately grounded in the emancipation of Latin America more than half a century earlier. Spain was the only big imperial power that lost its empire in the nineteenth century. Nowhere else in the colonial world did the colonized have such examples of achieved liberation before their eyes. Here one sees a situation wholly different from that of the twentieth-century New World, where Spanish became the "eternal" majoritarian master over all the indigenous languages in Latin America, and over an equally "eternal" oppressed minority in the United States. No emancipation visible on the horizon in either case.

Nonetheless, as indicated above, there are instructive reticences in Isabelo's youthful work, marked by the uneasy pronominal slippages between *I* and *they*, *we* and *you*. He was always thinking about two audiences, even when writing for one and a half. "The worst of men is the wretch who is not endowed with that noble and sacred sentiment which they call patriotism," he wrote. Spanish was not for him a national language, merely international. But was there a national language to which it could be opposed? Not exactly. The local languages with the largest numbers of speakers—Ilocano in the north, Tagalog in the middle, and Cebuano in the south—were all relatively small minority languages, and only just starting to burst into print. Was there a clear-cut *patria* to which his own language could be attached? A hypothetical Ilocano-land? He never spoke of it as such. Besides, there were those Aetas and Igorots, with their own languages, who were his *hermanos*. There were also those Tagalogs who, his investigations had shown him, were not a "race distinct" from the Ilocanos; but he knew, as the discoverer of this truth, that as yet few Tagalogs or Ilocanos were aware of it. This state of fluidity thus led him back, at twenty-three years old, to the obscurely bordered culture out of which he grew, and which he sensed he had partly outgrown. Ilocano popular knowledge, or culture, thus came to its young patriot as something to be investigated from the outside, as well as to be experienced from within, to be displayed to the whole world, but also something to be corrected—of course, by the Ilocanos themselves. His mother tongue, Ilocano, thus became something to be translated, yet partly untranslatable. And at some points it even slipped quietly away beyond the sunlit horizon of the Enlightened young bilingual himself.

2

Allá . . . Là-bas

Sunlit, but exactly why? Perhaps the best way to understand is to contrast Isabelo's temperament, experience, and work with those of his distant Tagalog cousin José Rizal, which this chapter begins to do.

Isabelo was an ebullient, practical, hugely energetic man, not much given to introspection. He got married when he was twenty, and his first wife had already given successful birth six times when she died in tragic circumstances in the early spring of 1897. (Subsequently, he married in succession a Spanish woman and a Chinese, both of whom died in childbirth, and both of whom gave birth nine times.)[1] With a large family to feed, he busied himself with successful literary and cultural journalism, folklore studies, and various small-business sidelines, until the outbreak of the Philippine Revolution in 1896, to which he was initially a surprised spectator. Even though his hostility to the Orders was patent, his writings do not seem ever to have got him to any serious political trouble. He was a *provinciano* who had made good in the colonial capital, and he was generally satisfied with his life. He did not go to Europe till the summer of 1897, at the age of thirty-three, and it was, as we shall see, entirely against his will—he was sent, in chains, to the torture fortress of Montjuich in Barcelona. The Europe he knew as a youngster came to him through the post—letters, books, and magazines from friendly academics, amateur folklorists, and journalists on the other side of the globe. Radiant progress was at hand.

Rizal, three years older, could not have been less sunlit: brooding, sensitive, endlessly introspective, impractical, and quite aware of his genius. He got married, perhaps, only on the night of his execution, and had no children. He left for Europe in 1882, shortly before his twenty-first birthday,

---

1. See Llanes, *The Life*, pp. 6–8, 13–15, 20–24.

and stayed there—first in Spain, then in France, Germany, England, and Belgium—for most of the next ten years. A natural polyglot, he acquired English, and German, and even some Italian. Without a doubt, he knew Europe better and more widely than any of his countrymen. He made plenty of personal friends in the professional ethnological circles of Western Europe, but most of his early published writing consisted of elegantly polemical articles on political subjects relating to the condition of his colonized *patria*. Then he turned novelist, publishing *Noli me tangere* in 1887, and *El Filibusterismo* in 1891, most likely the only "world-class" novels created by an Asian in the nineteenth century. Overnight, as it were, he became the most controversially famous "native" in his country.

In a limited sense, these novels came out of the blue. Prior to *Noli me tangere* only one novel—very bad indeed—had ever been written by a Filipino.[2] But the situation looks rather different if one reflects on their appearance in a wider context.

TRANSNATIONAL LIBRARIES

Until the middle of the nineteenth century the production of "great novels" was largely a French–English duopoly. After that, the boundaries of what Pascale Casanova has agreeably called "la république mondiale des lettres" began rapidly to globalize.[3] The astonishing *Moby Dick* of Melville (b. 1819) appeared in 1851, followed by the scarcely less amazing *The Confidence Man* in 1857; the *Oblomov* of Goncharov (b. 1812) also appeared in 1857, followed by the *On the Eve* (1860) and *Fathers and Sons* (1862) of Turgenev (b. 1819). Eduard Douwes Dekker (b. 1820) published *Max Havelaar*, the first major anticolonial novel, in 1860. The year 1866 saw the publication of *Crime and Punishment* and *War and Peace* by Dostoievsky (b. 1821) and Tolstoi (b. 1828). Then the Third World started to kick in with *Memorias póstumas de Bras Cubas* (1882) by Brazil's Machado de Assis (b. 1839). Rizal's own generation included Poland's Conrad (b. 1857), Bengal's Tagore (b. 1861), and Japan's Natsume (b. 1867), though their major novels were only published after those of the ill-fated Filipino. Seen from this angle, Rizal's works still seem precocious, but not at all magically eremitic.

Casanova makes a strong argument that historically writers on the periphery of the World Republic of Letters have found their originality in trying to break into the Capital of Letters by challenging its premises in different styles.

---

2. Pedro Paterno, four years older than Rizal, published his *Ninay* in 1885.
3. Pascale Casanova, *La République mondiale des lettres* (Paris: Éditions du Seuil, 1999).

The remainder of this chapter will be devoted to outlining how and where Rizal went about this task. It has to be conceded at the start that the evidence external to the novels is rather skimpy. Although Rizal kept up a huge correspondence, of which a surprisingly large part has been preserved, as well as diaries, and various unpublished pieces on literary matters, he was generally tight-lipped about other writers, novelists in particular: his comments comprise a youthful short essay, in French, on Corneille's originality, a later short piece from Berlin (again in French, written in 1887) on Daudet's *Tartarin sur les Alpes*, a few sentences on Eugène Sue and Douwes Dekker, some admiring passages on Schiller, and quotations from Heine.[4]

The records of two personal libraries offer some indirect additional indications. The library that Rizal himself brought back from Europe included texts by Chateaubriand, A. Daudet, Dumas *père* (5), Hugo, Lesage, Sue (10), Voltaire, and Zola (4) for France; Bulwer-Lytton, Defoe, Dickens, and Thackeray for England; Goethe and Hoffman for Germany; Manzoni for Italy, Douwes Dekker for the Netherlands, and Cervantes for Spain. His correspondence makes it clear that he had also read Andersen, Balzac, Hebel, and Swift.[5] This list is unlikely to represent fully what he had with him in Europe, since he knew his books would be thoroughly inspected by the colonial customs and police on his return home. But it shows unmistakably how central to his novelistic reading was France.

Recently, the books and papers left behind after the death of the medical doctor and distinguished philologist Trinidad Pardo de Tavera have been catalogued and made available to researchers at the Ateneo de Manila University. Rizal was a close friend of Pardo, in whose palatial rooms he stayed for part of the seven months he spent in the French capital in 1885–86.

---

4. The two French literary essays, along with a short text "Dimanche des Rameaux" (Palm Sunday)—on the history of Christianity's rise when it was a religion for the poor, and its decay when it fell into the hands of the rich—are on microfilm at the National Library of the Philippines. The irregular handwriting, and the title, "Essai sur Pierre Corneille", give one the feeling that this text dates from his schooldays, though intelligent references to Voltaire's "magnifique" *Commentaire sur le théâtre de Corneille*, and Lessing's *Hamburgische Dramaturgie* may indicate otherwise. The other two come from Rizal's unpublished notebooks "Cuadernos de médica clínica," with the Palm Sunday meditation signed and dated Berlin 1887. The originals appear to be held at the Ayer Library in Chicago.

5. See Esteban A. De Ocampo, *Rizal as a Bibliophile* (Manila: Bibliographical Society of the Philippines, Occasional Papers, No. 2, 1960). De Ocampo catalogued not only the contents of the now deceased library, but also books and authors mentioned in Rizal's correspondence. Thanks to Ambeth Ocampo (no relation), the leading authority on late-nineteenth-century Philippine history, I learned that De Ocampo's list was incomplete; a substantial number of additional library cards, in Rizal's hand, existed in Manila's López Museum Library.

In Pardo's flat. Rizal is in the back row, second from left.

This was the period when he started composing *Noli me tangere*. In Pardo's list France is represented by About (2), Adam, Balzac, Banville (2), Barbusse, Barrès, Bibesco, Bourget (2), Farrère (3), Flaubert, France (5), Hugo, Lorrain, Maupassant (2), Molière (collected works in 6 volumes), Prévost, and Zola; Spain by Alarcón, Baroja (2), Blasco Ibáñez (10), Galdós (16), and Larra; Russia by Andreyev (6), Chekhov (3), Dostoievsky (3), Gorki (4), and Turgenev; and the Anglo-Saxons merely by Conan Doyle (2), Haggard, O. Henry (4), Kipling, Sinclair, and Thackeray (collected works in 22 volumes). Once again, French authors are completely dominant.[6] The main differences

---

6. Pardo lived until 1925. Of the ninety-three books of fiction listed, those for which publishers and publication dates are provided come from the twentieth century—after Rizal's death. Only four go back to the period before Rizal went home for good in 1891. But at least 30 percent of the items have no publication dates. It is seems likely that before going home, Pardo left behind in Paris, or gave away to friends, the library he had assembled there, and that once in Manila he re-ordered books he was attached to, as well as buying new ones. Thus the Ateneo catalogue cannot tell us what Rizal might have read when he stayed with Pardo, but does give us a good picture of Pardo's cosmopolitan tastes. It is notable that Pardo's collection included almost no poetry, and virtually nothing from antiquity, while Rizal's, as we shall see, had plenty of both.

between the two libraries are the absence of Germany in Pardo's, and the peculiar near-absence of Spain in Rizal's.

With this suggestive, but inconclusive background, it is time to see what Rizal's novels themselves may reveal. There are several surprises in store.

NITROGLYCERINE IN THE POMEGRANATE

For all its satirical brilliance and the synoptic picture it gives of late-nineteenth-century colonial society in the Philippines, *Noli me tangere* can be said—up to a point—to be realist in style. A wealthy young *mestizo*, Crisóstomo Ibarra, returns to his country after years of study in Europe, with the intention of marrying his childhood sweetheart Maria Clara and starting a modern secular school in his home town. By the end of the novel these dreams are in ruins, thanks to the machinations of reactionary, lustful members of the Orders, and to the corruption and incompetence of the colonial administration. Maria Clara, who is revealed to be the child of an adulterous Franciscan friar, retires to the nameless horrors of a convent, and Ibarra himself seems to have perished, gunned down by the regime after being framed by the Orders for a revolutionary conspiracy.[7]

El Filibusterismo is much stranger. The reader gradually discovers that Ibarra did not die after all—his noble alter ego, Elias, sacrificed his own life to save him. After many years of wandering in Cuba and Europe, and having accumulated untold riches as a jewel merchant, Ibarra returns to his homeland in the bizarre disguise of "Simoun," a gaunt figure with long white locks and deep-blue spectacles that conceal the upper part of his face. His aim is to corrupt further an already corrupt regime, to the point that an armed uprising will occur that will destroy the colonial system and liberate Maria Clara. The climax of the narrative is a plot to detonate a huge nitroglycerine bomb, concealed in a jeweled lamp shaped as a pomegranate, at a grand wedding attended by the entire colonial elite. The conspiracy, however, goes awry. Maria Clara is discovered to be already dead, and Simoun, gravely wounded, dies on a lonely shore before he can be apprehended. Nothing in "real" Philippine history remotely corresponds to Simoun and his outré scheme. One could perhaps think (not entirely amiss, as will be shown later) that the novel was proleptic fiction, set in a time as yet to come—although no other Filipino would write the future like this for more than a century. What inspired Rizal to write *Noli me tangere*'s sequel in such a peculiar way?

---

7. I have written two essays on *Noli me tangere*, both republished in my *The Spectre of Comparisons* (London: Verso, 1998), so will treat it only tangentially in this chapter.

A LEGACY FROM BALTIMORE?

For the title of the book I finished in 1998, I mistranslated a brilliant phrase that occurs early on in *Noli me tangere*: "el demonio de las comparaciones." Rizal used the phrase to describe the young Ibarra's eerie experience on seeing again the seedy Jardín Botánico of Manila, and perversely finding himself helplessly imagining in his mind's eye the grand botanical gardens he often visited in Europe. It is as if he can no longer see what is in front of him simply as a familiar object. But the *demonio* also works on the author himself, who is writing in Paris and Berlin about a young man *allá* ("yonder, yes yonder, yonder, yonder") in Manila, who is thinking about . . . *allá*, that is, Berlin and Paris.[8] Ravished by this complex image, I completely overlooked one crucial thing. *Noli me tangere* is full of scorching epigrams and witty reflections, but there is no other phrase that is both eerie and unsatirical like this.

About that time my brother Perry, also struck by the phrase, wrote to me suggesting a possible source: a prose poem by Mallarmé (1842–98) entitled "Le Démon de l'analogie" (The Demon of the Analogy), probably first composed in 1864, when Rizal was three years old, published in *La Revue du Monde Nouveau* in 1874 as "La Penultième" (The Penultimate), and again on March 28, 1885 in *Le Chat Noir*, with the original title restored.[9] Perhaps, he suggested, Rizal might have been inspired by the poem, since he came to live in Paris only three months later.

My initial reaction to this suggestion was disbelief. Though Rizal started learning French at the age of twelve, when he entered the Ateneo, the Jesuits' elite secondary school in Manila, it seemed unlikely that he would have been able to tackle so difficult and esoteric a text. But later the suggestion seemed at least worth looking into. It transpired that Mallarmé's title was a creative homage to "Le Démon de la perversité," Baudelaire's translation of Edgar Allan Poe's story "The Imp of the Perverse."[10] This tale was first published

---

8. See the exchange about this oscillation between Jonathan Culler and myself, contained in Jonathan Culler and Pheng Cheah, eds, *Grounds of Comparison* (New York: Routledge, 2003), at pp. 40–41, 45–6, and 228–30.

9. See Bradford Cook, trans., *Mallarmé: Selected Prose Poems, Essays and Letters* (Baltimore: The Johns Hopkins University Press, 1956), pp. 2–4, for a reasonable English version; the notes on the text, pp. 108–10, include a brief publication history. Cook points out its remarkable affinities with the monomaniacal story "Berenice" of Edgar Allan Poe (1809–49), which can be found in his *Tales* (Oneonta: Universal Library, 1930), pp. 219–38.

10. Poe, *Tales*, pp. 455–61. It will be recalled that Poe's story, told in the first person, is that of a man who commits a perfect murder, but then is so driven by the urge to proclaim his own brilliance that he ends up confessing to the crime. The term "imp" has nothing imposing or Christian about it, and is best translated into French as *lutin*. Baudelaire's decision to use *démon* gives the imp a grand and *ci-devant* Catholic aura.

in barbarous Baltimore in 1839 as part of Poe's *Tales of the Grotesque and the Arabesque*, and then by Baudelaire in the second volume of his Poe translations.[11] An odd chain of possibilities then loomed up—from Poe's neurotic-psychological imp, through Baudelaire's quasi-theological demon and Mallarmé's uncanny source of poetic inspiration, to the political imagining of a colonized Rizal-in-Europe. But had Rizal read Baudelaire or Poe? Neither in De Ocampo's catalogue (see note 5), nor among Rizal's cards at the López Museum Library was there any mention of Poe, Baudelaire, or Mallarmé.

A STUDENT OF HOMEOPATHY

Then came the second accident: the arrival on my desk of a draft article from the pioneering Gay Studies scholar Neil Garcia, of the University of the Philippines. Garcia had asked himself whether Rizal was gay, and answered his own question negatively by saying, *à la* Foucault, that in the 1880s gayness did not yet exist in the Philippines. Garcia also seemed to feel that as a Third World *provinciano*, Rizal must have been sexually pretty innocent.[12] But the article called serious attention to a short passage from the chapter in *El Filibusterismo* titled "Tipos Manileños" (Manila Types).[13] There, at the splashy opening night for a travelling *French* vaudeville troupe, the cynical student Tadeo regales his country bumpkin cousin with scandalous gossip (mostly made up) about members of the Manila elite in the audience. At one point Tadeo comments thus:

---

11. Baudelaire's Poe translations were published as *Histoires extraordinaires* in 1856, and *Nouvelles Histoires extraordinaires* in 1857. "Le Démon de la perversité" was the opening tale in the second volume. This book, along with Baudelaire's Introduction, is reprinted in his *Oeuvres complètes* (Paris: Louis Conard, 1933), vol. 7. The genius of *Les Fleurs du mal* first encountered Poe's writing early in 1847, and was so exhilarated that he devoted much of the next sixteen years of his life to translating it. See Patrick F. Quinn, *The French Face of Edgar Poe* (Carbondale: Southern Illinois University Press, 1954), pp. 9, 14, and 101.

12. It is possible that Rizal was indeed so when still a boy in Manila. But the presence in his personal library of Pierre Delcourt's *Le vice à Paris* (4th edition, Paris, 1888), Dr P. Garnier's *Onanisme* (6th edition, Paris, 1888), Philippe Ricord's *Traité des maladies vénériennes* (Brussels, 1836), and Vatsyayana's *Le Kama Soutra* (Paris, 1891) indicates that his medical studies and other readings over the next decade left him quite a sophisticate.

13. The Latin words below are a witty play on the famous motto, *similia similibus curantur*, of the founder of systematic homeopathy, the German physician Christian Friedrich Samuel Hahnemann. In his library Rizal had a copy of *Exposition de la doctrine médicale homéopathique*, a French translation (Paris, 1856) of Hahnemann's standard work. José Rizal, *El Filibusterismo* (Manila: Instituto Nacional de Historia, 1990), p. 162.

> Ese respectable señor que va elegantemente vestido, no es médico pero es un homeópata sui generis: profesa en todo el similia similibus . . . El joven capitan de caballería que con él va, es su discípulo predilecto.

> That respectable gentleman, so elegantly dressed, is no doctor but a homeopathist of a unique type; he professes in everything the principle of like-with-like. The young cavalry captain arriving with him is his favorite disciple.

The gossip is catty, but not shocked; moreover, the insinuation of homosexuality flies past the country boy who knows no Latin, and also does not understand the meaning of the word *homeópata*. In other words, Tadeo appears really to be addressing not a country boy but some rather sophisticated readers.

Who were they? This question became still more pressing when I consulted the big facsimile edition of the original *El Filibusterismo* manuscript. For Rizal had first written, and then crossed out, the following phrase: "profesa en el amor el princ. . . similia similibus gaudet."[14] If we take *princ* to be *principio*, then we can translate the whole phrase as "he professes in matters of love the principle that like rejoices in like", or "like gains happiness from like." *Gaudet* is a strong word in Latin, expressing gladness, happiness, even rapture. One can easily see why Rizal thought better of this formulation. Artistically speaking, it absolutely did not fit the cynicism of the character Tadeo, who never speaks of *amor*. But culturally and morally speaking, it would surely have been scandalous in the Philippines of the friars. Besides, were there really prominent men in late-colonial Manila who showed up at big public events with their good-looking

---

14. José Rizal, *El Filibusterismo*, facsimile edition (Manila: National Historical Institute, 1991), p. 157b (overleaf); *-bus* is a superscript, and the final *a* of *similia* looks like a write-over of *s*. Probably, then, the true original was the grammatically correct *similis simili*.

15. Yet writing about the school year 1877–78, when Rizal was sixteen and still a student at the Ateneo, Felix Roxas recalled that the lads there, after studying Virgil and Fénélon, put on a play about the gods and goddesses of Olympus. Probably it was one they made up themselves, since neither Virgil nor Fénélon were dramatists. (The Frenchman, trained by Jesuits, and allied with them in the struggle against Jansenism, almost certainly came to the Ateneo boys through his theological "novel" *Télémaque*. In the Filipino student world of Madrid in the 1880s, where everyone had a jocular nickname, the serious would-be doctor Isidro de Santos was called *el joven telémaco*. See Nick Joaquín, *A Question of Heroes* [Manila: Anvil, 2005], p. 44.)

Needless to say all the roles in the play, male and female, were played by the teenage boys. Puberty being puberty, Roxas wrote, passionate affairs developed, till one of the various love letters being handed about was intercepted by the prying Fathers. See *The World of Felix Roxas*, translated by Angel Estrada and Vicente del Carmen (Manila: Filipiniana Book Guild, 1970), p. 330. This book is an English translation of columns Roxas wrote in Spanish for *El Debate* between 1906 and 1936.

military boyfriends? It does not seem too likely.[15] (Yet one remarkable earlier source pictures a quite visible trade in young male prostitutes).[16]

On the other hand, Garcia did not mention an equally curious passage in the following chapter, titled "La función" (The Show), which describes the vaudeville performance and the various characters' reactions to it. The troupe stages one scene of merry-making in the servants' quarters by *servantes*, *domestiques*, and *cochers*. The first, clearly female, are probably

16. This source is the redoubtable Puerto Rican revolutionary and "Antillean" nationalist, Dr Ramón Betances, who, as will be seen in Chapter 5, became in the mid-1890s a crucial link between the armed nationalist uprisings in Cuba and the Philippines. In 1877, while taking temporary refuge from the Spanish colonial authorities in the small Danish colony of St Thomas (sold to the United States in 1917 as part of the Virgin Islands), Betances wrote two satirical pieces for *La Independencia*, organ of the Cuban and Puerto Rican exiles in New York, entitled "La autonomía en Manila," which appeared in the issues of September 29 and October 27. [Taken from Haraldo Dilla and Emilio Godínez, eds., *Ramón Emeterio Betances* (Habana: Casa de las Américas, 1983), pp. 205–10. The editors "modernized" the original spelling.] In the second of these texts appears the following sneer at Domingo Morriones, newly appointed Captain-General of the Philippines (1877–80): "no habrá dejado de recibir el subsidio de las prinsesas. Las casas de princesas de Manila, como la esclavitud en Cuba, son de 'institución española, con aprobación del arzobíspado;' y no son precisamente princesas las que en ellas figuran sino príncipes originiarios del imperio de la flor de medio, príncipes chinos, jóvenes de 16 a 10 años, que se pavonean en los carruajes por las calles con aire femenil y trajes de mujer o poco menos, llevándose desvergonzademente a su casa a los miserables que tienen el descaro de seguirlas o seguirlos. Las casas de princesas pagan cuatro mil pesos por año a la ciudad, razón suficiente para que opusiera el señor arzobispo a la supresión de ese otro tráfico humano, reclamada por un abogado criollo, reformista indignado, que fue a parar con su indignación y sus reformas al presidio de Marianas. Pero este negocio es de miserable rédito; y no es imposible que Morriones haya entregado el pico y demás enseres de las princesas a los frailes, buenos para el caso." [And he will not have failed to receive the subsidy of the princesses. The houses (brothels) of the princesses in Manila are, like slavery in Cuba, "Spanish institutions, approved by the archiepiscopacy." It is not exactly princesses who appear in these houses, but rather princes originating from the Celestial Empire, Chinese princes, boys aged ten to sixteen, who parade like peacocks along the streets in carriages, with an effeminate air and in women's clothes or something not far from that, shamelessly bringing to their houses the wretches who have the brazenness to be after them (female) or them (male). The houses of the princesses pay 4,000 pesos a year to the city, a reason sufficient for Mr Archbishop to oppose the suppression of yet another form of traffic in human beings. When an outraged reformist creole lawyer protested about this, he paid for his outrage and his reforms with imprisonment in the Marianas. But this business actually brings in a miserable amount; and it is not impossible that Morriones will have handed over the princesses, lock, stock, and barrel, to the friars, well-suited for the affair.] If this is true—and the 4,000 pesos do not sound like false coin—it means these Chinese prostitutes were swanning about in Manila when Rizal was a sixteen-year-old schoolboy there. Big-city teenage schoolboys being what they are, it does not seem likely that his classmates were unaware of the traffic. Research in Manila's municipal accounts, if they still exist for that period, seems warranted.

kitchen staff; the second, of less explicit gender, are probably housemaids. The third group, however, are, as coachmen, unmistakably male. All the groups, however, are played by actresses, the last in teasing drag. Towards the end of the chapter, the nameless narrator limns the jealousy felt by the beautiful, opportunist *mestiza* Paulita Gómez, as she watches her current beau, the student Isagani, in the audience.

> Paulita se ponía más triste cada vez, pensando en como unas muchachas que se llaman *cochers* podían ocupar la atención de Isagani. *Cochers* le recordaba ciertas denominaciones que las colegialas usan entre sí para explicar una especie de afectos.

> Paulita felt more and more depressed, thinking about how some of these girls, called *cochers*, might occupy the attention of Isagani. The word *cochers* reminded her of certain appellations which convent-school girls use among themselves to explain a species of affection.[17]

The masculine noun, along with the obvious sexual implications of being a "rider," make it clear what "species of affection" is intended. One could go further and argue that a certain sexual–sociological reality is involved, since the explanation of the French word as (nun-evading) teenage argot is the narrator's gloss—notice the sudden switch to the generalizing present tense of *usan* ("they" use among themselves).

It is interesting that this passage does not appear in the facsimile, which means that Rizal inserted it at the last minute. Why? Neither the "homeo-pathist" nor the "coachmen" are important to the narrative, and they are never mentioned again. *Acte gratuit?* It seems improbable. Were the passages inserted for a Filipino readership? Possibly, but more than a century would pass before any Filipino author again referred to male or female homo-

---

17. *El Filibusterismo* (1990), p. 173. Emphasis in the original text.

18. I have no doubt that part of the explanation lies in the impact of American colonialism and the educational apparatus it set up. For the secular imported schoolteachers, and for the (later) Catholic clerics from places like Boston and Baltimore, classical literary culture was completely foreign. But those youngsters educated by Spanish Jesuits in Rizal's generation were trained to be fluent in classical Latin. De Ocampo's list shows this very clearly. We find in the Calamba library: Caesar, Cicero, Horace, Livy, Lucretius, Ovid, Plautus, Tacitus, and Thucydides. (In his correspondence, Rizal also speaks of Aeschylus, Plutarch, Sophocles, and Xeno-phon, I suspect all in translation.) Pagan classical Latin poetry in particular was suffused with descriptions of, or references to, amorous relations between males, both human and divine. Horace wrote humorously, and Virgil tenderly, about boys they had loved. Rizal does not mention Plato, but it is hard to think that he had never read the *Symposium*. Even if the friars censored, or tried to censor, what the Filipino youngsters read, there was no way to prevent them from seeing in their imaginations a highly civilized culture in which Christianity, with its peculiar sexual cont'd over/

sexuality in this allusive, but offhand manner.[18] Another possibility is that in these passages Rizal was thinking of his European readers.[19]

LÀ-BAS

In any case, Rizal's mention of homeopathy struck a chord in my failing memory. I dimly recalled a novel where homosexuality and homeopathy came together—the bizarre, scandalous, avant-garde *À rebours* (Against Nature) by the half-Dutch, half-French novelist Joris-Karl Huysmans (1848–1907), which I had read, half-secretly, when I was about sixteen. It turned out that my memory was only 50 percent correct: homosexuality was there, and homeopathy too, but in quite unrelated contexts. Had Rizal ingeniously put them together? But Huysmans's name did not show up in De Ocampo's little book or in the López Museum's library cards (nor, for that matter, in Pardo de Tavera's francophile personal library). Besides, though originally published in 1884, *À rebours* was not translated into Spanish until around 1919 (with a foreword by Vicente Blasco Ibáñez), long after Rizal's death.[20] The first English-language version came out at almost the same time.[21] If Rizal had read *À rebours*, he had to have done so in the original French. Perhaps it was a sheer fluke that Huysmans and Rizal had put homeopathy and homosexuality together in novels written

---

18 *cont'd* obsessions, was entirely absent. The arrival of the Americans closed the gates to this magical ancient world. (No Filipino writer after Rizal would joke about the Diana of Ephesus with her "numerous breasts.") Here is one sadly unnoticed piece of damage that the philistine North Americans inflicted on the generations after Rizal's.

19. My "Forms of Consciousness in *Noli me tangere*," *Philippine Studies*, 51:4 (2003), pp. 505–29, a statistical study of the novel's vocabulary, makes a strong argument for Rizal having aimed partly at a general European readership. The most telling evidence is the narrator's heavy use of everyday Tagalog words, accompanied by paraphrases in Spanish, which cannot have been intended for Tagalog-speaking readers, or indeed for Spanish old-timers in the colony, but rather for Europeans who did not know much about the Philippines. The Tagalog words seem to have been inserted in part to assure such readers that despite the author's Spanish name he was a genuine native informant.

20. Huysmans's *À rebours* was put out by Prometeo publishers in Valencia, under the title *Al revés* (n.d.).

21. *À rebours* was originally published in Paris by Charpentier in May 1884. See Robert Baldick's introduction to his translation of the work as *Against Nature* (London: Penguin Classics, 1959), p. 10. The first English-language version, I believe, was *Against the Grain* (New York: Lieber and Lewis, 1922). This version was bowdlerized of its erotic passages, and contains a dishonest, oily introduction by none other than the fake-radical sexologist Havelock Ellis, who also got the original's date of publication wrong by five years. Subsequent editions restored the censored sections.

Joris-Karl Huysmans

less than seven years away from each other. But it seemed sensible to keep reading.

À rebours has a single, aloof central character, the rich, elegant aristocrat Des Esseintes, who is so appalled by the dominant crass bourgeoisie of the French Third Republic, the corruption of the Catholic Church, the shadiness of the politicians, the low quality of popular culture, etcetera, etcetera, that he retreats into a private world of aesthetic fantasy, cultivating strange sexual experiences, avant-garde literature, rococo antiquarianism, and "mediaeval" Christian mysticism. He also builds himself a weird, expensive home designed to expel Nature, which he regards as now *passé*. No real flowers, for example, but artificial blooms made of rare and strange jewels; a pet tortoise slowly dying under the weight of a carapace entirely studded with gems. One cannot help but recall that Simoun, the central figure in *El Filibusterismo*, draws his singularity, his wealth and his power, from trafficking in rare and antique precious stones. Another coincidence?

Maybe. But there were other much stronger correspondences. In the long chapter where Des Esseintes's avant-garde literary preferences are laid out, special praise is given to Huysmans's close friend Mallarmé; and in a list of the nobleman's favorite texts by the great poet, "Le Démon de l'analogie" is singled out for mention.[22] Baudelaire's "Le Démon de la perversité" and Poe are mentioned too.[23] If Rizal's French was not up to managing the original prose poem, could he not have got an interesting idea for his *Noli me tangere* simply from reading Mallarmé's title inside *À rebours*? But the most striking coincidences between the work of Huysmans and Rizal turned out to be with *El Filibusterismo*, rather than with *Noli me tangere*. I will mention just three, all of which involve sex of different types.

FLAUBERT AND A FUTURE MURDERER

First is the scene in *À rebours* where a near-impotent Des Esseintes takes as a short-term mistress a young female ventriloquist. To get himself in the mood, he purchases two statuettes, one of polychrome terracotta representing the classical Chimaera, a mythical female monster combining a lion's head, a goat's body, and a serpent's tail, and the other, made of black marble, representing the also-female, also monstrous Sphinx. These are placed at the far end of the bedroom, which is illuminated only by the dim glow of embers in a coal-grate fire. The woman in bed with Des Esseintes, coached beforehand by her lover, then gives voice to the two statuettes' sepulchral conversation, including a famous phrase from Flaubert's *La Tentation de Saint Antoine* (The Temptation of Saint Anthony): "Je cherche des parfums nouveaux, des fleurs plus larges, des plaisirs inéprouvés" (I seek new perfumes, ampler blossoms, untried pleasures).[24] At this point, as hoped and planned, Des Esseintes's virility comes back to life.

In the extraordinary eighteenth chapter of *El Filibusterismo*—it is called "Supercherías" (Trickeries)—Simoun coaches Mr Leeds, a skillful American (*yankee*) prestidigitator and ventriloquist, in a scene reminiscent of Hamlet's use of the players to jolt his stepfather's guilty conscience.[25] Mr Leeds makes

22. Joris-Karl Huysmans, *À rebours* (Paris: Fascquelles, n.d., but c. 1904), p. 244.

23. *Ibid.*, p. 235.

24. See Gustave Flaubert, *La Tentation de Saint Antoine* (Paris: A. Quentin, 1885); the text appears there as volume 5 of the author's *Oeuvres complètes*. Among the last of Saint Anthony's torments is a vision of the bank of the Nile on which the two mythical beings, Chimera and Sphinx, converse. It is curious that Flaubert thought that the Sphinx was male. Was it because the word in French is grammatically masculine? The quoted sentence is spoken by the Chimaera on p. 254.

25. Rizal attended a performance of *Hamlet* in Madrid on April 26, 1884. Entry for that date in his *Diario en Madrid, 1 enero á 30 junio 1884*, in *Diarios y memorias. Escritos de José Rizal*, Tomo I (Manila: Comisión del Centenario de José Rizal, 1961), p. 127.

the mummified head of an ancient male Egyptian speak of millennia-past horrors endured at the hands of scheming priests—crimes that exactly replicate those once inflicted on the young Ibarra and his doomed love Maria Clara by the lustful, conniving Dominican, Father Salví. This Dominican has been lured into attending the show, and now faints in superstitious terror. The curious thing is that Mr Leeds summons the clearly male mummy head to speak by using the single word *¡Esfinge!* (Sphinx!).[26] What is purely sexual–literary in Huysmans seems to have been transformed by Rizal, cross-gender, into the psychological–political.

Next, there is the curious scene where Des Esseintes picks up a teenager off the street, and takes him to a very expensive brothel.[27] There he pays for him to be initiated by Vanda, an experienced and seductive Jewish prostitute. While the boy is busy losing his putative virginity, Des Esseintes chats with the madam whom he knows very well. Says Madame Laure:

> "Alors ce n'est pas pour ton compte que tu viens, ce soir . . . Mais où diable as-tu levé ce bambin?" "Dans la rue, ma chère." "Tu n'es pourtant pas gris," murmura la vielle dame. Puis, après réflexion, elle ajouta, avec un sourire maternel: "Je comprends; mâtin, dis donc, il te les faut jeunes, à toi." Des Esseintes haussa les épaules, "Tu n'y es pas; oh! mais pas du tout," fit-il; "la vérité c'est que je tâche simplement de préparer un assassin."

> "So it's not on your own account that you've come tonight . . . but where the devil did you pick up that baby?" "On the street, my dear." "Yet you're not drunk," murmured the old woman. Then, after a moment's reflection, she added, with a maternal smile: "Ah! I understand; come on, you rascal, tell me, you need them young." Des Esseintes shrugged his shoulders. "You're off the mark. It's nothing like that," he went on, "the truth is that I am simply preparing a murderer."

Having denied any sexual interest in the lad, he then explains his scheme. He will pay for the boy's sessions with Vanda for about six weeks, and at that point will cut him off. By then, the boy will be sexually addicted, and to pay for further sessions will turn to burglary and thus eventually to murder. Des Esseintes's ultimate purpose is to create "un ennemi de plus pour cette hideuse société qui nous rançonne" (one enemy more for this hideous society which holds us to ransom). This is, however, merely a moral/immoral and aesthetic gesture. One more corrupted teenager will not in himself change anything in France.

---

26. Rizal, *El Filibusterismo*, p. 135. Or was Mr Leeds an admirer of Flaubert?
27. *À rebours*, pp. 103–6, part of chapter 6, which was wholly censored in the Havelock Ellis-prefaced New York translation of 1922.

But in *El Filibusterismo*, Simoun's basic project is intended to change everything. He says this to the young medical student Basilio, who has felt helpless against the clerical murderer of his little brother, whose death had driven his mother insane:

> Víctima de un sistema viciado he vagado por el mundo, trabajando noche y día para amasar una fortuna y llevar á cabo mi plan. Ahora he vuelto para destruir ese sistema, precipitar su corrupción, empujarle al abismo á que corre insensato, aun cuando tuviese que emplear oleadas de lágrimas y sangre . . . Se ha condenado, lo está y no quiero morir sin verle antes hecho trizas en el fondo del precipicio.

> Victim of a vicious system, I have wandered throughout the world, laboring night and day to amass a fortune and bring my plan to fruition. Now I have returned to destroy this system, precipitate its corruption, and push it to the abyss towards which it insensately hurtles—even if I have to make use of torrents of tears and blood. There it stands, self-condemned, and I do not wish to die before seeing it shattered to pieces at the bottom of the precipice.[28]

Meanwhile he will use his vast wealth to corrupt further the whole "ransom-holding" colonial order—inciting it to greater greed, vaster embezzlements, worse cruelties and deeper exploitation, to bring on the cataclysm. As noted earlier, his final plot is to place a huge nitroglycerine bomb, hidden inside a fantastic Huysmanesque jeweled lamp in the shape of a pomegranate, in the midst of a wedding party attended by all Manila's top colonial officials. Meantime, Julí, Basilio's beloved fiancée, has committed suicide to avoid succumbing to the goatish friar Padre Camarro, and the boy is now psychologically ready to become "one more enemy of this hideous colonial society." He is quickly convinced by Simoun to get his personal revenge by helping to organize a pitiless massacre of any adult male not supporting the "revolution".[29] This is a political project, not an aesthetic gesture, and reminds us that the 1880s and 1890s were the heyday of spectacular assassinations, in Europe and the USA, committed by despairing and hopeful anarchists. The linkages will be discussed in detail in a later chapter.

UNTRIED PLEASURES

Finally, there is the episode in *À rebours* in which Des Esseintes picks up an attractive teenage boy and has a sexual relationship with him for several months, which is described summarily as follows:

---

28. *El Filibusterismo*, p. 46.
29. *Ibid.*, chapters 30, 33, and 35.

Des Esseintes n'y pensait plus sans frémir; jamais il n'avait supporté un plus attirant, et un plus impérieux fermage; jamais il n'avait connus des périls pareils, jamais aussi il ne s'était plus douloureusement satisfait.

Des Esseintes could never think of it again without shuddering; never had he endured a more alluring, and a more imperious captivity; never had he experienced such perils, never too had he been more painfully satisfied.[30]

One should not take these sentences out of context. Des Esseintes, like Huysmans himself, is heterosexual, with a long string of mistresses. The affair with the boy appears to be part of a Flaubertian search for *plaisirs inéprouvés*.

There is no equivalent to this episode in *El Filibusterismo*, and Simoun appears to be almost asexual. Yet it may suggest a context for the half-bowdlerized description of the elegant "homeopathist" and his favorite disciple. The account in *À rebours* of Des Esseintes's avant-garde tastes in poetry praises not only Mallarmé in the highest terms, but also Paul Verlaine (1842–96); and in a preface written for a reissue of the novel in 1903, Huysmans declared that he would have awarded Arthur Rimbaud (1854–89) the same accolade had he published a collection of his poems by the year *À rebours* originally came out. But Rimbaud's epoch-making *Les Illuminations* only appeared two years later, in 1886, just before *Noli me tangere*, and well after Rimbaud had abandoned poetry and Europe.[31]

Verlaine and Rimbaud had been "notoriously" tempestuous lovers in the 1870s, and some of their poems made clear references to their sexual

30. *À rebours*, pp. 146–8; the passage quoted is on p. 147.

31. Rimbaud's flight from Europe is usually associated with the ten years he spent mainly as a business agent in Aden, and later a gunrunner for Menelik in Harar. But his first real journey out of Europe took place in 1876, when he went to the Netherlands Indies as a mercenary recruit to the Dutch colonial military. He was certainly aware that three years earlier the colonial regime had begun what would eventually prove to be a brutal thirty-year campaign to conquer the people of Acheh. Arriving in Batavia from Aden on July 20, he had two weeks of boot camp there before being sent to central Java. A fortnight later he deserted, and managed to elude the authorities long enough to strike some kind of bargain with the Scottish captain of an undermanned vessel shipping sugar back to Europe. Disguised as a sailor, "Mr Holmes," he endured a grueling ninety-day voyage to Cork, via the Cape of Good Hope, before turning up in France in early December. The barracks in Tuntang where he served for that fortnight—in the cool hills behind the port of Semarang—still placidly exist. He was back in Aden by June 1879. (My thanks to Joss Wibisono for this information, and the references below.) It is nice to imagine 20-year-old Rizal waving to the 28-year-old Rimbaud from the deck of the *D'jemnah* in the early summer of 1882, as the ship moored off Aden before heading up the Red Sea toward Europe. See Graham Robb, *Rimbaud* (London: Picador, 2000), chapter 25; Wallace Fowlie, *Rimbaud: A Critical Study* (Chicago: University of Chicago Press, 1965), pp. 51ff.

The KNIL barracks in Tuntang, in the hills south of the port of Semarang, Java, where Rimbaud served for a fortnight in July 1876, before deserting.

relationship. Verlaine was a lifelong friend of Huysmans, and besides, in avant-garde literary circles it was a point of honor to disdain bourgeois, official, and good-Catholic conceptions of morality.[32] Given Rizal's sojourn in Paris in the second half of 1885, mid-point between the equally sensational *À rebours* and *Les Illuminations*, and his later frequent visits, his allusions to male and female homosexuality in *El Filibusterismo* are likely to have been stimulated in part by his perusal of Parisian books and periodicals. Lesbian affections, furthermore, were very chic in nineteenth-century French literature from the time of Balzac on. Conceivably, then these passages represent a certain claim to membership in Casanova's "république mondiale des letters."

Last, it is perhaps worth noting that prior to *À rebours*, Huysmans had published sketches of Parisian society—in the sober vein of his early literary teacher Zola—

32. Incidentally, in those days Paris—like London, Berlin, and Barcelona—already had its organized underground world of male and female homosexual bars and cruising areas, which a touristy Huysmans visited on several occasions with his homosexual friend, the writer Jean Lorrain. See Ellis Hanson, *Decadence and Catholicism* (Cambridge, MA: Harvard University Press, 1997), chapter 2 "Huysmans Hystérique," esp. at p. 149.

under the title *Types parisiens*, corresponding in name, if not in tone, with *El Filibusterismo*'s satirical "*Tipos manileños*". And it is agreeable that Rizal's second novel came out in the same year that Huysmans published his next avant-garde bombshell, the satanical *Là-bas*—which translates nicely into Spanish as *Allá*.

THE LUXURY OF FRENCH

So much for Huysmans, except to observe that *À rebours*, coming out in May 1884, was a huge *succès de scandale*, enraging especially the Catholic clergy and *bien-pensant* bourgeois society.[33] The 24-year-old Rizal arrived in Paris fourteen months later, and stayed there till January 1886, when he left for Germany. *À rebours* was still the literary talk of the town. We know little of what Rizal did in Paris except to take classes with a then-famous ophthalmic surgeon. But he lived with close Filipino friends, not only the philologist Trinidad Pardo de Tavera but also the painter Juan Luna, who had lived in the magical city longer, and were more fluent in French.[34]

Rizal once said that he had written one quarter of *Noli me tangere* while in Paris.[35] He later seriously considered writing his second novel in French, to reach a world audience. In a memoir of his time with Rizal in Berlin, Máximo Viola recalled:

> Y cuando quise saber la razón de ser de aquel lujo innecesario del francés, me explicó diciendo de que su objecto era escribir en adelante en francés, caso de que su *Noli me tangere* fracasara, y sus paisanos no respondieran a los propósitos de dicha obra.

33. Huysmans himself recalled in his 1903 preface that the book "tombait ainsi qu'un aérolite dans le champ de foire littéraire et ce fut et une stupeur et une colère" (fell like a meteorite into the literary fairground of literature; there was both stupefaction and fury). His amusing description of all the different, contradictory hostilities he had aroused can be found on pp. 25–6.

34. Rizal's competence in French has yet to be seriously studied. In his *Diario de viaje. De Calamba à Barcelona* (1882), entry for May 12, he noted shipboard that he was reading Walter Scott's *Carlos el Temerario* (*Quentin Durward*) in a French translation. Scott's vocabulary is rich and complex, so that to read him in French would have required some real ability at reading, even if not necessarily speaking or writing, the language. See Rizal, *Diarios y memorias* (cited in note 25), p. 47. But eight years later, in a letter from Brussels to his bosom friend the Austrian ethnologist Ferdinand Blumentritt, dated June 28, 1890, he wrote that he was studying French hard under the best teacher around. See *Cartas entre Rizal y el Profesor Fernando Blumentritt, 1890–1896*, in *Correspondencia epistolar* (Manila: Comisión del Centenario de José Rizal, 1961), Tomo II, Libro 2, Parte 3, pp. 668–71. Was he studying speaking and writing only?

35. León Ma. Guerrero, *The First Filipino, a Biography of José Rizal* (Manila: National Historical Institute, 1987), p. 121. The book spends only two pages on Rizal's stay in Paris. One reason for this may be the very remarkable paucity of letters from Rizal to anyone, including his family, over those seven months.

When I asked him the reason for this needless luxury of French, he explained to me that his purpose was to write from then on French in the event that his *Noli me tangere* proved to be a failure, and his countrymen did not respond to the objectives of the work.[36]

In a letter of July 4, 1890, Blumentritt wrote to Rizal: "Ich sehe mit Sehnsuche den Buche entgegen, dass Du französich schreiben wirst, ich sehe voraus, dass es ein ungeheures Aufsehen erregen wird" (I eagerly await the book that you are to write in French; I foresee that it will provoke a colossal sensation).[37] In the end, of course, *El Filibusterismo* was written in Spanish, not French. It was printed in 1891 in Ghent, only forty miles from Ostend, where, three years earlier, in 1888, James Ensor had finished his extraordinary proleptic anarchist-revolutionary painting *Christ's Entry into Brussels, 1889*, which has a very Rizalean mixture of biting social satire, caricature, romanticism, and rebellion. Definitely a coincidence, but a nice one.

WRITING REVENGE

A quite different insight came to me as I was doing research on the great Dutch writer Eduard Douwes Dekker (pen name Multatuli) (1820–87) and his bombshell anticolonial novel *Max Havelaar*, which was first published in 1860, and translated into German, French, and English in the 1860s and 1870s. It remains one of the first anticolonial novels based on concrete experience in a colony. *Max Havelaar* is also, among other things, about a young, idealistic hero (like Ibarra of *Noli me tangere*) who tries to defend the oppressed natives, and who is then politically and financially destroyed by a cabal of corrupt colonial bureaucrats and sinister native chiefs. The novel can be understood as Douwes Dekker returning fire on the powerful enemies who had not only forced him out of the colonial civil service to return home in penury, but were continuing a brutal exploitation of the Javanese peasantry.

Rizal ran across *Max Havelaar* late in 1888 while in London, probably in the quite good English translation. He was reading it shortly after *Noli me tangere* had come out and Douwes Dekker himself had died. In a December 6th letter Rizal wrote thus to Blumentritt:

Das Buch Multatuli's, welche ich dir senden werde, als bald wie ich es bekommen, ist ausserordentlich reizend. Kein Schweifel [Zweifel], ist es meinem weit überlegen. Nur, da der Verfasser selbst ein Niederländer ist, so sind die Angriffe nicht so heftig

36. See Viola's *Mis viajes con el Dr Rizal*, in *Diarios y memorias*, p. 316.
37. Letter contained in *Cartas entre Rizal y el Profesor Fernando Blumentritt, 1890–1896*, p. 677.

wie meine; aber es ist viel künstlicher, viel feiner, obgleich nur eine Seite von dem Niederländischen Leben auf Java entblösst.

Multatuli's book, which I will send you as soon as I can obtain a copy, is extraordinarily exciting. Without a doubt, it is far superior to my own. Still, because the author is himself a Dutchman, his attacks are not as powerful as mine. Yet the book is much more artistic, far more elegant than my own, although it only exposes one aspect of Dutch life on Java.[38]

Rizal thus recognized the affinities between his own novel and Douwes Dekker's, though they were written a quarter of a century apart. There is a very strong probability that the young Filipino found in *Max Havelaar* an example of how a novel could be powerfully written to take anticolonial political, and personal, revenge. Evidence for this argument will be developed in the following chapter, where *El Filibusterismo* is analyzed in more detail.[39]

THE CHILDREN OF RODOLPHE

A fine article by Paul Vincent not only makes explicit comparisons between *Max Havelaar*, *Noli me tangere* and *El Filibusterismo*, but points out that Douwes Dekker, contemptuous of the Dutch literary world of his time, revered *Don Quixote* and *Tristram Shandy*, and was inspired mainly by Walter Scott in English and Victor Hugo, Dumas *père*, and Eugène Sue in French. Vincent also comments that the heroes Max Havelaar and Crisóstomo Ibarra clearly descend, by separate lines, from the "socialist" aristocrat Rodolphe whom Sue (1804–59) made the hero of his 1844–45 blockbuster *Les Mystères de Paris*.[40] Like Rizal and Douwes Dekker, Sue started out as a dandy, but he underwent a political conversion around 1843, which made him an ardent (Proudhonian) socialist, and an energetic enemy of Louis Napoléon, the biggest French imperialist of them all, who drove him to exile, penury, and death three years before Rizal was born.[41]

---

38. Letter contained in *Cartas entre Rizal y el Profesor Fernando Blumentritt, 1888–1890* in *Correspondencia epistolar*, Tomo II, Libro 2, Parte 2, p. 409.

39. As we shall discover, between 1889 and 1891 Rizal's family was financially ruined by an alliance between the colonial regime and the Dominicans. His father, his elder brother Paciano, two sisters, and two brothers-in-law were exiled to remote parts of the archipelago.

40. Paul Vincent, "Multatuli en Rizal Nader Bekeken" (Further Reflections on Multatuli and José Rizal), *Over Multatuli*, 5 (1980), pp. 58–67.

41. A witty, intelligent and sympathetic biography of Sue is Jean-Louis Bory, *Eugène Sue, le roi du roman populaire* (Paris: Hachette, 1962). A good recent edition of the 1,300-odd-page novel was published in 1989 by Éditions Robert Laffont in Paris.

Lithograph from Le Juif Errant [The Wandering Jew], *imagining Java.*

Sue benefited from, and exploited, the innovation of *romans-feuilleton*, novels serialized in competitive daily newspapers, which created huge new markets for novelists. (His works were rapidly translated into all the major European languages.) Newspaper publishers encouraged gifted writers to keep readers hooked from issue to issue by artful suspense, intrigue, exotica, undying tragic loves, revenge, satire, and panoramic views of all levels of society. Composing this kind of serialized novel meant holding multiple plots together, usually by means of an unnamed, omniscient narrator, rapid and abrupt shifts from milieu to milieu and time to time, and quite often a moralizing populist politics.[42] (Needless to say these *romans-feuilleton* were mostly suppressed under Louis Napoléon.) Sue's second great hit, *Le Juif*

---

42. See Charles Bernheimer, *Figures of Ill Repute: Representing Prostitution in Nineteenth Century France* (Cambridge, MA: Harvard University Press, 1989), p. 47; and Paolo Tortonese, "La Morale e la favola: Lettura dei *Misteri di Parigi* como prototipo del *roman-feuilleton* [Morality and the Tale: a Reading of the *Mystères de Paris* as protoype of the *roman-feuilleton*]" (mimeo, n.d.). (My thanks to Franco Moretti for giving me a copy of this text.) The pioneer editor was Émile de Girardin who in 1836 started serializing Balzac's *La vieille fille* in his new newspaper *La Presse*.

errant (The Wandering Jew), which appeared over 1845 and 1846, especially interested me because its sprawling structure is held together by a satanic Jesuit, whose tentacles stretch as far as Siberia, North America and . . . Java![43] Rizal's novels have almost all these structural and thematic elements, though neither was serialized. But it will be recalled that in his library there were ten works by Sue, far more than by any other writer. This did not mean that he was not shrewdly critical of his predecessor.

Dumas *père* (1803–70) was another master of the *roman-feuilleton*, and his *Le Comte de Monte Cristo*—the story of Edmond Dantès, ruined and imprisoned for many years by a conspiracy of his enemies, who reappears, disguised as the Count of Monte Cristo, to take vengeance on them—is, as it were, those of Ibarra and Simoun rolled into one. Coincidence? Unlikely. In his *Memorias de un estudiante de Manila*, written under the pen name P. Jacinto in 1878, sixteen-year-old Rizal recalled that he had read *El Conde de Montecristo* at the age of twelve, "saboreando los sostenidos diálogos y deleitándose en sus bellezas, y siguiendo paso à paso à su héroe en sus venganzas" (savoring its sustained dialogues, delighting in its charms, and following step by step the hero and his revenges).[44] But neither Sue nor Dumas was much interested in the depredations of colonialism and imperialism, and their characters' revenges are basically personal and metropolitan.

---

43. The text available to me is a three-volume 1889 English translation, running to over 1,500 pages, and published in London and New York by George Routledge and Sons. This edition has terrific nineteenth-century-style illustrations. The Jesuit's agents include both a shady Dutch colonial businessman and a skillfully murderous Thug on the lam from India. (East India Company Governor-General William Bentinck had launched an extermination campaign against the Thugs, a stratum of professional robbers and murderers who typically killed their victims by strangulation, in 1831, a little more than a decade before *Le Juif errant* began to be serialized.) But the Proudhonian socialist took Dutch rule in the Indies completely for granted.

Rizal tells us that he bought a Spanish translation of this immense work for 10 pesetas, while paying another 2.50 pesetas for works by Dumas and Horace. See the entry for January 6, 1884, in his *Diario de Madrid*, in *Diarios y memorias*, p. 114. On January 25, he recorded that he had just finished the book, and offered this pithy comment. "Esta novela es una de las que me han parecido mejor urdidas, hijas únicas del talento y de la meditación. No habla al corazón como el dulce lenguaje de LAMARTINE. Se impone, domina, confunde, subyuga, pero no hace llorar. Yo no sé si es porque estoy endurecido." [This novel is one of those which have struck me as the most consciously contrived, unique children of talent and premeditation. It does not speak to the heart like the sweet language of LAMARTINE. It imposes itself, dominates, confounds, and subjugates, but does not make [me] weep. I don't know if the reason for this is that I have become hardened]. *Ibid.*, p. 118.

44. *Ibid.*, p. 13.

LAUGHTER AND SUICIDE

And "Mother Spain"? Earlier in this chapter, attention was drawn to the absence of any Spanish novels, aside from *Don Quixote*, in Rizal's personal library, and their heavy presence in that of his philological friend Trinidad Pardo de Tavera. Part of the explanation is the difference in life span between the two men. Blasco Ibáñez (b. 1867) and Pío Baroja (b. 1872) who figure prominently in Pardo's library, were of Rizal's generation, but did not become famous until well after he died. Pardo, however, survived his friend by thirty years. But this kind of explanation cannot be applied to the case of Benito Pérez Galdós (1843–1920), the so-called Spanish Balzac, often said to be the country's greatest novelist after Cervantes. What Sue was for Rizal's library, Galdós was for Pardo's. Is it really conceivable that Rizal never read a single item of Galdós's colossal novelistic output? It is certain that in his voluminous writings he never mentioned the older man's name. But many scholars have pointed to thematic similarities between *Noli me tangere* and Galdós's *Doña Perfecta*, published in 1876, when the Filipino was fourteen years old. *Doña Perfecta*, a short novel by Galdós's standards, is indeed about a politically innocent liberal engineer who is destroyed by the religious fanaticism of his eponymous aunt, with the Church behind her. *Noli me tangere* is in every respect vastly superior. But it is by no means implausible to speculate that Rizal had partly in mind just this "anticolonial" project, to beat the most famous metropolitan novelist on his own terrain, without, of course acknowledging anything of the sort. All the more satisfying, perhaps, in that Galdós, though a liberal, had nothing to say about Spanish imperialism. Hence, as a Filipino anticolonialist, Rizal, in turn, had nothing to say about Galdós.[45]

But then there is Rizal's unquenchable laughter, something extremely rare in anticolonial literature. This laughter—which is not just a matter of razor-sharp epigrams and mordant sallies, but so suffuses both novels that the reader often feels like giggling out loud—cannot be traced to Hugo, Dumas, Sue, or Galdós, for none of whom was laughter a strong suit. Douwes Dekker could be killingly funny, but Rizal only read him after *Noli me*

45. Over 1884–85, Leopoldo Alas (pen name Clarín)—nine years older than Rizal—published his most important novel, *La Regenta* (The [Lady] Regent), a strongly anticlerical, penetrating study of social life in a provincial Spanish cathedral town. It produced howls of rage in clerical and *bien-pensant* circles. Rizal was studying in Madrid till the late summer of 1885, when he left for France and Germany, so he would certainly have known about the novel, even if he did not have time to read it. But it is never mentioned in his writings. As in the case of Galdós, this silence might be deliberate; but *La Regenta* is also absent from Pardo de Tavera's library, an indication that may be more telling.

tangere was published. Part of Rizal's laughter came from the miserable comedy of colonialism itself. In the Epilogue to *Noli me tangere*, the 25-year-old Filipino wrote:

> Viviendo aún muchos de nuestros personajes, y habiendo perdido de vista á los otros, es imposible un verdadero epílogo. Para bien de gente, mataríamos con gusto á todos nuestros personajes, empezando por el P. Salví y acabando por Da. Victorina, pero no es posible . . . Que vivan! El país y no nosotros los ha de alimentar al fin

> Since many of our characters are still alive, and having lost sight of others, a true epilogue is not possible. For the good of the public, we would happily kill off all our personages, starting with Padre Salví and finishing with Doña Victorina, but this is not possible . . . let them live! In the end, the country, and not we, will have to feed them[46]

As I have said elsewhere, this kind of authorial play with readers, characters and "reality," is quite uncharacteristic of most serious nineteenth-century European fiction, but reminds one instantly of Machado de Assis's *Memorias póstumas de Blas Cubas*, published only five years earlier.[47] The novel came to the Filipino, as to the Brazilian, from . . . *allá*. It was a miraculous import, with which it was possible to play, as Debussy would do with the gamelan music of the Javanese.

At the same time it is known that, after Cervantes, the Spanish writer to whom Rizal was most attached was Mariano José de Larra, who was born in 1809 and killed himself twenty-eight years later.[48] During his brief life, the francophile, liberal-radical writer stepped back and forth across the blurry divide between journalism and fiction, politics always there. Everything could be mocked, but not long-distance. Larra's hilarious, sharply char-

---

46. *Noli me tangere*, p. 350.

47. Benedeict Anderson, *The Spectre of Comparisons* (London: Verso, 1998), p. 231.

48. In a letter to his close friend Mariano Ponce, written in London on June 16, 1888, Rizal described Larra as "[d]el mejor prosista español de este siglo" (Spain's greatest writer of prose in this century). In an earlier letter, sent from San Francisco on April 30, he had asked Ponce to buy him Larra's complete works and post them to London, but had received only a selected works. In the June 16 letter, Rizal went on to say: "como tengo la costumbre de preferir las obras completas á las escogidas, tratándose de los grandes autores, le suplicaría me remitiese las Obras Completas . . . Conservaré sin embargo ésta con mucho gusto para ir haciendo comparaciones entre las diversas ediciones. Mi razón . . . es porque creo que en los grandes hombres todo es digno de estudio, y que es muy difícil decir en absoluto cuáles sean las mejores ó las peores." [as I am in the habit of preferring, where it concerns great authors, the collected works to just selections, I would plead with you to send me the Collected Works . . . However, I will keep this volume with great pleasure, in order to make comparisons between various editions. My reason . . . is that I believe that with regard to great men everything is worthy of study, and that it is very difficult to state absolutely which are better and which are worse]. *Epistolario Rizalino*, vol. 2, 1887–1890 (Manila: Bureau of Printing, 1931), pp. 7–8, 12–14.

acterized portraits of every stratum of Madrid society under the ferocious reactionary Fernando VII, including unforgiving mimicry of each, must have shown Rizal what it was possible to emulate and surpass for the dilapidated society of colonial Manila.

COLLABORATION AND EMULATION

The basic contrast between the work of Isabelo de los Reyes and Rizal lay in the very genres that they adopted. In the world of global ethnology and folklore studies, to which Isabelo attached himself, the basic norms were professional and cooperative. Emulation was by no means excluded, but it was subordinated to what all participants understood as a world enterprise to which each gave his or her own contribution. Isabelo thought there was nothing strange in dedicating his *magnum opus* to ethnological colleagues in Spain, and liberally citing the texts of English, Portuguese, Italian, and Spanish folklorists in his footnotes. "Colleagues" indeed can be said to be the key word in studying his relationship to Europe.

But novelists do not have colleagues, and the norms basic to the novel genre are profoundly competitive, whether in terms of originality or of market popularity. Almost one fifth of the sixty-four chapters in *Noli me tangere* begin with epigraphs, which, if one wished, could be thought of as shadow footnotes. But these are all taken from poets, dramatists, philosophers, the Bible, and the vast, enigmatic world of popular sayings; and they come in Spanish, Italian, Latin, and even Hebrew. Not one is from a novelist. Yet one cannot doubt the author's ambiguous debt to Sue and Larra, Dumas and Douwes Dekker, Galdós and Poe, Huysmans and Cervantes—and doubtless others. Rizal's originality lay in the manner in which he transposed, combined, and transformed what he had read.[48] If the analysis in this

---

48. This maybe the appropriate moment to bring up something Rizal wrote in a letter to Blumentritt from London on November 8, 1888. He told his friend that the problem in the Philippines was not really a lack of books. Booksellers actually did good business. In Calamba itself, a small town with between five and six thousand people, there were six small libraries, and in his own family's collection there were more than a thousand volumes. "Doch die meisten Bücher die sie verkaufen, sind religiös und narcotisch. Viele haben kleine Bibliotheken, zwar nicht grosse, denn die Bücher sind sehr theuer, man liesst Cantú, Laurent, Dumas, Sue, Victor Hugo, Escrich, Schiller und ander mehr." [Yet most of the books they sell are religious and narcotic. Many people have small libraries, not large, since books are very expensive. People read Cantú (a then-famous Italian Catholic writer on world history), Laurent (perhaps the great French chemist Auguste Laurent), Dumas, Sue, Victor Hugo, Escrich, Schiller, and many others]. See *Cartas entre Rizal y el Profesor Fernando Blumentritt, 1888–1890*, in *Correspondencia epistolar*, Tomo II, Libro 2, Parte 2, pp. 374–80.   cont'd over/

chapter is correct, one could say that in his novels the imp-demon of Poe–
Baudelaire–Mallarmé became the *demonio de los comparaciones* haunting the
colonized intellectual; Dumas's "sustained dialogues" were remade as urgent
debates about the paths to freedom; Sue's panorama of the social structure of
Paris was refigured into a synoptic diagnosis of the ills of colonial society,
and so on. But nothing shows Rizal's creativity better than the manner in
which the avant-garde aesthetic of Huysmans was borrowed from and
radically transformed to stimulate the political imagination of young Filipino anticolonial nationalists to come.

---

48 cont'd   Another international point should also be made. The persons who built
the 1,000-book family library were obviously Rizal's parents. We can get an idea of
their broad culture from four letters sent home by Rizal between June 21 and August
2, 1883 during his first trip to Paris. He describes going to Nôtre-Dame, and being
reminded of Victor Hugo's novel of the same name. He loves the Titians, Raphaels
and Vincis in the Palais Luxembourg. He makes a pilgrimage to the tombs of
Rousseau and Voltaire at the Panthéon. He wanders round the Louvre, casually
noting that part of it was burned by the Commune in 1871, and admiring the Titians,
Correggios, Ruisdaels, Rubenses, Murillos, Velasquezes, Riveras, Van Dykes, Raphaels and Vincis, as well as the Venus de Milo. He even goes to the Musée de Grevin
to see the waxworks of Hugo, "Alphonso" Daudet, "Emilio" Zola, Arabi (Pasha),
Bismarck, Garibaldi, and Tsars "Alejandro" II and III. The striking thing is that he
explains none of these names, and obviously feels no need to do so. His parents are
already perfectly familiar with them. See *Cartas á sus padres y hermanos*, in Tomo I of
Escritos de José Rizal cited in note 25, pp. 90–106.

In the World-Shadow
of Bismarck and Nobel

By the time *El Filibusterismo* was published (1891) Rizal had been in Europe for almost ten years, and had learned the two master-languages of the subcontinent—German and French—as well as some English. He had also lived for extended periods in Paris, Berlin, and London. He subtitled his second major fiction *novela filipina* with good political reason, as will be shown later on. But, seen from another angle, it is *Noli me tangere* that is *filipina*, while *El Filibusterismo* could well be termed a *novela mundial*. The former has no characters who are not either colonizers or colonized; but in the latter, we have already noted the appearance of a French vaudeville troupe in Manila, as well as that of Mr Leeds, the *verdadero yankee*, who is said to be fluent in Spanish because of long residence in South America. A key character is the vastly rich "Chinaman" Quiroga, who plans to set up a local consulate for his *nación*. Furthermore, the book is littered with casual references to Egypt, Poland, Peru, Germany, Russia, Cuba, Persia, the Carolines, Ceylon, the Moluccas, Libya, France, China, and Japan, as well as Arabs and Portuguese, Canton and Constantinople.

Yet, compared with *Noli me tangere*, which has been translated into a good number of languages and is widely known and loved in the Philippines, *El Filibusterismo* is relatively unregarded. At one level, this neglect is easy to understand. The novel has no real hero, while *Noli me tangere* has at least one, and perhaps three. Women play no central role, and are barely sketched as characters, while three of the most powerfully imagined figures in *Noli me tangere* belong to what Rizal called the "bello sexo." The plot and subplots of *El Filibusterismo* are stories of failure, defeat, and death. The moral tone is darker, the politics more central, and the style more sardonic. One might say that if the Father of the Philippine Nation had not written it, the book would have had few readers in the Philippines, let alone elsewhere, up till today. Yet it is an astonishing work in many ways. For Filipino intellectuals and scholars it has been a puzzle, not least because they have been distressed by its apparent lack of correspondence with what is known about Philippine colonial society in the 1880s. The temptation therefore has been to analyze it "morally" in terms of its author's real-life ambivalence toward anticolonial revolution and political violence (which will be touched on later). But at least some of these difficulties may be reduced if we consider the text as global, no less than local.

To create such a multicentered perspective, the narrative technique must inevitably be that of *montage*. The analyst must begin with the political experience of the young Rizal before he set off to Europe in 1882. Afterward? Three intersecting "worlds." The first, only in time, is the inter-state world-system of 1860–90, which was dominated by Bismarck. Crushing Prussian military victories over Austro-Hungary at Königgrätz in 1866, and over France at Sedan in 1870, not only made his Prussia the master of continental Europe and created the German Empire, but put an end to monarchism in France, destroyed the temporal power of the Papacy, and launched his country as a late-comer imperialist in Africa, Asia, and Oceania. Rizal's *Noli me tangere* was published in Berlin only three years before the world-arbiter finally fell from power. Yet at the same time, on the periphery, post-Tokugawa Japan and post-Civil War America were preparing themselves to overthrow, from different directions, Europe's world-hegemony.

The second world was that of the global Left. Thanks in part to Bismarck, 1871 saw something that has never happened again—the fall of the (then) symbolic "capital of world civilization" into the hands of its populace. The Paris Commune sent reverberations all over the planet. Its savage suppression by a French government far more afraid of the *communards* than of Bismarck, followed by the death of Marx, opened the way for the rise of international anarchism, which up to the end of the century was the main vehicle of global opposition to industrial capitalism, autocracy, latifundism, and imperialism. To this upsurge, the Swedish businessman-scientist Alfred Nobel unwittingly made a signal contribution by inventing the first-ever weapon of mass destruction readily available to energetic members of the oppressed classes almost anywhere across the globe.

Third was the narrower world of the decaying, residual Spanish empire into which Rizal was born. The metropole itself was wracked by dynastic civil war, fierce competition between ethno-regions, class conflicts, and ideological struggles of many kinds. In the far-flung colonies, stretching from the Caribbean through northern Africa to the rim of the Pacific, anticolonial movements, led by that of Cuba, were steadily increasing in

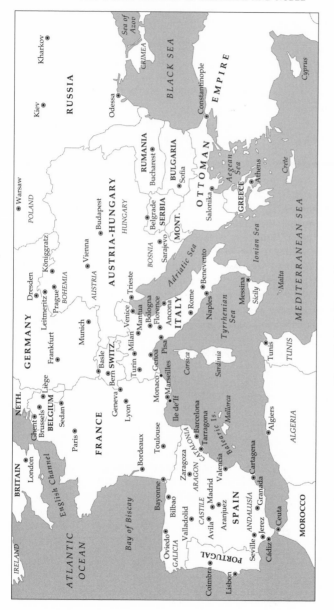

Three Worlds 1: The Mediterranean

vehemence and social support, while at the same time beginning to have serious contacts with one another.

As the chapter proceeds towards its concluding political analysis of *El Filibusterismo*, the intercalation between these worlds becomes more and more intricate, and requires a crosscutting between Spain, France, Italy, Russia, the Caribbean, the United States, and the Philippines—even if this tries the reader's patience.

PASSAGE TO EUROPE

In 1833 a dynastic crisis occurred in Spain that gave rise to two successive civil wars and haunted the country to the end of the century. In that year the ferociously reactionary Fernando VII, imprisoned and deposed by Napoléon, but restored by the Unholy Alliance after 1815, died, leaving the crown to his only child, the three-year-old Infanta Isabel; her Neapolitan mother became Regent. Fernando's younger brother Carlos, however, disputed the succession, claiming that the 1830 public abrogation of the Salic law prohibiting women from becoming sovereigns was a manipulation designed to rob him of his inheritance. Raising an army in the ultraconservative North (Navarre, Aragon, and the Basque Country), he opened a war that lasted the rest of the decade and ended only in an uneasy truce. The Regent and her circle turned, for financial as well as political reasons, to the liberals for support, and by a measure of far-reaching consequences, as we shall see, expropriated the property of all the powerful Orders. At sixteen, Isabel was married off to the "effeminate" Duke of Cádiz, and soon became accustomed to finding her pleasures elsewhere. On coming of age, she moved away from her mother's policies, fell under the sway of some diehard conservative clerics, and presided over an increasingly corrupt and ramshackle regime.

In the last months before this regime finally fell, in September 1868, the Queen ordered the deportation of a number of her republican enemies to the Philippines, where they were incarcerated on the fortified island of Corregidor in Manila Bay. In the exhilaration that followed her abdication and flight to France, some well-off, liberal-minded Manileño creoles and mestizos, including Joaquín Pardo de Tavera, Antonio María Regidor, and José María Basa—the latter two later to become good friends of Rizal—organized a public subscription on behalf of the suffering prisoners.[1] In June 1869, the rich and liberal Andalusian General Carlos María de la Torre took over as the new Captain-General, and horrified much of the Peninsular colonial elite

---

1. William Henry Scott, *The Unión Obrera Democrática: First Filipino Trade Union* (Quezon City: New Day, 1992), pp. 6–7.

by inviting creoles and mestizos into his palace to drink to "Liberty," and strolling about on the streets of Manila in everyday clothes. He then proceeded to abolish press censorship, encouraged freedom of speech and assembly, stopped flogging as a punishment in the military, and ended an agrarian revolt in Manila's neighboring province of Cavite by pardoning the rebels and organizing them into a special police force.[2] The following year, the liberal Overseas Minister Segismundo Moret issued decrees putting the ancient Dominican University of Santo Tomás under state control and encouraging friars to secularize themselves, while assuring them, if they did so, of continued control of their parishes in defiance of their religious superiors.[3] The same exhilaration set off what became a ten-year insurrection (1868–78) in Cuba under the capable leadership of the well-to-do landowner Carlos Manuel de Céspedes, who at one point controlled the eastern half of the wealthy colony.[4]

But in Madrid, with the decision to install Amadeo of Savoy as the new (unpopular) sovereign, the political winds started to shift.[5] In December 1870, prime minister General Juan Prim y Prats, who had led the assault on Isabel and then largely engineered Amadeo's accession, was assassinated. Accordingly, in April 1871, de la Torre was replaced by the conservative General Rafael de Izquierdo, who had Moret's decrees suspended, and then abolished the traditional exemption from corvée labor for workers in the naval shipyards of Cavite. On February 20, 1872 a mutiny broke out there in which seven Spanish officers were killed. It was quickly suppressed, but Izquierdo followed up by arresting hundreds of creoles and mestizos—secular priests, merchants,

2. Guerrero, *The First Filipino*, pp. 9–11.

3. John N. Schumacher, SJ, *The Propaganda Movement, 1880–1895*, rev. ed. (Quezon City: Ateneo de Manila Press, 1997), p. 7.

4. Guerrero observes that the war, ending in an armed truce, cost Spain 700 million pesos, and 140,000 casualties (mainly through disease), the pledge of autonomy and other reforms, a general amnesty, and a humiliating agreement with the United States permitting Cubans to acquire North American citizenship. *The First Filipino*, p. 283. Developments in Cuba will be treated in more detail in Chapter 4.

5. It will be recalled that the succession crisis created by Isabel's flight became the *casus belli* for the Franco-Prussian War. The Spanish cabinet, looking for a suitable replacement, decided to approach Prince Leopold, a distant cousin of the Prussian king, and Bismarck, seeing all the advantages to having a Hohenzollern on the throne in Madrid, pressured Leopold into accepting the invitation. When the news leaked to Paris, the French foreign minister lost his head. He rushed to Ems, where Wilhelm I was vacationing, and demanded not only Leopold's withdrawal, but a public declaration that no further Hohenzollern candidate would be put forward. Unwilling to be humiliated, Wilhelm refused. Bismarck, on receiving a telegraphed account of the meeting, doctored it to make Paris's demands seem more peremptory, and Wilhelm's rejection more brusque, than they really were. Publication of the doctored telegram did exactly what the Iron Chancellor hoped—it caused Louis-Napoléon foolishly to declare war.

lawyers, and even members of the colonial administration.[6] Most of these people, including Basa, Regidor, and Pardo, were eventually deported to the Marianas and beyond. But the regime, abetted by some conservative friars, decided to make a terrifying public example of three liberal, secular priests. After a brief kangaroo trial, the creoles José Burgos and Jacinto Zamora, and the aged Chinese mestizo Mariano Gómez, were garroted in the presence of, it is said, forty thousand people. Rizal's beloved ten-years-older brother Paciano, who had been living in Burgos's house, was forced to go into hiding and forswear any further formal education.[7]

Six months later, on September 2, almost 1,200 workers in the Cavite shipyards and arsenal went on the first recorded strike in Philippine history. Numerous people were arrested and interrogated but the regime failed to find an arrestable mastermind, and eventually all were released. William Henry Scott quotes Izquierdo's ruminations on this unpleasant surprise. Since "more than a thousand men could not share exactly the same thoughts without some machiavellian leadership," the general concluded that "the International has spread its black wings to cast its nefarious shadow over the most remote lands." Unlikely as this perhaps sounds, the fact is that the International had only been banned by the Cortes in November 1871, and the Bakuninist Madrid section had made special mention in the maiden issue (January 15, 1870) of its official organ *La Solidaridad*, devoted to arousing the workers of the world, of "Virgin Oceania and you who inhabit the rich, wide regions of Asia."[8]

Many years afterward Rizal wrote: "Sin 1872, Rizal sería ahora jesuita y en vez de escribir *Noli me tangere*, habría escrito lo contrario" (Had it not been for 1872, Rizal would now be a Jesuit, and instead of writing *Noli me tangere* would have written its opposite).[9] With Paciano on the blacklist, Rizal's prime family name, Mercado, would have closed for little José any chance of a good education; he was therefore enrolled at the Ateneo under the secondary family name Rizal. In 1891, he dedicated *El Filibusterismo* to the memory of the three martyred priests. When asked in 1887 by his Austrian friend the ethnologist Ferdinand Blumentritt what the meaning was of the odd word *filibustero*, he replied:

Das Wort Filibustero ist noch auf den Philippinen sehr wenig bekannt worden; die

6. Like others of his generation, Izquierdo was sure that the natives were incapable of insurrection on their own. Creoles and mestizos, not natives, it was thought, had cost Spain its continental American empire, and were the main force behind Céspedes's alarming contemporary successes in Cuba.

7. *Ibid.*, pp. 8–9; Guerrero, *The First Filipino*, pp. 3–6, 13.

8. Scott, *The Unión Obrera Democrática*, pp. 6–7.

9. Rizal, letter to his friend Mariano Ponce and staff members of *La Solidaridad*—1890s organ of the Filipino nationalists in Spain—as quoted in Guerrero, *The First Filipino*, p. 608, at note 13. My translation.

niedrige Bevölkerung kennt es noch nicht. Als ich dieser Wort zum ersten Mal hörte, war es in 1872, wann die Hinrichtungen stattgefunden haben. Ich erinnere mich noch das Erschrecken welches dieses Wort weckte. Unser Vater hat uns verboten dieses Wort auszusprechen . . . ein gefährlicher Patriote, welcher in junger Zeit aufgehängt wird, oder ein eingebildeter Mensch!

The word *filibustero* is still very little known in the Philippines; the common people as yet are unaware of it. The first time I heard it was in 1872 [he was then eleven years old] when the executions took place. I still remember the terror it aroused. Our father forbade us ever to utter it . . . [It means] a dangerous patriot who will soon be hanged, or a presumptuous fellow![10]

It turns out the word was politically coined around 1850 on one surprising shore of Céspedes's Caribbean, and from there drifted, via Cuba and Spain, across the Indian Ocean to Manila.[11]

---

10. *The Rizal–Blumentritt Correspondence, Vol. 1, 1886–1889* (Manila: National Historical Institute, 1992), fifth and sixth unnumbered pages after p. 65. Letter of March 29, 1887, from Berlin.

11. F[ernando] Tarrida del Mármol, "Aux inquisiteurs d'Espagne," *La Revue Blanche*, 12:88 (February 1, 1897), pp. 117–20. On p. 117 he wrote, of the "inquisiteurs modernes" in Spain, that "leurs procédés sont toujours les mêmes: la torture, les exécutions, les calomnies. Si le malheureux qu'ils veulent perdre demeure à Cuba, c'est un flibustier; si dans la péninsule, un anarchiste; si aux Philippines, un franc-maçon" [The methods of these modern Inquisitors are always the same: torture, executions, slanders. If the wretched person whom they mean to destroy lives in Cuba, he is called a filibuster; if he lives in the Peninsula, an anarchist; if in the Philippines, a freemason]. We shall run into the redoubtable Tarrida later on. Suffice it here to say that he knew what he was talking about, since he was born in Cuba in 1861—the year also of Rizal's birth—and said of himself in the above article "je suis cubain." See George Richard Esenwein, *Anarchist Ideology and the Working Class Movement in Spain, 1868–1898* (Berkeley: University of California Press, 1989), p. 135.

How the term *filibuster*, derived from the Dutch *vrijbuiter* (later the English *freebooter*), which originally meant "buccaneer" or "pirate," became a positive, fully political word, is an interesting matter. A significant turning-point can probably be found in chapter 52 ("Les flibustiers désolent les mers d'Amérique. Origine, moeurs, expéditions, décadence de ces corsairs") of Raynal and Diderot's exhilarating *Histoire philosophique et politique des établissements & du commerce des Européens dans les deux Indes* (Geneva: Libraires Associés, 1775). Without glossing over the buccaneers' ruthlessness, the authors nonetheless wrote admiringly of their love of liberty and their self-created code of honor. "Filibuster" in the full political sense seems to have been created around 1850 by the creoles of New Orleans, who used it to describe the variegated mercenaries and idealists who joined the Venezuelan Narciso López in that city for four successive attempted invasions (1848–50) of Cuba, to throw off the Spanish yoke and insure the island's annexation by the United States. People like the notorious American adventurer William Walker, who briefly made himself president of Nicaragua in the mid-1850s, were *cont'd over/*

In the late spring of 1882, the twenty-year-old Rizal left his country to study in Spain, concealing his plan from his parents, but supported by his adored brother Paciano and a sympathetic uncle. How was this possible? The Mercados were a cultivated, Spanish-and-Tagalog-speaking family of mixed "Malay," Spanish, and Chinese descent. They were the most prosperous family in their town of Calamba (today an hour's drive south of Manila), yet their wealth was fragile, as they did not own much land, but rented substantial tracts from the huge local Dominican hacienda. In 1882, world sugar prices were still high, but would crash in the depression that lasted from 1883 to 1886. The family would always send what money they could to José, but it was never enough, and the youngster usually found it hard make ends meet.

In any case, early in June, Rizal disembarked from the Dutch luxury vessel *D'jemnah* at Marseilles, before proceeding to Barcelona and then to Madrid to enrol as a student at Central University.[12] The first disagreeable downward shock was, as he wrote to his family:

> Yo me paseaba por aquellas calles anchas y limpias adoquinadas como en Manila, llenas de gente, llamando la atención de todo el mundo, quienes me llamaban

---

11 cont'd already proudly calling themselves "filibusters." Most likely the word traveled to Manila in the baggage of high-ranking military officers who had served in the Caribbean before being assigned to the Philippines. Four of the last five captains-general in the archipelago, Valeriano Weyler (1888–91)—born to Prussian parents in Mallorca—Eulogio Despujol (1891–93), Ramón Blanco (1893–96), and Camilo Polavieja (1896–97) had all won their repressive spurs in the Caribbean, Despujol in Santo Domingo, the others in Cuba.

It is a strange historical irony that López—who offered command of his second expedition to both Jefferson Davis and Robert E. Lee—was notorious for his "severity" towards blacks, allied himself with the Southern slavocracy and Northern expansionists, and recruited men mainly among veterans of the Mexican War—found posthumous patriotic rehabilitation thanks to his public garroting in Havana. The red-white-and-blue, star-and-stripes flag he designed for annexationist purposes remains Cuba's national flag today. See Hugh Thomas, *Cuba, The Pursuit of Freedom* (New Brunswick, NJ.: Harper & Row, 1971), pp. 212–17.

12. In his *Diario de viaje. De Calamba á Barcelona*, included in *Diarios y memorias*, p. 57, the twenty-year-old Rizal wrote that (Rimbaud's) Aden "me recordó el infierno de Dante" (reminded me of Dante's *Inferno*). From a letter sent home from Barcelona on June 23, we know he stopped off to enjoy the pleasures of Pompeii and Herculaneum, and admired from on deck the island of If, where Edmond Dantès had been so long incarcerated. *Cartas entre Rizal y los miembros de la familia, 1886–1887*, which are in *Correspondencia epistolar* (Manila: Comisión del Centenario de José Rizal, 1961), Tomo II, Libro I, pp. 20–21.

José Rizal as a young boy.

chino, japonés, americano, etc: ninguno filipino. ¡Pobre país! ¡Nadie tiene noticia de tí!

I walked along those wide, clean streets, macademized as in Manila, crowded with people, attracting the attention of everyone; they called me Chinese, Japanese, American [that is, Latin American], etc., but not one Filipino! Unfortunate country—nobody knows a thing about you! [13]

In Madrid, he was to be asked by fellow students whether the Philippines was owned by the United Kingdom or by Spain, and another Filipino whether it was very far from Manila.[14] Yet the overwhelming Spanish ignorance of, and indifference to, his country was soon to have useful consequences. In the

---

13. *One Hundred Letters of José Rizal* (Manila: National Historical Society, 1959), p. 26. Letter of June 23, 1882 from Barcelona. These letters were not available when the big *Correspondencia epistolar* was published.

14. "Que nos tomen por chinos, americanos ó mulatos y muchos aun de los jóvenes estudiantes no saben si Filipinas pertenece á los ingleses ó los españoles. Un día preguntaban á uno de nuestros paisanos si Filipinas estaba muy lejos de Manila." *Ibid.*, p. 85. Letter home from Madrid dated January 29, 1883.

A sketch of the port of Aden, by José Rizal.

colony—but the Spanish state never called either the Philippines or Cuba a colony, and contained no Colonial Ministry—racial hierarchy, embedded in law, modes of taxation, and sumptuary codes, was of overriding importance to everyone. Peninsulars, creoles, Spanish and Chinese mestizos, "Chinese," and *indios* were italicized social strata. In the Philippines, the word *filipino* referred to the creoles alone. In Spain, however, Rizal and his fellow students quickly discovered that these distinctions were either unknown or seen as irrelevant.[15] No matter what their status was back home, here they were all *filipinos*, just as the Latin Americans in Madrid in the late eighteenth century were *americanos*, no matter if they were from Lima or Cartagena, or if they were creoles or of mixed ancestry.[16] (The same process has produced the

15. In the first-class *Avant-Propos* she wrote to her new French translation of *Noli me tangere*, Jovita Ventura Castro noted that it was only after 1863 that students from the Philippines were permitted to enrol in metropolitan universities. The first to enrol were creoles physically indistinguishable from Spain-born Spaniards. Multi-colored mestizos and indios seem only to have arrived in the later 1870s. They were thus something visibly new. See *N'y touchez pas!* (Paris: Gallimard, 1980); the edition was sponsored by Unesco.

16. See my *Imagined Communities* (London: Verso, 1991), p. 57.

José Rizal during his student years at Madrid Central University.

contemporary American categories "Asians," and "Asian Americans".) On
April 13, 1887, Rizal would write to Blumentritt thus:

> Wir müssen alle der Politik etwas opfern, wenn auch wir keine Lust daran
> haben. Dies verstehen meine Freunde welche in Madrid unsere Zeitung
> herausgeben; diese Freunde sind alle Jünglingen, creolen, mestizen und
> malaien, wir nennen uns nur Philippiner.

> All of us have to make sacrifices for political purposes, even when we have
> no inclination to do so. This is understood by my friends, who publish our
> newspaper in Madrid; these friends are all youngsters, creoles, mestizos, and
> Malays, (but) we call ourselves simply Filipinos.[17]

What they "are" (colonially) is contrasted to what they "call themselves"
(publicly) in the metropole. But there is actually a further elision, since many
of these mestizos were Chinese not Spanish. (Indeed the Chinese mestizos

---

17. See *The Rizal–Blumentritt Correspondence, 1886–1889*, p. 72. It is important
to recognize that the German word *Philippiner* is uncontaminated by the ambiguities
surrounding *filipino*. It is clearly and simply (proto)national.

vastly outnumbered Spanish mestizos in the Philippines.)[18] The political *esfuerzo* involved probably explains why their newspaper called itself hopefully—and unmindful of the International—*La Solidaridad*. Thus one can suggest that Filipino nationalism really had its locational origins in urban Spain rather than in the Philippines.

For four years Rizal studied hard at Madrid's Central University. By the summer of 1885, he had received his doctorate in philosophy and letters, and would have done the same in medicine if his money had not run out. After Rizal's execution at the end of 1896, Miguel de Unamuno, who though three years younger than the Filipino entered the philosophy and letters faculty two years before him, and graduated in 1884, claimed, perhaps truthfully, that he had, so to speak, seen him around during those student days.[19] But for the purpose of this investigation, the most significant event occurred at the beginning of Rizal's senior year (1884/85) when Miguel Morayta, his history professor and Grandmaster of Spanish Masonry, delivered an inaugural address that was a blistering attack on clerical obscurantism and an aggressive defense of academic freedom.[20] The scholar was promptly excommunicated by the Bishop of Ávila and other mitre-wearers for heresy and for besmirching Spanish tradition and culture. The students went on a two-month strike in Morayta's behalf, and were quickly supported by fellow students at the big universities in Granada, Valencia, Oviedo, Sevilla, Valladolid, Zaragoza, and Barcelona.[21] The government then sent in the police, and many students were arrested and/or beaten up. Rizal later recalled that he had only escaped arrest by hiding in Morayta's house and assuming three different disguises.[22] As we

18. It is very striking that the words *mestizo chino* do not occur in *Noli me tangere* at all, and only once, in passing, in *El Filibusterismo*. There are plenty of characters whom one can assume are such mestizos, but Rizal is careful not to mention their give-away surnames. Sadly enough, Spanish prejudices against the Chinese were imbibed rather heavily by the young anticolonial elite.

19. Mentioned in the Mexican Leopoldo Zea's illuminating introduction to the Venezuelan edition of *Noli me tangere* (Caracas: Biblioteca Ayacucho, 1976), p. xviii, citing the "Elogio" (Eulogy) by the Basque philosopher, essayist, poet and novelist Miguel de Unamuno y Jugo in W.E. Retana, *Vida y escritos del Dr José Rizal* (Madrid: Victoriano Suárez, 1907).

20. Morayta particularly enraged the hierarchy by stressing that the Rig-Veda was much older than the Old Testament, proclaiming that the Egyptians had pioneered the idea of retribution in the afterlife, and discussing in sceptical terms the Flood, and a Creation which Rome still insisted had taken place in 4404 BC. Manuel Sarkisyanz, *Rizal and Republican Spain* (Manila: National Historical Institute, 1995), p. 205.

21. Rizal, *El Filibusterismo*, endnotes, pp. 38–9. The editors add that congratulations and supportive protests came in from students in Bologna, Rome, Pisa, Paris, Lisbon, Coimbra, and various places in Germany.

22. See the animated account Rizal gave his family in a letter of November 26, 1884, in *One Hundred Letters*, pp. 197–200.

shall see later, this experience, transformed, became a key episode in the plot of *El Filibusterismo*.

There is only one other event from the student years that is here worth underscoring: Rizal's first vacation in Paris in the spring of 1883. We have described earlier in some detail the excited letters he wrote to his family from the French capital. There is nothing remotely comparable for Madrid. Paris was the first geographical–political space that allowed him to see imperial Spain as profoundly backward: economically, scientifically, industrially, educationally, culturally, and politically.[23] This is one reason why his novels feel unique among anticolonial fictions written under colonialism. He was in a position to ridicule the colonialists rather than merely to denounce them. He read Eduard Douwes Dekker's *Max Havelaar* only after he had published *Noli me tangere*, but one can see at once why he enjoyed the Dutchman's take-no-prisoners style of satire.

By the time he graduated he had had enough of the metropole; he spent most of the next six years in "advanced" northern Europe. There are perhaps parallels with José Martí, eight years older than Rizal, who studied in Spain in the middle 1870s and then left it for good, spending much of the rest of his life in New York.

BISMARCK AND THE NEW
GEOGRAPHY OF IMPERIALISM

At this point we must temporarily leave 24-year-old Rizal in order to look schematically at the three worlds in which he found himself situated in the 1880s—the time of *Noli me tangere*'s publication and the planning of *El Filibusterismo*.

---

23. According to the 1860 census, most of the adult working population was occupationally distributed as follows: 2,345,000 rural labourers, 1,466,000 small proprietors, 808,000 servants, 665,000 artisans, 333,000 small businesspeople, 262,000 indigents, 150,000 factory workers, 100,000 in the liberal professions and related occupations, 70,000 "employees" (state functionaries?), 63,000 clergy (including 20,000 women), and 23,000 miners. Jean Bécarud and Gilles Lapouge, *Anarchistes d'Espagne* (Paris: André Balland, 1970), vol. I, pp. 14–15. Forty years later, in 1901, Barcelona alone had 500,000 workers, but half of them were illiterate. See J. Romero Maura, "Terrorism in Barcelona and Its Impact on Spanish Politics, 1904–1909," *Past and Present*, 41 (December 1968), p. 164.
Schumacher goes so far as to claim a level of equality in illiteracy between metropole and colony "unique in the history of colonization." (In 1900, illiteracy among people over ten years old in Spain was 58.7 percent. The American-organized census of 1903 showed a figure of 55.5 percent for the Philippines—this figure takes into account various local languages, Spanish, and American.) *The Propaganda Movement*, p. 304, note 9.

Otto von Bismarck

Having routed the armies of the Austro-Hungarian empire at Königgrätz in 1866, the Iron Chancellor repeated this triumph in 1870 at Sedan, where Louis-Napoléon and 100,000 French troops were forced to surrender. This victory made possible the proclamation he engineered in January 1871—at Versailles, not Berlin—of the new German empire, and the annexation of Alsace-Lorraine. From this point on until the ruin of the Great War, imperial Germany was the dominant power on the European continent. In the 1880s, reversing an earlier policy, Bismarck began to interest himself in competing with Britain and France in extra-European imperial adventures—primarily in Africa, but also in the Far East and in Oceania. It is this last that connects most directly with Rizal's trajectory.

A look at any atlas will show why. Situated broadly across the crow's flight from Hawaii to the Philippines lies a triangle of archipelagoes, with the Marianas at the northern apex and the Carolines and the Marshalls at the southwest and southeastern apices. The Marianas are roughly 1,400 miles due east of Manila, the westernmost Carolines about 600 miles due east from the southern Philippine island of Mindanao, and the Marshalls another 1,600 miles further east. From early imperialist times, when the Papacy had declared the Pacific a *mare clausum* for the rulers of the Spanish empire, up to the Napoleonic Wars, these archipelagoes had been generally regarded as under Spanish suzerainty. In fact Spain had little interest in them, except as coaling stations and as places to exile political troublemakers. Insofar as they were administered at all, the task was left to the Captain-General of the Philippines. But in 1878 Germany took the liberty of establishing a coaling station of its own in the Marshalls, following in the sea-steps of private commerce. In 1884, Berlin annexed northeast New Guinea (about 800 miles due south of the central Carolines), hitherto run by a private company. The following year it moved to claim the Carolines by raising the imperial flag on the island of Yap. Fearful of German power, the Spaniards hurried to crush local resistance to the hasty extension of Madrid's "sovereignty," and appealed to the Papacy to mediate. Rome confirmed this sovereignty, but the Germans won trade and coaling privileges, and through a deal with London took control of the Marshalls. The following year the Solomons were partitioned between the United Kingdom and Germany. In 1889, Samoa was made a tripartite protectorate under American, UK, and German joint control.[24] (Echoes of all this imperialist hubbub are clear in *El Filibusterismo*, where the good-hearted *indio* student Isagani is divided between his sympathy for the repressed native islanders and his solidarity with Spain against the menacing Germans.) Rizal was under no illusions about Bismarck personally, but he was enormously impressed by Germany, which with its Protestant sobriety, its orderliness and discipline, its impressive intellectual life and its industrial progress, made a salutary contrast to Mother Spain. He was certainly happy to have his first novel published, not in Madrid, but in Bismarck's *Hauptstadt*.

In France, the Prussian triumph at Sedan was followed by a brutal siege of Paris from which the shaky post-Louis-Napoléon government fled to Bordeaux, only to reappear at Versailles to sign a humiliating armistice and, later, treaty. In March 1871 the Commune took power in the abandoned city and held it for two months. Then Versailles, having capitulated to Berlin, seized the moment to attack and in one horrifying week executed roughly 20,000 *communards* or suspected sympathizers, a number higher than those killed in the recent war or during Robespierre's Terror of 1793–94. More than 7,500 were jailed or deported to distant places such as New Caledonia and Cayenne. Thousands of others fled to Belgium, England, Italy, Spain,

---

24. See the useful chronology on pp. 63–4 of Karl-Heinz Wionsek, ed., *Germany, the Philippines, and the Spanish–American War*, translated by Thomas Clark (Manila: National Historical Institute, 2000).

and the United States. In 1872, stringent laws were passed that ruled out all possibilities of organizing on the Left. Not till 1880 was there a general amnesty for exiled and imprisoned *communards*. Meantime, the Third Republic found itself strong enough to renew and reinforce Louis-Napoléon's imperialist expansion—in Indochina, Africa, and Oceania. A fair number of France's leading intellectuals and artists had either participated in the Commune (Courbet was its quasi-minister of culture, Rimbaud and Pissarro were active propagandists) or were sympathetic to it.[25] The ferocious repression of 1871 and after was a key factor in alienating these milieux from the Third Republic and stirring their sympathy for its victims at home and abroad. We shall look at this development in more detail later.

Sedan also caused the withdrawal of the French garrison in Rome, which had guaranteed the Papacy's dwindling territorial sovereignty, and its replacement by the forces of the new, increasingly repressive and inefficient Kingdom of Italy. The by now completely reactionary Pio Nono, aka Giovanni Mastai-Ferretti, deprived of all temporal power, declared himself and his office incarcerated, and struck back politico-spiritually with the threatened excommunication of any Catholic participating in the Kingdom's political institutions. This stance persisted until the happy concordat with Mussolini at the end of the 1920s. Italian imperialism of a mediocre sort began in East Africa, while rural misery in the South was so great that between 1887 and 1900, half a million Italians left the country every year. Rizal visited Rome briefly in 1887 but seems not to have noticed anything but antiquities.

On his return to Europe in February 1888 via the Pacific, Rizal made a brief stop in mid-Meiji Japan, and was impressed by its orderliness, energy, and ambition, and appalled by the rickshaws. It was gratifying, of course, to see a non-European people protect its independence and make rapid strides towards modernity. Though he spent a short time in Hong Kong, China itself seems to have been off his map. He reached San Francisco at election time, when anti-Asian demagogy was at its height. Enraged at being kept for days on board ship for "quarantine" purposes—the ship held about 650 Chinese, very useful for racist anti-immigration campaigning—he hurried across the continent as rapidly as he could. Nothing was less likely to impress him than the corruption of the Gilded Age, the post-Reconstruction repression of black former slaves, the brutal anti-miscegenation laws, the lynchings, and so on.[26] But he was already foreseeing American expansion across the Pacific. He then settled contentedly in

---

25. See the vivid account and superb analysis in Kristin Ross, *The Emergence of Social Space: Rimbaud and the Paris Commune* (Minneapolis: University of Minnesota Press, 1988); also James Joll, *The Anarchists* (Cambridge, MA: Harvard University Press, 1980), pp. 148–9.

26. See the detailed description in Guerrero, *The First Filipino*, p. 198.

London to do research on early Philippine history at the British Museum, and seems to have taken no interest in the gradually growing crisis over Ireland. (Living on Primrose Hill, was he aware that Engels was ensconced close by?)

But this apparently calm world of conservative political dominance, capital accumulation, and global imperialism was at the same time helping to create another kind of world, more directly related to Rizal's fiction. Indeed, already in 1883, he had sensed the direction of things to come.

> Europa amenazada continuamente de una conflagración espantosa; el cetro del mundo que se escapa de las temblorosas manos de la Francia caduca; las naciones del Norte preparándose á recogerlo. Rusia cuyo emperador tiene sobre sí la espada de Nihilismo como el antiguo Damocles, esto es Europa la civilizada . . .

> Europe constantly menaced by a terrifying conflagration; the scepter of the world slipping from the trembling hands of declining France; the nations of the North preparing to seize it; Russia, over the head of whose emperor hangs the sword of Nihilism, like Damocles in Antiquity, such is Europe the Civilized.[27]

LE DRAPEAU NOIR

The year Rizal was born, Mikhail Bakunin escaped to western Europe from Siberia where for a decade he had been serving a life sentence for his conspiratorial activities against tsardom in the 1840s. The following year, 1862, Turgenev published *Fathers and Sons*, his masterly study of the outlook and psychology of a certain type of Nihilist. Four years later, a Moscow student named Karakozov attempted to shoot Alexander II, and was hanged with four others in the great public square of Smolensk.[28] That same year Alfred Nobel took out a patent on dynamite, which though based on highly unstable nitroglycerine was both simple to use, stable, and easily portable. In March 1869 the 22-year-old Nihilist leader Sergei Nechayev left Russia; he met Bakunin in Geneva, where they coauthored the sensational *Catechism of a Revolutionary*, and returned to Moscow a few months later. Bakunin kept up (strained) relations with the Nihilist leader despite the notorious murder of a skeptical student follower, later fictionalized by Dostoievsky in *The Possessed*.[29]

---

27. *One Hundred Letters*, p. 174. Letter home from Madrid, dated October 28, 1883. Spain seems not worth mentioning!

28. For a *tableau vivant*, see Ramón Sempau, *Los victimarios* (Barcelona: Manent, 1901), p. 5. For an impressive listing of successful and failed *attentats* in Russia between 1877 and 1890, see Rafael Núñez Florencio, *El terrorismo anarquista, 1888–1909* (Madrid: Siglo Veintiuno de España, SA, 1983), pp. 19–20.

29. The *groupuscule* was characteristically named The People's Retribution. Nechayev fled back to Switzerland, but was extradited in 1873, and sentenced to twenty years in prison. In 1882 he was "found dead in his cell" *à la* Baader-Meinhof.

Alexander II's assassination by Narodnaya Volya revolutionaries in St Petersburg on March 1 1881.

The nihilist leader Sergei Nechayev.

Towards the end of the 1870s, by which time the Nihilists were being succeeded by small clusters of *narodniki* as the clandestine radical opposition to the autocracy, political assassination, successful and failed, had become quite common in Russia. 1878: in January, Vera Zasulich shot but failed to kill General Fyodor Trepov, military governor of St Petersburg; in August, Sergei Kravchinski stabbed to death General Mezentsov, head of the Tsar's secret police. 1879: in February, Grigori Goldenberg shot to death the governor of Kharkov, Prince Dmitri Kropotkin; in April, an attempt by Alexander Soloviev to kill the Tsar in the same manner failed; in November, Lev Hartmann's attempt to mine the imperial railway carriage proved abortive. 1880: Stepan Khalturin successfully blew up part of the Imperial Palace—8 died, 45 were wounded. Nobel's invention had now arrived politically. Then on March 1, 1881—fifteen months before Rizal landed in Marseilles—the spectacular bomb-assassination of the Tsar occurred, by a group calling itself Narodnaya Volya (the People's Will), an event that reverberated all over Europe.[30] (The assassination of US President Garfield a few months later was barely noticed.)

The storms of Russia were to have profound effects across Europe. They can be symbolically represented in one epoch by Bakunin (born in 1814), who died in 1876, and, in a second, by Prince Pyotr Kropotkin (born in 1842), who escaped from a Tsarist prison to western Europe that same year.

The Communist International's first two congresses, held in peaceable Switzerland in 1866 and 1867, went ahead quietly enough with Marx in the central position. But Bakunin's influence was strongly felt at the third congress held the following year in Brussels, and Bakuninists were already a majority at the fourth congress, held in Basle in 1869. The fifth congress was supposed to assemble in Paris, but Sedan made this impossible. By the time it was finally held, in 1872 in The Hague, it was hopelessly divided. In the year of Bakunin's death it was dissolved, though Bakuninist congresses

---

30. Núñez, *El terrorismo*, pp. 66–7; Norman Naimark, *Terrorists and Social Democrats: The Russian Revolutionary Movement under Alexander III* (Cambridge, MA: Harvard University Press, 1983), chapter 1; Derek Offord, *The Russian Revolutionary Movement in the 1880s* (Cambridge: Cambridge University Press, 1986), chapter 1; and especially David Footman, *Red Prelude*, second edition (London: Barrie & Rockleff, 1968), *passim*. The first bomb failed to touch the Tsar. Realizing this, a figure whom Sempau names "Miguel Ivanovitch Elnikof," but who was actually Ignatei Grinevitsky, came close enough before throwing a second bomb that he was killed along with his victim. An early suicide bomber, one could say. A valuable feature of Footman's book is a biographical appendix on fifty-five Narodnaya Volya activists. Thirteen were executed, fourteen died in prison, fourteen more survived imprisonment, eight escaped abroad, four committed suicide during or after their *attentats*, and two went to work for the secret police.

continued to be held till 1877.[31] That same year the word *anarchist* in its technical-political sense was coined, and spread rapidly and widely (though it was also obvious that there were competing and crosspollinating currents of thought about anarchism's aims and methods).[32]

Anarchism's emphasis on personal liberty and autonomy, its typical suspicion of hierarchical ("bureaucratic") organization, and its penchant for vitriolic rhetoric made its appeal especially great under political conditions of severe repression by rightwing regimes. Such regimes found it much easier to smash trade unions and political parties than to keep track of, penetrate, and destroy dozens of self-generated autonomous *groupuscules*. Anarchist theory was less contemptuous of peasants and rural labour than mainstream Marxism was then inclined to be. One could argue that it was also more viscerally anticlerical. Probably these conditions help to explain why revolutionary anarchism spread most successfully in still heavily peasant, Catholic post-Commune France, Restoration Spain, and post-unification Italy, Cuba—and even Gilded Age immigrant-worker America—while prospering much less than mainstream Marxism in largely Protestant, industrial, semidemocratic northern Europe.

In any event, at the end of the bleak 1870s there arose in intellectual anarchist circles the theoretical concept of "propaganda by the deed," spectacular *attentats* on reactionary authorities and capitalists, intended to intimidate the former and to encourage the oppressed to re-prepare themselves for revolution. Historians tend to mark the beginning of this new phase by the almost comically unsuccessful uprising of April 1877 in Benevento, northeast of Naples, organized by two young Neapolitans, Errico Malatesta and his rich friend Carlo Cafiero (who had earlier bankrolled Bakunin from the safe northern shore of Lake Maggiore), and twenty-five year old Sergei Mikhailovitch Kravchinski aka Stepniak (1852–95), who had joined the 1875 Bosnian

---

31. See the succinct account in Jean Maitron, *Le mouvement anarchiste en France* (Paris: Maspéro, 1975), vol. I (*Dès origines à 1914*), pp. 42–51.

32. Maitron offers some interesting data in this regard. The single most important theoretical anarchist publication was Jean Grave's *Le Révolté*, first published in safe Geneva in February 1879 with a print run that rose from 1,300 to 2,000 before Grave felt it was possible to relocate it to Paris (in 1885) and rename it *La Révolte*. By 1894, when it was smashed by the state in the wake of President Sadi Carnot's assassination, it had a 7,000 print run, with subscribers in France, Algeria, the United States, Ukania, Switzerland, Belgium, Spain, Italy, Holland, Rumania, Uruguay, India, Egypt, Guatemala, Brazil, Chile, and Argentina. No Russians. Its "apache" opposite number, Emile Pouget's satirical *Le Père Peinard* ("*Bons bougres, lisez tous les dimanches*"), had a slightly narrower stretch, which nonetheless, given that it was written in Parisian argot, is even more startling: Algeria, the United Kingdom, Tunisia, Argentina, Belgium, Spain, the United States, Italy, Switzerland, and Monaco. *Le mouvement*, pp. 141–6.

Errico Malatesta

uprising against the Turks, and would go on, as we have seen, to kill the head of the Tsar's secret police.[33] Put on trial, the two Italians were acquitted in the cheerful atmosphere created by the young Umberto I's

---

33. See the detailed account in Nunzio Pernicone, *Italian Anarchism, 1864–1892* (Princeton: Princeton University Press, 1993), pp. 118–28. Bakunin had settled in Florence in 1864, but moved to Naples in 1865, staying in the area till 1867. (He wrote to a Florentine follower: "There is infinitely more energy and genuine political and social life [here] than in Florence.") He instituted the first Italian section of the International there, and Malatesta was one of his earliest recruits. Malatesta recalled later that the Russian "was the man who brought a breath of fresh air to the dead mill-pond of Neapolitan traditions, who opened the eyes of youths who approached him to vast new horizons." In fact, the Mezzogiorno was a good place to start revolutionary activity since its heavily peasant economy had been ruined by the free-trade policies of Cavour and his successors, while its political class had come to feel they had no less been conquered by the House of Piedmont (in the aftermath of the Italian Reunification of 1861) than they had earlier been suppressed by the Spanish Bourbons. Pernicone also gives an excellent account of how Bakunin completely outmanoeuvred Marx and Engels in Italy, with the help of some stupidities of Engels and Mazzini's hysterical attacks on the Commune, for which there was huge sympathy among Italian progressives. As Bakunin put it pithily, Mazzini "has always wanted *the People for Italy*, and not *Italy for the People*." Ibid., pp. 17, 27, 44–53, and 24.

accession to the throne in 1878. (The same ambience allowed the young anarchist cook Giovanni Passanante to get off lightly when he narrowly failed to kill the young king with a knife etched with the words *Long Live the International Republic*.)[34] Two months after the Benevento affair, Andrea Costa, a close collaborator of Malatesta, gave a talk in Geneva theorizing the new tactic. In early August, Paul Brousse published an article in the radical *Bulletin de la Fédération Jurassienne* explaining that words on paper were no longer enough for awakening the *conscience populaire*; the Russians had shown the need to be just as ruthless as the Tsarist regime. The gentle Kropotkin then swung into action in the December 25, 1880 edition of *Le Révolté*, theoretically defining anarchism as "la révolte permanente par la parole, par l'écrit, par le poignard, le fusil, la dynamite . . . Tout est bon pour nous qui n'est pas la légalité" (permanent revolt by means of the spoken word, writing, the dagger, the gun, and dynamite . . . For us everything is good which is outside legality).[35] It remained only for *Le Drapeau Noir* to publish clandestinely on September 2, 1883 a "Manifeste des Nihilistes Français" in which the claim was made that:

Depuis trois ans que la ligue existe, plusieurs centaines de familles bourgeoises ont payé le fatal tribut, dévorées par un mal mystérieux que la médicine est impuissante á définir et á conjurer.

In the three years of the League's existence, several hundred bourgeois families have paid the fatal tribute, devoured by a mysterious sickness that medicine is powerless to define and to exorcise.

Revolutionaries were urged to continue the insinuated campaign of mass poisonings (Rizal had just made his first happy trip to Paris a few months before).[36] These were all signs that some anarchists were thinking about a new kind of violence no longer solely targeted, *à la Russe*, against state leaders, but rather against those regarded as class enemies.

We shall look in more detail later at cases of "early terrorism" by young anarchists. But a quick glance at the spate of spectacular assassinations that erupted in the twenty years prior to the onset of the Great War will show some interesting features.

---

34. Joll, *The Anarchists*, pp. 102–5.
35. Maitron, *Le mouvement*, pp. 77–8.
36. *Ibid.*, p. 206.

Table 1 Assassinations

Date	Victim	Place/Method of Assassination	Assassin	Political Orientation	Nationality
1894	Sadi Carnot	Lyon/Stabbed	Sante Jeronimo Caserio	Anarchist	Italian
1897	Cánovas	Santa Águeda/Shot	Michele Angiolillo	Anarchist	Italian
1898	Elizabeth	Geneva/Stabbed	Luigi Luccheni	Anarchist	Italian
1900	Umberto I	Monza/Shot	Gaetano Bresci	Anarchist	Italian
1901	McKinley	Buffalo/Shot	Leon Czogolsz	Anarchist	Polish
1903	Alexander	Belgrade/Shot	Soldiers	Nationalists	Serbian
1904	Von Plehve	St Petersburg/Bombed	E.Z. Sazonov	Social Revolutionary	Russian
1905	Sergei	St Petersburg/Bombed	Kaliayev	Social Revolutionary	Russian
1908	Carlos/Luiz	Lisbon/Shot	Alfredo Costa and Manuel Buiça	Radical republicans	Portuguese
1909	Ito	Harbin/Shot	An Jung-geun	Nationalist	Korean
1911	Stolypin	St Petersburg/Shot	Dmitri Bogrov	Anarchist	Russian
1913	George	Salonika/Shot	Alexander Schinas	Unclear, said to be "mad"	Greek?
1914	Franz Ferdinand	Sarajevo/Shot	Gavrilo Princip	Nationalist	Serbian

The first thing to notice is that all the major states are on the list, except for the United Kingdom and Germany within Europe, and China and the Ottoman Empire outside.[37] Second, the anarchist assassinations of 1894–1901 were copycatted by radical nationalists thereafter. Third, while the nationalists typically killed their own rulers, anarchist assassins served their cause across national boundaries. Lastly, the prominence of Italians among the anarchists is very striking, and seems to confirm Pernicone's reference to "the unique role played by Italians as missionaries of the anarchist ideal. Political refugees and emigrants, they established libertarian enclaves among

37. In fact there were two genuine anarchist attempts to kill Kaiser Wilhelm I in 1878, by Max Hödel on May 11, and by Karl Nobiling on June 2 (Pernicone, *Italian Anarchism*, p. 148). Another was uncovered after an explosion at police headquarters in Frankfurt. Its purported "anarchist" leader, August Reinsdorf, was quickly executed, while police chief Rumpf was assassinated shortly afterward: a murky affair, in which the manipulative hand of Rumpf is quite probable. In the years 1883 to 1885, there were bomb plots in London against the Tower, Victoria Station, and the House of Commons. See Núñez, *El terrorismo*, p. 18. These "events" were quickly reflected in Henry James's *Princess Casamassima* (1886), and much later in Conrad's *The Secret Agent* (1907) and *Under Western Eyes* (1911). Mention should also be made of the May 1882 Fenian assassination of Lord Cavendish, the new Chief Secretary for Ireland, and his undersecretary, though their status was well below that of the figures mentioned above, and though the Fenians, like the nationalists who killed Franz Ferdinand, were far from being anarchists.

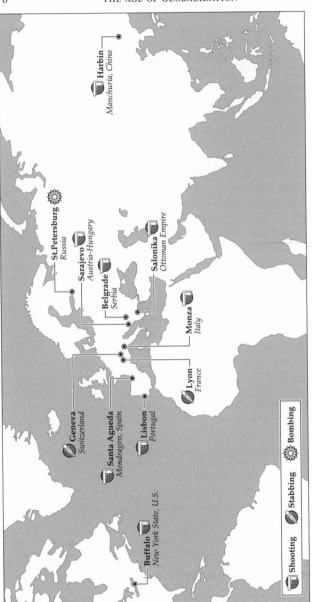

Harbin
Manchuria, China

St.Petersburg
Russia

Sarajevo
Austria-Hungary

Belgrade
Serbia

Salonika
Ottoman Empire

Monza
Italy

Geneva
Switzerland

Santa Agueda
Mondragon, Spain

Lisbon
Portugal

Lyon
France

Buffalo
New York State, U.S.

Shooting   Stabbing   Bombing

Assassinations

Police Photographs of François Ravachol after his arrest in March 1892

Vera Zasulich (left); Sante Caserio, the assassin of French president Sadi Carnot, in captivity, June 1894 (right)

*The shooting of President William McKinley by the Polish anarchist Czogolsz at
the Pan-American Exposition in Buffalo, New York, on September 6 1901.*

Italian communities in France, Switzerland, England, Spain, the United
States, Argentina, Brazil, Egypt and Tunisia."[38] Malatesta himself spent the
years 1885–89 proselytizing in and out of Buenos Aires.[39]

And Rizal? He had left Spain in 1885, well before the first wave of
anarchist "outrages" began there in 1888. The same is true of his time in

---

38. Pernicone, *Italian Anarchism*, p. 3. A supplementary, and contemporary,
explanation is provided by Francesco Nitti, then a professor of political economy at the
University of Naples, and much later prime minister, who amusingly lamented: "We
must add that in the schools of Italy, an error never to be too much deplored, they make
an apology for regicide. Unlearned teachers do not explain the difference between
martyr and murderer. The history of ancient Rome is full of murders of tyrants or
aspirants to tyranny. An individual becomes thus the avenger and deliverer of society. I
take up by chance a manual of history, used in a great number of Italian schools. It is
astonishing to observe how many tyrannicides they justify, from Brutus to Agesilao
Milano. There is praise for all. There was a time when Italy, especially Central Italy, was
full of little tyrants; the regicide became an emancipator. The tradition has been
unfortunately perpetuated. Even the poets, in like manner, have not refused to applaud
political murder, not only the less odious regicides, but also the worst 'Italian Anarchists.'" *North American Review*, 167:5 (November 1898), pp. 598–607, at p. 607.

39. *Ibid.*, p. 7.

A contemporary sketch of Luigi Luccheni's assassination of Empress Elisabeth of Austria, September 1898 (left); Cánovas (right)

On February 4, 1905, Grand Duke Sergei Alexandrovich's carriage was bombed by Ivan Kaliayev in Moscow.

Paris. Most of his post-1885 experience in Europe was in Germany, England, and Belgium, countries where anarchist activity was fairly insignificant. But he was an avid reader of newspapers, and followed world political trends with eager interest. The obvious question that arises is: did he actually know any European radicals personally? The evidence is circumstantial, but interesting.

In his old age, Rizal's good friend Trinidad Pardo de Tavera wrote an article describing his close relations with two generations of Russian Nihilists in Paris. He said that like many others he had been an admirer of Alexander II.

> También admiraba la osadía y el enorme sentimiento de responsabilidad de los nihilistas de quienes tenía referencias que me parecían muy apasionados por proceder de mi profesor de ruso, Michael [Mikhail] Atchinatski, famoso nihilista condenado ya en aquello época tres veces á la pena de muerte por atentados contra la vida de aquel mismo Tsar.

> Yet at the same time I admired the daring and the enormous sense of responsibility of the Nihilists, about whom I had information that seemed to me all the more moving in that it came from my professor of Russian, Michael Atchinatski, a famous Nihilist whom at that time had already been three times sentenced to death for attempts on the life of that same Tsar.

The "terrible Nihilist" had fled to Paris to escape the hangman, but, alas, Pardo commented, tuberculosis killed him only three months after his great enemy's destruction.

The rest of the article was devoted to two Russian girls to whom Pardo had been introduced by his professor of medicine, the "famous Tardieu." When the surprised Filipino ventured that they would have very little in common, the great man replied thus:

> Lo sé, lo sé, pero son vuestros hermanos espirtuales, de pueblos dominados por las tiranías religiosas y políticas, y presentes aquí en este patria, porque unos y otros venían en la seguridad de nuestra libertad.

> I know, I know . . . But they are your spiritual sisters. All of you come from countries dominated by religious and political tyrannies, and are here now in this country because you have reached the safety of our liberty.

Pardo went to visit the pair quite often and became fond of them. Both were from well-off families in Kazan, and had gone to St Petersburg to study medicine. There they became active Nihilists in their spare time, denouncing the Tsarist autocracy, police terror, and "Siberia." As the Okhrana closed in on them, their parents summoned them to go home, threatening to cut off funds if they did not, but the girls, each about twenty years old, decided to flee to Paris and continue their studies there. Terribly poor, they survived on odd jobs and occasional translations. Under surveillance by the French police and the Russian embassy, they never complained, and tenderly looked after dying older Nihilists they knew. Pardo commented that no one could doubt the goodness of their hearts and their altruism, and this won them "el aprecio y el respeto de los estudiantes de todas las Facultades que constituyen el pueblo soberano del Arrabal Latino" (the admiration and respect of the students of all the Faculties who constitute the sovereign country of the Latin Quarter). They stayed in Paris until the accession of Nicholas II in 1894, when they returned home. But the following year they were tried for participation in an *attentat* against the new tsar, and were sentenced to life imprisonment in Siberia. Maria Michaelovna Lujine died on the way there, of the tuberculosis she had contracted in Paris, and Luise Ivanovna Krilof died a few months later, killed by the same disease, in the prison of Tobolsk.[40]

Pardo's Russian teacher was dead before Rizal arrived in Europe, but he would surely have heard about the famous Nihilist from his friend. And it seems most unlikely that he would not have visited the rooms of the two Russian girls, along with Pardo, and chatted with them over the samovar always kept hot for guests. What is much less clear is whether they were strictly Nihilists. One suspects that in a Paris probably not very well informed about the intricate development of new subversive undergrounds in Russia, the term "Nihilists" served to cover a wide range of such groups.

CACIQUE SPAIN

Rizal's third world was that of Spain and its once-vast empire—what was left in the 1880s was only Cuba, Puerto Rico, the Philippines, the Marianas and Carolines, Spanish Morocco and the Berlin-acquired, goldless Rio de Oro. In the nineteenth century, this world was unique in the zigzag of insurrectionary explosions in the metropole and in the colonies. (One will not find anything

40. See Pardo's "Las Nihilistas," *The Women's Outlook* (Manila), November 10, 1922. Pardo's uncle Joaquín (who had cared for him after his father's early death), moved to Paris in 1875, after four years of exile in the Marianas, and summoned his nephew to join him. Like Rizal in Madrid, he studied both medicine (Sorbonne) and letters (École Nationale des Langues Orientales Vivantes), graduating in 1885. Though specializing in the languages of the Malay world, he knew both Russian and Sanskrit. For an astute account of Pardo's chequered political career and intellectual contributions, see Resil Mojares' just published *Brains of the Nation, Pedro Paterno, T.H. Pardo de Tavera, Isabelo de los Reyes, and the Production of Modern Knowledge* (Quezon City: Ateneo de Manila University Press, 2006), pp. 121–252.

remotely comparable till after the Second World War. For France: the fuse was set by Ho Chi Minh's political and Vo Nguyen Giap's military victory at Dien Bien Phu, and set alight by Algeria's FLN revolt leading to the collapse of the Fourth Republic, De Gaulle's return to power, and the OAS's retaliatory terrorism. For Portugal: military failures in Angola, Mozambique, and Guiné-Bissau led to the bloodless coup against Salazarist autocracy in Lisbon in April 1974.) It is worthwhile considering briefly the main features of this interactive zigzagging, for it was a phenomenon on which José Rizal was well informed, and by which his thinking was shaped.

In 1808, the odious future Fernando VII had organized a military revolt in Aranjuez which accomplished its main aim, the forced abdication of his father, Carlos IV. But Napoléon, at the height of his power, took this opportunity to send troops into Spain (occupying Madrid), on the pretext of a major intervention in Portugal. Fernando, who had rushed to Bayonne to negotiate legitimization of his succession with the Secretary of the World-Spirit, was immediately imprisoned. Joseph Buonaparte was then put on the Spanish throne. Resistance and rebellion broke out almost simultaneously in Andalusia and in Hidalgo's Mexico. In 1810, a liberal-dominated Cortes met in Cádiz, which produced in 1812 Spain's first constitutional order. The colonies, including the Philippines, were given legislative representation.[41] Napoléon's defeat brought Fernando back to power in Madrid with the full support of the Unholy Alliance. In 1814, he refused to recognize the constitution, inaugurated a new reactionary absolutism, and, in spite of a ruined economy, attempted to arrest the American revolutions for whom nationalism and in-Spain-repressed liberalism were the two main principles. Fernando failed completely in continental Spanish America, but held the loyalty of slave-owning Peninsulars and creoles in the Spanish Caribbean—who were out of Bolívar's charismatic orbit, and petrified by the successful slave revolution in Haiti.

And the Philippines? The Sarrat revolt of 1815, named from a township in the Ilocano-populated northwest corner of Luzon, was quickly and violently repressed. In 1820, a military revolt in Andalusia, headed by the mayor of Cádiz, forced Fernando briefly to accept a liberal constitutional order. But Castlereagh's London, Metternich's Vienna, Alexander I's Petersburg, and Fernando's kinsman in Paris would have none of this. A French military expedition restored autocracy in 1823, the mayor of Cádiz

---

41. The Philippines kept this representation in all subsequent constitutional moments, until its rights were abolished—well after the collapse of the South American empire—in 1837. Rizal told his friend Blumentritt that his maternal grandfather had in fact sat as a Philippine representative in this metropolitan legislature. See *The Rizal–Blumentritt Correspondence*, vol. 1, third unnumbered page after p. 268 (Letter of November 8, 1888, from London).

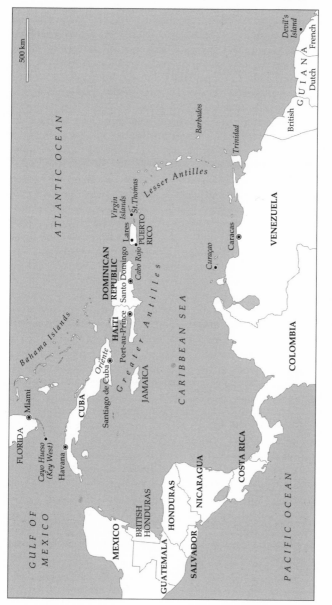

Three Worlds 2: The Caribbean

was hanged, drawn, and quartered, and hundreds of liberals and republicans were executed, brutally imprisoned or forced to flee for their lives. That same year, and in response to these events in the metropole, a creole-led mutiny occurred in the colonial military which came within an ace of seizing Manila, and would have done so had it not been betrayed from within.[42] Its leader, the mestizo Captain Andrés Novales, had earlier fought for Madrid against the South American independence movements.[43]

One can easily detect a comparable conjuncture in the years 1868–74. Isabel's regime was overthrown in September 1868 by a military–civil coup in which General Prim y Prats, the machiavellian liberal politician Práxedes Sagasta, and the conspiracy-minded radical republican Manuel Ruiz Zorilla were key players. We have already seen the consequences of this explosion in Cuba and the Philippines. But in Spain itself the next six years were ones of extraordinary political turbulence. Prim y Prats's assassination at the end of 1870 doomed the monarchy of Amadeo of Savoy, which led to the proclamation of a Spanish Republic on February 11, 1873. The new regime lasted in reality only eleven months—during which time it experienced four Swiss-style rotating presidents—till the generals moved in (guided behind the scenes by the sly Andalusian conservative politician Antonio Cánovas del Castillo), dissolving the Cortes in January 1874, and restoring the Bourbon monarchy in the person of Alfonso XII at the end of that year. Among the key reasons for this *démarche* was, as one might have surmised, the imminent threat posed by Céspedes's Cuban revolt to the integrity of what was left of the old Spanish empire. Meantime, however, there was an extraordinary effervescence in the Spanish public sphere. Republicans were briefly legal for the first time in living memory. Bakuninian and Marxian radicalism gained their first political footholds, and in the widely popular "cantonalist" political movement of 1873 for radical decentralization of the polity many young anarchists and other radicals got their first experience of open, mass politics.

With this background we can now consider Restoration Spain as Rizal encountered it at the beginning of the 1880s. Its dominant politician, Antonio Cánovas del Castillo, was born in 1828—the same year as Tolstoi—to a petit bourgeois family in Málaga. A prolific and accomplished historian, he was

---

42. D.G.E. Hall, *A History of South-East Asia*, 3rd edition (London and New York: St Martin's Press, 1968), p. 721. For details on these commotions, typically organized by creoles, see Sarkisyanz, *Rizal*, pp. 76–9.

43. Luis Camara Dery, "When the World Loved the Filipinos," *Kasaysayan*, I:4 (December 2001), p. 57. Foolishly, he also proclaimed himself Emperor of the Philippines. Interestingly, Mojares, *Brains*, p.412, reports that some of the rebel officers were Mexicans.

also a devious and ruthless politician.[44] A liberal cabinet minister at thirty-two, he moved quickly to the right after the fall of Isabel, and became the key architect of the Bourbon Restoration. His ambition, aside from accumulating power, was to create a stable order, in a state notorious for decades for its chaotic inner life. Order meant ending the country's civil wars and eliminating caudillism; in this he was successful during his life, but they returned with a vengeance later. It also meant repressing the radical Left and any signs of serious anticolonial separatism in the empire. In effect, one could see him as a sort of Spanish Bismarck. After Cánovas's assassination in 1897, the ex-Reichskanzler would say: "He was the only European with whom I could have a conversation."[45] But Cánovas recognized that Bismarckianism depended on royal favor, and so was ultimately ephemeral. Deeper and more lasting order he detected in the United Kingdom, where power passed safely back and forth between conservative and liberal elites in a systemic way, while industrialization advanced headlong, and imperialism by leaps and strides. This is why he was wont to say that he was a great admirer of British parliamentary government, and why he proceeded to set up, with the help of Sagasta, a peculiar parody of the Gladstone–Disraeli duumvirate. Schumacher has pithily described a corrupt, cacique-ridden regime which lasted essentially till the end of the century: "[T]he two leaders permitted the entire system to be vitiated through managed elections . . . As more serious crises came to be resolved, each would yield power to the other and the successor government would *then* proceed to manage an election in which a respectable minority of candidates would be elected with a scattering of outstanding republicans and Carlists to give verisimilitude to the Cortes."[46] Salvador de Madariaga put the same judgment in local terms. Canovism, he observed, was intended to create a "bullfight" politics, where elections were manipulated, caciquism was the order of the day, and the Cortes was a monumental theater, which could play in classical, gypsy, or musical comedy genres depending on Cánovas's direction and script.[47] The Spanish Disraeli ruled in 1875–81, 1883–85, 1890–92, and 1895–97, while his Gladstone filled most of the spaces in between. The worst domestic and colonial repressions typically occurred under Cánovas, while timid reforms were occasionally accomplished under Sagasta.

---

44. His ablest lieutenant towards the end of his career, the future prime minister Antonio Maura, said of him: "Da frío oírlo y espanto leerle" (Listening to him made one shiver, and reading him feel terrified). Frank Fernández, *La sangre de Santa Águeda. Angiolillo, Betances y Cánovas* (Miami: Ediciones Universal, 1994), p. 4.

45. *Ibid.*, p. 1.

46. Schumacher, *The Propaganda Movement*, pp. 21–2. My italics.

47. Fernández, *La sangre*, p. 5.

THE ORDERS: DISPOSSESSED AND POSSESSED

For what follows next, it is crucial to understand Cánovas's policies toward the generally reactionary Spanish Church. In 1836, the Regent's first minister, Juan Mendizábal, had decreed and carried out the expropriation of all the property of the religious Orders in Spain; during Glorious 1868, Antonio Ortiz, head of the Gracia y Justicia ministry, had abolished the Orders themselves—in metropolitan Spain. Mendizábal was no Thomas Cromwell, so that the Orders were compensated by being put on the state's payroll. The clerical properties were put up for auction, and, especially in rich rural Andalusia, were snapped up by members of the nobility, high civilian and military officials, and wealthy bourgeois, many of them absentee owners. Relatively mild Church exploitation was succeeded by ruthless agribusiness methods. Hundreds of thousands of peasants lost access to land, and swelled the numbers of paupers, half-starved day laborers, and the "bandits" for which the region became famous after 1840. The Andalusian Cánovas made no attempt to roll back what Mendizábal had decreed, though he sought and secured strong Church backing against the rising tide of liberalism, Masonry, republicanism, socialism and anarchism.[48] (It was he who in 1884 sent the police into Central University at the call of the bishops.) Nor did he restore the independent position of the Orders, who, after all, were directly responsible to Rome not to himself. But there was one striking exception to all these changes—and that was the colonial Philippines.

It had begun centuries earlier, in the time of Felipe II. The conscience of the aging monarch had been sufficiently stung by the revelations by de las Casas and others of the inhuman depredations of the conquistadors in the Americas that he decided to entrust his last major imperial acquisition largely to the religious Orders, who indeed managed the relatively peaceful conversion of the bulk of the local population. The remote Philippines had no "lay" attractions comparable to Potosí, and so the Orders largely ran the colony, especially outside Manila. In the course of time, the Dominicans and Augustinians especially acquired vast properties both in Manila real estate and in hacienda agriculture.[49] Furthermore, from the start the Orders had

---

48. On Mendizábal and Ortiz, see *ibid.*, p. 134, note 16. More generally on the consequences of the confiscation of Order properties, especially in Andalusia, see Bécarud and Lapouge, *Anarchistes*, pp. 14–20.

49. The exception was the Jesuits, expelled from his realms by Carlos III in 1768. A coalition of the monarchs of France, Spain, Portugal, and Naples successfully pressured Clement XIV to suppress them worldwide in 1773. Pius VII brought the Order back to legal life in 1814, but its members had lost a lot of ground. In the Philippines they did not reappear till 1859, and for a long time were the poor relations of their clerical rivals.

insisted on carrying out conversions via the dozens of native languages (only then would conversions be deep and sincere, it was claimed) which they assiduously attempted to learn. This monopoly on linguistic access to the natives gave them an enormous power which no secular group shared; fully aware of this, the friars persistently opposed the spread of the Spanish language. Even in Rizal's time, it has been estimated that only about 3 percent of the population of the archipelago had any command of the metropolitan language, something unique in the Spanish empire (with the partial exception of ex-Jesuit Paraguay). In the nineteenth century the Spanish political class understood this situation very well, and, perhaps rightly, reckoned that without the Orders Spanish rule in the Philippines would collapse.[50] Hence the only Order-controlled seminaries tolerated in Spain after Ortiz's *démarche* were there simply to provide new young friars for the Philippines. At the same time, many friars traumatized by their 'defenestration' in Spain headed off for safety and power on the other side of the world. Thus, in the Cánovas era, friar power was as peculiar to the Philippines as slavery was to Cuba. But slavery was finally abolished in 1886, while in Manila friar power was not seriously undermined till the collapse of the whole system in 1898. From another angle, one can see that Filipino

---

50. Compare the Netherlands East Indies, possession of another old empire in rapid decline. Serious education in Dutch only began there at the start of the twentieth century—after three hundred years of Dutch meddling in the archipelago, and after Spanish rule in the Philippines had collapsed. The great "multinational" East Indies Company which ruled for the first two centuries saw no reason to waste money on schools. The nineteenth-century colonial state was too busy exploiting the colony (to recover financially from the Napoleonic Wars and the huge Diponegoro rebellion of the 1820s) to do more than its predecessor. Training in native languages only began seriously in the 1870s, and concentrated only on Javanese. Besides, in the Netherlands itself, the ruling class was still using Dutch mostly to speak to maids and shopkeepers. Democratization, especially expansion of the suffrage, after 1880 began to put nationalist pressure on colonial policy, such that when a colonial educational system began to appear, the medium finally was Dutch. By the 1920s there was thus a small *ilustrado* nationalist elite—four decades later than in the Philippines—which did initiate nationalist and socialist agitation. But it was too late. The Japanese onslaught of 1942 put an administrative end to Dutch, and the last Indonesian novel of any signifiance written in Dutch was a product of the 1930s. Of the 70 million population of the colony in 1930, almost completely native, at best 0.5 percent understood the colonial language. But in the long meantime, from East India Company days, a kind of pidgin Malay was in use, not only in interisland commerce, but in the administrative practice of the rulers themselves. (The geographical location of the Indies on the highway of maritime transoceanic commerce compared favorably with the Philippines' marginal position.) When a vernacular press began to develop, from the 1890s, "Malay" so far outstripped its Dutch, Javanese, and Arabic competitors in the market that it was ready to be inscribed by young nationalists in 1928 as, not pidgin Malay, but the "Indonesian language." Dutch lingered on till the 1960s as the private language of the *ilustrado* elite, but no one spoke it in public after 1942.

anticolonial activists were inevitably faced with a hard choice which was not open to Cubans and Puerto Ricans: to reject Spanish or spread it. We shall see later on how this question shaped the narrative of *El Filibusterismo*.

BLACK WINGS

When an alarmed Captain-General Izquierdo suspected that the machinations of the International were behind the extraordinary Cavite strike of the autumn of 1872, what made the idea plausible to him? After Isabel fled Madrid in September 1868, Bakunin was much quicker off the mark than Marx. He immediately sent his close Italian friend, the ex-Mazzinist, ex-Garibaldist Giuseppe Fanelli, to Barcelona and Madrid to inform and organize the most advanced local radical activists.[51] In spite of the fact that Fanelli knew no Spanish, he had an instant and powerful impact. (Probably people in the Italian community in Barcelona helped out.) The Centro Federal de las Sociedades was formed early the following year, and sent two Bakuninist delegates to swell the Russian's majority at the Basle Congress of the International in September. Early in 1870 the Federación Regional Española (FRE), the Spanish section of the International, was publishing *La Solidaridad*, and a little later it held its first and only Congress in early-industrial Barcelona.[52]

Meantime, Marx's Cuban son-in-law, Paul Lafargue, who had been with the Commune in Paris, but then moved to Bordeaux to widen support for the Parisian insurrectionaries, finally fled across the Pyrenees with his family (his newborn baby died en route).[53] Once settled in Madrid (June 1871) under the alias Pablo Fargas, he followed Marx's instructions to combat the influence of the Bakuninists. But it was pretty late in the day. In December, the Cortes banned the International. During the year or so that Lafargue was in Spain,

---

51. On Fannelli and his background, see Pernicone, *Italian Anarchism*, pp. 19–20. Yet another Neapolitan, and an architect and engineer to boot, he had been prominent in revolutionary activities in Lombardy and Rome in 1848–49, and had fought with Garibaldi's Thousand in Sicily, who brought Bourbon rule in Southern Italy to its knees. Elected to the new national parliament in 1865, he refused to take part in the institution's deliberations, but used the railway pass that was a perquisite of office to tour the country incessantly, spreading radical propaganda.

52. Esenwein, *Anarchist Ideology*, pp. 14–18; Bécarud and Lapouge, *Anarchistes*, pp. 27–9.

53. How did a Cuban manage to have so fine a French name? His grandparents on both sides had been "French Haitians," and had moved to Cuba to escape Toussaint's revolution. One grandfather (Lafargue) was a small slave-owning planter and the other (Abraham Armagnac) a Jewish merchant. One grandmother was a Haitian mulatta, and the other a Jamaican Caribe. Both Paul and his parents were born in Santiago de Cuba. The family moved back to the grandparents' native Bordeaux in 1851, escaping this time from Cuban rebellion and Spanish repression. Paul carried a Spanish passport, and was bilingual in French and Spanish.

he had no luck in Barcelona, but he did help start a Marxist group in Madrid. Lafargue was the only pro-Marx "Spanish" delegate at the disastrous 1872 Congress of the International in The Hague. Not till 1879 was a semi-clandestine Marxist Socialist Party formed, and it did not come out of the closet till the rule of Sagasta in the early 1880s. Its organ, *El Obrero*, first appeared in 1882.[54] Many more years would pass before it became a central player in the politics of the Spanish Left. There is no special reason to think that Rizal ever heard of it while a student in Madrid.

But he was certainly well aware of what developed next, and we shall find traces of this in *El Filibusterismo*. Cánovas's six-year regime of repression was replaced by the milder Sagasta in 1881, very soon after the assassination of Alexander II, and after a meeting in London of various anarchists had moved to confirm the necessity of violent "propaganda by the deed." The change of government in Spain allowed the FRE top leadership, mostly Catalan, to believe the way was now open for wider, and legal, organizing of the working class, and in September it replaced the FRE by the FTRE (Federación de Trabajadores de la Región Española). Since this policy diverged from the radical resolutions approved in London, they did what they could to keep these decisions under wraps. But the news leaked out anyway. In spite of a spectacular increase in its affiliated membership—58,000 people in one year—tension grew quickly between the legalists in industrial Barcelona and the radicals with their base in rural Andalusia. At the 1882 Congress in Seville, most of the Andalusians broke away to form a group they called The Disinherited (Los Desheredados). 1883 was a difficult year in any case. A worldwide depression had set in, with especially severe consequences in Andalusia, where hunger and immiseration grew rapidly. Furthermore, Cánovas returned to power. A new wave of rural arson and robbery spread all over the prime minister's home region, causing real panic in many places.[55] The police arrested and tortured hundreds of people, anarchists, peasants, and bandits, claiming shortly thereafter to have uncovered a vast insurrectionary conspiracy called La Mano Negra [Black Hand].[56] Far from offering

---

54. Bécarud and Lapouge, *Anarchistes*, pp. 29–34; David Ortiz, Jr, *Paper Liberals. Press and Politics in Restoration Spain* (Westport, CT: Westwood Press, 2000), p. 58.

55. According to Bécarud and Lapouge, *Anarchistes*, p. 36, an earlier such wave had occurred in 1878–80.

56. Ramón Sempau observed that now "se renovaron prácticas olvidadas" [forgotten practices (i.e. of the Inquisition era) were renewed]. *Los victimarios*, p. 275. Two famous Spanish novels, published a quarter of a century later under a liberalized regime, afford fine evocations of the undergrounds of Barcelona and Andalusia in this period: Pío Baroja's *Aurora roja* (Red Dawn) and Vicente Blasco Ibáñez's *La bodega* (The Cellar), both originally published in Madrid in 1905.

its support, the FTRE, hoping to avoid repression, firmly disassociated itself from what it termed criminal activities. This stance did not help, and the organization declined steadily till its dissolution in 1888.[57] We shall see, however, that the specter of La Mano Negra and the Andalusian panic are reflected in the latter half of *El Filibusterismo*.

A BOSOM FRIEND

Sagasta returned to power in 1885, and held it until 1890. It was this government that finally abolished slavery in Cuba, enacted a rather liberal law on association which allowed radicals to start organizing legally once again, and substantially expanded press freedom. It even made some serious attempts at reforms in the Philippines. In 1887 the Spanish Penal code was extended to the archipelago, followed in 1889 by a similar extension of the Spanish commercial code, the law on administrative litigation, and the civil code, except with regard to marriage (the Church in the Philippines bitterly insisted on this). But it was exactly in July 1885 that Rizal left Spain more or less for good, proceeding to France and Germany, and busying himself with further medical studies and with the completion of his first novel. When it was published in the spring of 1887, he decided the time had come to return to the Philippines. Before doing so, however, he went to Austria to meet for the first and last time Ferdinand Blumentritt, his favorite correspondent and undoubtedly his closest friend and counsellor. As we shall see a lot of the Austrian scholar later on, it seems worth describing him and the nature of the friendship between the two men.

The son of a minor imperial official, Blumentritt was born in Prague in 1853 (thus eight years before Rizal), and lived there till he graduated from Charles University in 1877 with a degree in geography and history. He then moved to the also Bohemian town of Leitmeritz, where he taught at the non-classical secondary school for the rest of his career. His responsibilities—and a visible hypochondria—kept him from bodily travel outside Bohemia for the rest of his life. But while he was still a child, a paternal aunt who had married a Peruvian creole returned from Peru after her loyalist husband was killed by Bolívar's forces at the climactic battle of Ayacucho in 1824. The boy was enchanted by the exotic books and Spanish colonial paraphernalia in her house. Like Rizal a gifted linguist, he acquired early a reading knowledge of Spanish, Portuguese, Dutch, and English. Within the Spanish empire, he was especially fascinated by the Philippines, and published his first book about

---

57. See the succinct account of these developments in Núñez, *El terrorismo*, pp. 38–42.

the country in 1879. Three years later, just as Rizal was first arriving in Europe, Blumentritt's landmark *Versuch einer Ethnographie der Philippinen* appeared, the first systematic professional treatise on all the dozens of ethnolinguistic groups in Las Filipinas. More than two hundred publications followed over the next thirty years, covering the country's languages, history, geography, and politics. In effect, he rapidly became Europe's leading scholarly authority on the archipelago.

This was by no means the only reason that intelligent young Filipinos were drawn to him, and tried to enlist him in their cause. He was perfectly loyal to Emperor Franz Joseph, but Austro-Hungary was the one European empire where, as Musil sardonically put it, "the words 'colony' and 'overseas' had the ring of something as yet utterly untried and remote." A church-going Catholic, he had little time for the reactionary Spanish Church. A liberal constitutionalist and democrat in politics, he was immediately sympathetic to the plight of the Philippines. Not at all a pedant, he threw himself into municipal politics, organized amateur theatricals, enjoyed sketching, and honed a sharp and witty pen. He was even a good cook, and astonished Rizal when he arrived in Leitmeritz with a feast made up of all the main Filipino dishes. And his house felt like a combined library and museum crammed with Philippine artefacts.

The two short men were made for each other, and realized this soon after Rizal sent his first formal letter of self-introduction from Heidelberg in September 1886. Within eighteen months they had switched from *Sie* to *Du*. Rizal provided the older man with a torrent of information about the Philippines, especially his own Tagalog region; Blumentritt introduced him to relevant scholars in Berlin, Leiden, and London, and showed him sources on early Philippines history of which the Filipino had no knowledge. By 1891 it was natural for Rizal to ask his friend to write the foreword to *El Filibusterismo*.[58]

THE FIRST HOMECOMING

On coming to power for the second time, Sagasta had appointed a new, relatively moderate Captain-General of the Philippines, Lt. Gen. Emilio Tererro y Perinat, who in turn relied heavily on two capable anticlerical subordinates, both of them Masons: the civil governor of Manila, José Centeno García, a mining engineer with republican sympathies, and an

---

58. These paragraphs are partly drawn from the first three short chapters of Harry Sichrovsky, *Ferdinand Blumentritt: An Austrian Life for the Philippines* (Manila: National Historical Institute, 1987), which is a translation of *Der Revolutionär von Leitmeritz*, originally published in Vienna in 1983.

unusual twenty years of experience in the Philippines; and the director-general of civil administration, Benigno Quiroga López Ballesteros, a younger man who had once been a liberal deputy in the Cortes. (Centeno would appear, unnamed but honored, in *El Filibusterismo*.) The two men vigorously enforced laws that took municipal justice away from the mayors and gave them to new justices of the peace, and likewise reassigned the provincial governors' judicial powers to judges of the first instance. The intended effect of both measures was to cut back the power of the friars, who had traditionally held undisputed sway over local government via control of local executives.[59]

Rizal was aware of this promising atmosphere. After leaving Blumentritt, he did a quick tour of Switzerland, visited Rome, and then set sail from Marseilles. He was back in Manila by August 5, 1887. News of *Noli me tangere* (and a few copies) had preceded him, and he found himself a famous, and infamous, man. The Orders and the Archbishop of Manila demanded that the book be prohibited as heretical, subversive, and slanderous, and that the author be severely punished. But, perhaps to his own surprise, Rizal was summoned to a tête-à-tête with Terrero himself, who said he wanted to read the novel, and asked for a copy. We do not know what the Captain-General thought of it, but the novel was not banned under his rule.[60] After a few days in Manila, Rizal returned home to Calamba to be with his family, and open a medical practice. Then his many enemies went to work. In a letter to Blumentritt of September 5, 1887 he wrote this:

> man droht mich jeden Tag . . . Mein Vater lässt mich nie allein spazieren, noch bei einer anderen Familie essen; der Alte fürchtet und zittert. Man hält mich für einen deutschen Espion oder Agent; man sagt ich sei Bismarck Agent, Protestant, Freimason, Zauberer, Halbverdammte Seele u.s.w. Darum bleibe ich zu Hause.

> I get threats every day . . . My father never lets me go for a walk alone, or dine with another family. The Old Man is terrified and trembles. People take me for a German spy or agent; they say I am an agent of Bismarck, a Protestant, a Freemason, a sorcerer, a half-damned soul, etc. So I stay at home.[61]

---

59. Compare Guerrero, *The First Filipino*, pp. 178–80, with Schumacher, *The Propaganda Movement*, pp. 109–14.

60. Guerrero, *The First Filipino*, p. 180.

61. *The Rizal–Blumentritt Correspondence*, vol. 1, fifth unnumbered page following p. 133. Bismarck was seen as an ogre in clerical circles because of his decade-long *Kulturkampf* of the 1870s, intended to coerce German Catholics into giving their first loyalty to the Reich. (It was partly his reaction to the promulgation of Papal Infallibility.) But there was also wider fear of his designs on Spanish Oceania. It seems that in 1885 the Reichskanzler had announced that the imperial navy would ensure the safety of German entrepreneurs in the Carolines. Spanish troops were sent off hurriedly to put down resistance there to the full imposition of Madrid's sovereignty.

Worse was to follow. As noted earlier, Rizal's family wealth rested on the extensive lands it leased from the local Dominican hacienda. From the time of the 1883–86 depression the friars had started raising rents steeply, even as world sugar prices collapsed. Furthermore, they appropriated other lands to which, the townspeople felt, they had no just claim. About the time that Rizal returned, various tenants, including relatives of Rizal, stopped paying rent, and appealed to Manila to intervene on their behalf. Suspecting that the Dominicans were cheating on their taxes, Terrero sent a commission to investigate, but then did nothing. At this point the friars went on the attack by getting court orders for evictions. Rizal's family was deliberately chosen as the main target. Both sides went up the legal hierarchy over the next four years, even to the Supreme Court in Spain, but unsurprisingly the Dominicans prevailed. In the meantime members of Rizal's family were evicted from their homes, and other recalcitrant townspeople were soon treated the same way. By then Rizal himself had been advised by everyone to leave the country, since he was suspected of masterminding the resistance. It appears that the Captain-General himself passed the word that he could protect the young novelist no longer. Accordingly, in February 1888, Rizal left the country, sailing first to Japan for a quick first-hand look at a rapidly self-modernizing independent Asian power, then to the United States for a few days, and finally to England.

At about the same time, Terrero's term in office ended, and the Sagasta government, under heavy political pressure from conservatives at home and in the colony, made the fateful decision to appoint in his stead General Valeriano Weyler, a man with a reputation for severity while serving previously in Havana, and in the middle 1890s to become world-notorious, thanks to the American press, as the "Butcher of Cuba."[62] Terrero's liberal

62. Weyler (b. 1838) spent almost all of the first ten years (1863–73) of his career in the Caribbean. It will be recalled that the First Dominican Republic had successfully broken away from Haiti in 1844, but in 1861, at President Pedro Santana's initiative, had been taken back into the Spanish empire. In 1863 a popular revolt broke out—aided by Haiti—against this treason. Weyler was among the first young officers to be sent from Cuba to crush the insurrection. Pressured by the US, and by military reverses, Madrid was forced two years later to withdraw its troops and recognize the Second Dominican Republic.

Weyler made his reputation as an outstanding officer (he was the youngest man of his time to achieve the rank of general) by his successes against the Céspedes revolt in Cuba. He earned the soubriquet "el Sanguinario" by his leadership of ruthless hunter units (*cazadores*) composed of lumpen or criminal volunteers. Even his fervent admirer concedes that he killed more prisoners than any other Spanish officer. On his return to Madrid, he was assigned the task of smashing the Carlist forces in Valencia, and accomplished it successfully—without Cuban-style methods. See the hilarious *franquista* hagiography by General Hilario Martín Jiménez, *Valeriano Weyler, de su vida y personalidad, 1838–1930* (Santa Cruz de Tenerife: *cont'd over/*

advisers were quickly dismissed or transferred. In 1891 Weyler would be the man who finally "solved" the problem of tenant recalcitrance in Calamba by sending in a detachment of artillerymen to burn several houses to the ground, and forcibly clear lots "illegally" occupied. In *El Filibusterismo* Weyler appears, unnamed, as the central target of Simoun's Fabergé bomb. It is not surprising then that Rizal delayed his final return to the Philippines until after the grim general's term was over.

A SCHISM WITHIN ÉMIGRÉ NATIONALISM

During Rizal's first long sojourn in Europe his time had been mainly taken up by his studies and the composition of his novel. These were now well behind him, and he had to contemplate what to do next. Embittered by the disaster in Calamba, for which he felt himself deeply responsible, and totally disillusioned by Sagasta's sending of Weyler to Manila, he saw the answer as being to plunge more directly into nationalist (cultural) politics. His decision to live in London was partly spurred by the research collection of the British Museum to which Blumentritt and his scholarly friends had alerted him. From newspapers and journals he could observe the rising tide of nationalism within the dynastic empires of Europe, to say nothing of Cuba, the Ottoman empire, and the East. Central to all these nationalisms' articulation were the efforts of folklorists, historians, lexicographers, poets, novelists, and musicians to resurrect glorious pasts behind humiliating presents, and, especially, through replacing imperial languages by local vernaculars, to build and consolidate national identities. He had never forgotten the early shock of being misrecognized as a Chinese, Japanese, or *americano*, and of realizing that his country was basically unknown in Europe. Furthermore he was aware that unlike, for example, Malaya, Burma, India, Ceylon, Cambodia, and Vietnam, no precolonial written records in his country had survived European conquest. Such Philippine history as existed was mostly the product of members of the Orders, or, later, of racist Spanish conservatives. His concern in this regard was probably also stimulated—rivalrously—by the slightly younger Isabelo

---

62 *cont'd*   Ediciones del Umbral, 1998), chapters 2–6, and especially on dead prisoners p. 247. Hugh Thomas says that Weyler was military attaché in Washington during the American Civil War, and became an admirer of the ruthless Sherman. See his *Cuba*, p. 328. In his *El desterrado de París. Biografía del Doctor Ramón Emeterio Betances (1827–1898)* (San Juan: Ediciones Puerto Rico, 2001), p. 351, Félix Ojeda Reyes confirms this appointment, referring to Weyler's 1910 *Mi mando en Cuba.*

de los Reyes, whose landmark *El folk-lore filipino* had, as we have seen, won a prize at the Madrid Exposition of 1887.[63]

In the British Museum Rizal found what he was looking for: a very rare copy of the *Sucesos de las Islas Filipinas* of Dr Antonio de Morga, published in Mexico in 1609. Morga had arrived in the Philippines in 1595, at the age of thirty-four, to take up the positions of Justice of the Audiencia in Manila, and lieutenant-governor. He was a rarity in his time, an austerely honest colonial official whose realistic outlook was not clouded by clerical prejudices. After laboriously copying out this book by hand, Rizal decided to get it republished with extensive annotations and commentaries of his own, most of which were designed to show the relative reliability, by comparison with clerical chronicles, of Morga's more favorable account of native society—its level of civilization, its peaceful productivity, and its commercial relations with China, Japan, and parts of Southeast Asia. He managed to publish the book with Garnier in Paris, officially in 1890, but in fact late in 1889.[64]

---

63. It probably upset Rizal that Blumentritt had been corresponding with Isabelo. On April 30, 1888, he wrote irritably from San Francisco to his friend as follows: "Wie ich sehe, viele Folkloristen oder zukunftige Anthropologen tauchen in Ilokos auf. Da ist ein Herr Delosserre, mit dem Sie verkehren. Ich bemerke eine Sache: Da die meisten philippinischen Folkloristen Ilokaner sind, und weil diese das Epithet Ilokanisch gebrauche, werden die Anthropologen nach her angeben für ilocanische Gebräuche und Sitten was richtig Philippinisch sind; aber es ist unsere Schuld. Ich habe die Werke Isabelo's, überdessen Bemerkungen will ich Sie aufmerksam von Europa aus machen. Er sind einige Fehler darin, vielleicht weil er die tagalische Sprache nicht vollständig kennt." [As I observe, many folklorists or future anthropologists come from Ilocos. Here is Mr Delosserre (nom de plume of Isabelo) with whom you have dealings. I notice one thing: most of the Philippine folklorists are Ilocanos, and because they use the epithet "Ilocano," anthropologists will be led to classify as Ilocano customs and mores what are properly Filipino; but this is our fault. I have with me Isabelo's works, about which I will send you comments from Europe. There are some errors in it, perhaps because he does not fully understand the Tagalog language.] *The Rizal–Blumentritt Correspondence*, vol. 1, unnumbered page after 165. One notices the brusque tone of "with whom you have dealings." It is also telling that while Rizal called his first novel *"novela tagala,"* and evidently understood Ilocano not at all, this was fine, while poor Isabelo was criticized for using Ilocano to stand in for Filipino, and for not fully mastering Tagalog!

64. In his *First Filipino*, Guerrero has a lengthy and interesting discussion both of Morga's original and of Rizal's annotations (pp. 205–23). In 1890, Isabelo wrote an appreciative review of the book in *La Solidaridad*, but suggested that in some places Rizal's patriotism had led him into exaggerations. Rizal was livid, and wrote a scornful and acid rejoinder, basically accusing Isabelo of being a mere amateur dabbler. Juan Luna, a friend of both men, wrote to Rizal saying that though many of his points were right, an attack of this kind only made the Spaniards in Manila roar with laughter at the disunity in the Filipino camp; Isabelo did not really hit hard, and Rizal should have let it go. Letter of November 8, 1890. *Cartas entre Rizal y sus colegas de la propaganda* (Manila: José Rizal Centennial Commission, 1961), Tomo II, Libro 3, Parte 2a, pp. 587–8.

Though Rizal's *Morga* was not widely read then, or later, it clearly represents a turning point in Rizal's political trajectory. He was becoming a *filibustero*, a patriot determined one way or another on his country's full independence. (As we shall see, *El Filibusterismo* shows this new stance extremely clearly.) One consequence—given the prestige he had won among Filipinos by *Noli me tangere* and a spate of powerfully written articles published in various republican newspapers in Spain—was a growing schism within the overseas Filipino community in the metropole. Even during his student days in Spain, Rizal had frequently criticized his fellow countrymen there for frivolity, womanizing, idleness, gossipmongering, drunkenness, and the like. Although he retained a number of close friends in the Peninsula, his years away in northern Europe had deepened his irritation and sense of alienation.

Yet there was an interesting moment of partial reconvergence. At the end of 1888 a group of the more serious Filipinos in Barcelona had decided to take advantage of Sagasta's 1887 law liberalizing political space to form themselves into an energetic new political organization and to publish their own journal, to be called *La Solidaridad*. Barcelona's atmosphere was a significant element in these decisions. The influential anarchist journal *La Acracia* had already started publication in Barcelona in 1886, at the same time that in Madrid Pablo Iglesias's (Marxist) Socialist Party put out *El Socialista*. But in 1887, Barcelona's anarchists could finally have their own successful daily, *El Productor*.[65] Republican and anarchist organizations were proliferating along with many others. The Filipino initiatives were focused by the arrival in January 1889 of Marcelo del Pilar, the most capable

---

65. See Ortiz, *Paper Liberals*, pp. 57–60. Ortiz comments that these productions, as well as the later *La Revista Blanca*, showed that the lively anarchist press "surpassed the socialist press in intellectual rigor, circulation, and longevity." He also points out the massive new popularity of reading clubs where—given the widespread illiteracy of Barcelona's working class—readers (*lectores*) read out loud from the press. It is quite remarkable that two *El Productor*s appeared in the same year, one in Barcelona, and the other in Havana under the chief editorship of the energetic Catalan anarchist Enrique Roig y San Martín, whose Círculo de Trabajadores also issued a bimonthly Bakuninist magazine called *Hijos del Mundo*. I owe this information to an unpublished article "Leaves of Change: Cuban Tobacco Workers and the Struggle against Slavery and Spanish Imperial Rule, 1880s–1890s," by Evan Daniel (2003), at pp. 23–4. My thanks to Robin Blackburn and Evan Daniel for allowing me to read it. Daniel says that the Havana *El Productor* regularly reprinted articles from Barcelona's *La Acracia*, as well as translations from *Le Révolté* (in fact, by then it had been renamed *La Révolte*) and other non-Spanish anarchist periodicals, but does not mention its Barcelona twin, which is puzzling. Daniel also emphasizes the enormous importance of *lectores* for the many illiterate tobacco workers. All of this offers a striking contrast between Havana and Manila in this period: a vigorous and legal anarchist press could flourish in Cuba, while nothing remotely comparable would ever have been tolerated in the Philippines.

*Marcelo Del Pilar (centre), flanked by José Rizal (left)
and Mariano Ponce (right).*

Filipino politician of his generation. Del Pilar's elder brother, a native priest, had been arrested and deported to the Marianas in Izquierdo's repression of 1872, and Marcelo was an agile anti-friar and nationalist organizer under the permissive rule of Terrero, Centeno, and Quiroga. But after Weyler's arrival he knew he was a marked man, and so escaped to Spain. He immediately took over leadership of the Filipino activists and their new journal, eventually moving it to Madrid to be close to the center of state power. From then on, till his death in Barcelona in July 1896, he never left Spain.

   While Del Pilar's goal was certainly eventual Philippine independence, and while he actively promoted close ties with Manila and encouraged organizing there, he was convinced that the necessary first major steps had to be taken in Spain itself. "Liberal" cabinets, along with liberal and republican members of the Cortes, had to be lobbied by every means available to create the institutional spaces in which independence could eventually be achieved—while concealing this ultimate goal as much as possible. The tactical steps to be taken were basically to catch up with Cuba with a program of assimila-

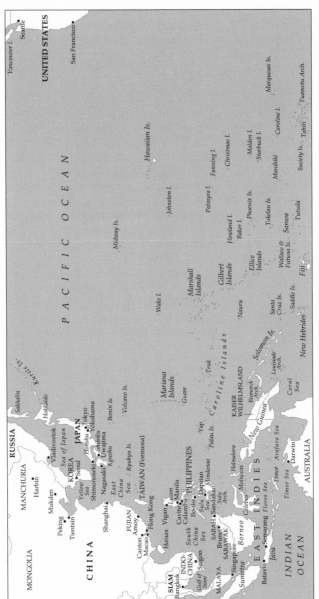

Three Worlds 3: The Pacific

tion. Cuba had long had representation in the Cortes, but the Philippines had lost this right in 1837. After the abolition of slavery in 1886, Cuba had basically the same legal system as Spain. The Caribbean colony was Spanish-speaking, its educational system was basically secular and state-provided, and the Church's political power was relatively little. Though Del Pilar was an accomplished writer in Tagalog (more so than Rizal, in fact), and though he privately discussed language policy in a future independent Philippines, he was sure that at this stage only assimilation and hispanicization would create the political atmosphere in which Madrid would permit the Philippines to assume Cuba's political status. Pushing through a serious state-sponsored Spanish-language educational system in the Philippines would also have the effect of destroying the foundations of the Orders' peculiar dominance in his country.[66] Del Pilar and his circle aggressively cultivated ties with the moderate liberal-republican press, polemicized against conservative news-papers and journalists, and seem to have steered well clear of the anarchist Left. There were tactical reasons for this caution, but the fact is that in an era innocent of scholarships for poor colonials, only the children of the wealthy and well-connected could afford to pursue an education in the metropole.

Though utterly different in temperament and talents, Rizal and Del Pilar respected one another, and for a time Rizal wrote energetically for the new journal. But gradually their relationship became more and more strained. Del Pilar was eleven years older than Rizal, had spent years in the risky business of organizing in the Philippines, and in Spain was a shrewd, indefatigable lobbyist for detailed, practical political reform of state policies towards his country. Like Blumentritt, in fact, with whom he was also on excellent terms, he saw no plausible alternative line of action. But his position had three

---

66. Schumacher's *The Propaganda Movement* provides an astute and generally sympathetic account of Del Pilar's life, ideas, goals, and political activities. The paragraph above is a wholly inadequate micro-version of his argument. This may be the place to say something brief about Cuban–Filipino contacts in Spain, such as they were. Most of the Filipinos who became Masons in the metropole joined lodges largely composed of Cubans, probably because the Cubans were more friendly and welcoming than the Spaniards. Rafael Labra, a senior creole Cuban member of the republican group in the Cortes (sitting for Puerto Rico and the Asturias in the weird Restoration manner), with a strong autonomist program, was not only intellectually influential through his voluminous writings on colonial questions, but also regularly attended and spoke at political banquets organized by Filipino activists. He had earlier headed the first abolitionist movement in Spain (in the 1860s!) (Thomas, *Cuba*, p. 240). Beyond this, the ties seem to have been rather limited until the mid-1890s. Cuba's political status was far in advance of that of the Philippines, its representatives in Spain were more likely to be Peninsulars and creoles (rather than mestizos or "natives"), and the problems of the two colonies were very different. I know of no Cuban who visited the Spanish Philippines until the 1890s, and no more than one or two Filipinos who, in the late colonial period, had seen Cuba at first hand.

liabilities. The first and biggest was that he had to show that his policies had significant results, otherwise disillusion was bound to set in. We can see the pattern in the Calamba affair, where he worked untiringly for the cause of Rizal's family and townspeople, but got nowhere. Second, the putative effectiveness of his lobbying depended on persuading Spanish politicians and publicists that the Filipino community in Spain was solidly behind him, which forced him to tolerate the gambling, womanizing, drinking and petty rivalries of which Rizal so sharply disapproved. Third, the editorial policy of *La Solidaridad* had to be the avoidance of anything that risked needlessly offending its Spanish readers, or being exploited by the rightwing press in Madrid. Rizal, on the other hand, away in northern Europe, had no practical political experience at all, either in the Philippines or in Spain. He did not have to produce practical results, tolerate what he regarded as the moral defects of many in the Filipino community, or worry much about the personal sensibilities of Spanish politicians and journalists he despised or detested. He was writing, he believed, for Filipino readers, not the Spanish public.

It is striking that in April 1890, when things were still going well for both men, Rizal returned the edited copy of one of his articles, saying he had made all the recommended changes, but adding one pregnant sentence: any changes were acceptable "samantalang hindi mababago ang pagiisip, o hindi masisira kaya ang takbo ñg pananalita" (just so long as my thinking is not altered, or, accordingly, my way of expressing myself isn't ruined). [67] But on May 26, he wrote to Del Pilar that he had decided for the time being to stop writing for *La Solidaridad*, rather implausibly explaining that readers needed a "rest" from his essays, and other Filipinos needed more chance to prove themselves. Eleven days later a deeply worried Del Pilar replied, also in Tagalog, to ask for a clear explanation of what he done wrong so that he could repent, adding, sadly: "Maniwala kang sa mga kasaliwaang palad na nag sususon-suson sa buhay ko ay hindi makapayag yaring loob sa ganitong pañguñgulila" (Believe me, amidst the accumulating miseries and misfortunes of my life, I cannot bear the prospect of being so orphaned). Evidently touched by this appeal, Rizal replied that Del Pilar was overreacting and not taking at face value his reasons for discontinuing contributions to *La Solidaridad*.

Ako'y sinisiglahan ñg malulungkot na pagiísip, bagama't di lubos ang aking paniwala. Niaong kabataan ko'y paniwala akong lubos na di ako sasapit sa

---

67. *Cartas entre Rizal y sus colegas*, p. 517. The entire letter is in Tagalog, unusual for Rizal, but clearly meant to convey intimacy and friendliness. It was written from Brussels, where Rizal had moved in late January, hearing from friends that the costs of living and of book-printing were much lower than in Paris. Here he started serious work on *El Filibusterismo*.

tatlong pung taon, aywan kung bakit gayon ang isipan ko. Mayroon na ngayong halos dalawang buan na halos gabi gabi'y wala akong ibang pangarap kundi ang mga patay kong kaibigan at kamaganak.

My imagination is stirred by melancholy thoughts. When I was a child, I was certain that I would not live to be thirty, I don't know why. It has been two months now that every night my dreams are only of dead friends and kin.[68]

As 1890 wore on, Del Pilar was too overworked to handle *La Solidaridad*, and made the tactical error of turning the job over to the vain and ambitious creole Eduardo de Lete, who in his teens had been a good friend of Rizal but was turning against him, perhaps out of jealousy of the huge prestige Rizal had gained by *Noli me tangere*. Always touchy, the novelist more and more felt that his writings were censored if they appeared in *La Solidaridad*, and ignored or belittled if they appeared elsewhere. A factional rivalry among so-called Pilaristas and Rizalistas was becoming visible, rooted in personal conflicts, but expressed in internal arguments over "assimilation" versus "separatism."

Things came to a head at the end of the year when Rizal came to Madrid to urge the community to establish a constitution for itself, and elect a leader who would have the power to set policy.[69] Apparently assured by letters he was getting from Manila that his writings were responsible for a major surge of patriotic activity, he seems to have been shocked when three successive ballots were divided almost equally between himself and Del Pilar, who had long been the *de facto* leader of the Filipinos in Spain. Finally, anxious to avoid a disastrous split, Del Pilar instructed his supporters to switch their votes to Rizal, who, annoyed by what had happened, then threatened to resign if a man he distrusted, but who was elected as one of two vice-leaders, was allowed to take up the position. Though formally triumphant, Rizal recognized that the unified support he had hoped for was a charade to mollify him, not a commitment to his goals. So he returned to Brussels, and resigned his position. In May 1891 he wrote to Del Pilar saying he would absolutely not write for *La Solidaridad* again, but would not oppose it. Instead he would busy himself with completing his new novel. Bitterness over this affair, which he himself had unwisely precipitated, had two different consequences. First, as we shall see, it centrally shaped the form and style of *El Filibusterismo*. Second, it greatly sharpened the hostility between the

---

68. *Cartas entre Rizal y sus colegas*, pp. 539–41, 547–51. The last two letters are dated June 8 and 11, 1890.

69. The complexities of the conflict between Rizal and Del Pilar are fully and impartially elaborated in the excellent chapter 12 of Schumacher's *The Propaganda Movement*.

Pilarista and Rizalista factions, both of which worked on their symbolic leaders out of variously good and discreditable motives.

It is noticeable that Rizal said nothing about all this to Blumentritt until October 9, on the eve of his final departure from Europe, and that the letter took the form of a defense of his decision to break with *La Solidaridad*, which had upset his friend.

Du möchtest dass ich einen Artikel auf die Solid: schriebe leider muss ich dir gestehen, dass ich die Abzicht habe keinen Artikel mehr für jene Zeitung zu arbeiten. Dass hätte ich dir früher sagen können, aber ich wollte die unannehmlichen Angriffe gegen mich dir verbergen. Es haben viele Sachen unter uns passirt. Du schreibst ja, und ich stimme ganz überein was du schreiben kannst. Was Blumentritt und Rizal thun können, das kann Blumentritt allein. Ich habe viele Entwürfe vorgeschlagen, die haben gegen mich einen geheimen Krieg zugeführt; sie nannten mich Idol, sie sagten ich sei Despote u.s.w. als ich die Philippiner zum Arbeiten bringen wollten. Darüber schrieben sie nach Manila, alle Sachen ändern, und sagten ich wollte so und so, was nicht genau wahr ist. Von Manchem weiss ich dass, ehe mein Filibusterismo in Druck gegangen, sagte er schon es taugte nichts und sei dem Noli tief unterliegend. Da sind viele geheime Kleinigkeiten als ob man wünschte, meinen kleinen Ruhm zu vernichten. Ich ziehe mich zurück um das Schisma zu verhindern: mögen Andere die Politik zuführen. Sie sagte Rizal sei eine zu schwere Personalität; gut, der Rizal weicht ab. Hindernisse sollen nicht aus mich kommen. Es kann möglich sein dass man dir das Geschehene anders erzählen als es gegangen, wie es schon passirt, aber du hast einen scharfen Blick, und versteht mehr als was man dir sagt.

You would like me write an article for *Soli*, but I must confess to you that my intention is not to work on any further article for that periodical. I could have told you this earlier, but I wanted to hide from you the disagreeable attacks against me. We have been through a lot together. You already write [for it], and I completely agree with what you can write. What Blumentritt and Rizal can do, Blumentritt can do on his own. I have suggested many projects, but they carried on a secret war against me; they call me "Idol," say I am a despot, etc., when I wished to get the Filipinos to work. They wrote about all this to Manila, twisting the facts, saying that I wanted this and that— which was hardly the truth. From various people I have learned that even before my *Filibusterismo* went to press, they were already saying that it was worthless and far inferior to the *Noli*. Many secret pettinesses are going on, as though they wished to destroy the little reputation that I have. I am withdrawing in order to forestall a schism; let others take the political lead. They said that Rizal is too difficult a personality; good then, Rizal goes his own way; obstacles ought not to come from me. It is possible that they are telling you another version of what has happened, but you have a sharp eye and you understand more than what you hear.[70]

70. *The Rizal–Blumentritt Correspondence, 1890–1896*, unnumbered pages between 416 and 417. The letter was sent from Paris on October 9, 1891.

Blumentritt's immediate reply has been lost, but one can infer its substance from a letter of July 4, 1892, which, for reasons we will come to later, Rizal probably never received. The Austrian was unusually blunt. He said all the letters he had received from Del Pilar had expressed great appreciation for Rizal. He himself had strongly urged both Pilaristas and Rizalistas to forget petty personal differences, and avoid conflicts which could only benefit the common enemy and weaken the movement. He was advocating not a full peace, but only an intelligent truce. Furthermore, he absolutely disagreed with Rizal's view of *La Solidaridad*, whose value was demonstrated by the fact that the enemy had recently established a fortnightly precisely to combat its influence. But, he added, one should not expect miracles from the periodical, let alone that it could achieve in four years what other peoples had taken four decades to accomplish. Filipinos should not despise it, since it defended the honor of their country and their people. "Perhaps my words are harsh and blunt, but my heart is tender and good, I will never abandon my poor Philippines; I shall not be a deserter."[71]

Rizal was increasingly certain that the whole assimilationist campaign was futile. Cuban representation in the Cortes was meaningless under the corrupt Cánovas–Sagasta electoral system. It had not stopped Spain from continued merciless exploitation of Cuban production through manipulated tariffs, monopolies, and subjection to Basque and Catalan business interests.[72] Besides, Rizal believed, there was no chance whatever, at the end of the nineteenth century, of turning millions of Filipinos into assimilated Spanish-speakers. Sagasta's sending of the brutal Weyler to Manila in 1888, and his own replacement by Cánovas in 1890, further deepened Rizal's conviction that nothing could be successfully achieved in Spain. The work of emancipation would have to be done back home.

It was in this frame of mind that he abandoned journalism in 1891 to focus entirely on *El Filibusterismo*, seeing it frantically through the press in August, after which he immediately headed home. If *Noli me tangere* was targeted at multiple audiences in Europe and the Philippines, *El Filibusterismo* was meant only for the latter. He sent a few copies to personal friends in Spain and elsewhere, but the rest of the entire edition was shipped to Hong Kong, where he intended to settle till Weyler's term was over. To his trusted older friend Basa, one of the deported victims of Izquierdo twenty years earlier, who had settled in Hong Kong and

---

71. *Ibid.*, pp. 47–8. The volume does not include Blumentritt's original German text.

72. When he heard from Mariano Ponce that his good-hearted but erratic comrade Graciano López Jaena was thinking of going to Cuba, he wrote back: "es inútil, Cuba está exhausta; es una cáscara de nuez" [It's pointless, Cuba is exhausted, it's an empty nutshell]. Letter of July 9, 1890, in *Cartas entre Rizal y sus colegas*, pp. 559–60.

become a successful businessman (and agile smuggler), he wrote an important letter from Ghent on July 9 entrusting the books to him, and urging complete secrecy in the face of clerical espionage which also stretched into the British colony. The letter is very bitter about his own extreme poverty, and the endless broken promises of financial help from rich members of the Filipino community in Spain.[73]

> Estoy cansado ya de creer en nuestros paisanos; todos parece que se han unido por amargarme la vida . . . ¡Ah! Le digo á V., que si no fuera por V., si no fuera porque creo que hay todavía verdaderos buenos filipinos, ¡me dan ganas de enviar al diablo paisanos y todo! ¿Por quién me han tomado? Precisamente, cuando uno necesita tener su espíritu tranquilo y su imaginación libre, ¡venirle á uno con engaños y mezquindades!

> I am tired of trusting in our fellow countrymen; they all seem to have joined hands to embitter my life . . . Ah! I tell you [frankly], that if it were not for you, if it were not that that I believe that there are still [some] genuinely good Filipinos, I would readily send fellow countrymen and all to the devil! What do they take me for? Exactly at the moment when one needs to keep one's spirit tranquil and one's imagination free, they come at one with intrigues and petty meannesses![74]

A MISSING LIBRARY?

Before turning to reconsider some of the puzzles that face the reader of Rizal's second novel, especially its apparently proleptic aspects, it is necessary to discuss briefly one serious investigative difficulty—the problem of Rizal's philosophical formation in the political sphere. The list of the books in his Calamba library includes no volumes by political thinkers after the time of Voltaire, Rousseau, and Herder, unless we include Herbert Spencer. The character of this list might reasonably be explained by the risks involved, especially for his family, in trying to bring books of contemporary political theory into the colonial police state. But Rizal's vast published correspondence within Europe shows a comparable absence. No mention of Constant, Hegel, Fichte, Marx, Tocqueville, Comte, Saint-Simon, Fourier, Bentham,

---

73. In fact the printing bill for *El Filibusterismo* was paid by a good friend, the wealthy Pampangueño Valentín Ventura. Rizal normally lived very simply, and was often regarded by his friends as a skinflint, but we have had occasion to notice that when traveling he usually went first-class and stayed at opulent hotels, less for their luxury than out of a colonial's pride.

74. *Epistolario Rizalino*, vol. 3 (1890–1892), ed. Teodoro M. Kalaw (Manila: Bureau of Printing, 1935), pp. 200–01.

Self-portrait of Juan Luna, aged 22.

Mill, Bakunin, or Kropotkin—only one-sentence casual allusions to Proudhon and Tolstoi. Is it possible that over the almost ten years he spent in Madrid, Paris, London, and Berlin, he managed to avoid or ignore all these influential political thinkers?

There is, so far, only one direct, if ambigous, clue—a letter of May 13, 1891, written to him in Brussels by his close friend in Paris, the painter Juan Luna. It is worth quoting at some length.

Mañana se inaugura el Salón del Campo de Marte. Es la primera vez que tengo los dos cuadros en la *cimaise* ó zócalo. Me puedo dar por satisfecho (por ahora) que sabes cómo mando yo los cuadros, como patatas al mercado. A mi cuadro del entierro le titulé *Les Ignorés* y como habrás visto me ocupo ahora de los humildes y desheredados. ¿Qué libro me aconsejarías que lea para inspirarme en lo mismo? De alguno que hubiese escrito en contra de este tan desnudo materialismo y de esta explotación infame del pobre; de la lucha del rico con el miserable! Estoy buscando un asunto digno de ser desarrollado en una tela de ocho metros. Estoy leyendo *Le Socialisme contemporaire* por E. de Lavelaye, en donde he recopilado las teorías de Carl Marx, Lasalle, [*sic*] etc., el socialismo católico, el conservador, el evangélico, etc. Me interesa muchísimo. Pero yo lo que quisiera es un libro que pusiera en relieve las miserias de nuestra sociedad contemporánea; una especie de Divina Comedia, un Dante que se paseare por los talleres en donde apenas se respira y en donde vería á hombres, chiquillos y mujeres en el estado más miserable que imaginar se puede. Chico, yo mismo he ido á ver un fundición de hierro; he pasado allí cinco horas y créeme que por más duro que tenga uno el corazón, el espectáculo que yo vi allí me ha impresionado muchísimo. Nuestros compatriotas con todo lo malo que hacen allí los frailes, son felices comparados con esta miseria y muerte. Había un taller en donde se molía arena y carbón, éste al convertirse en polvo finísimo por la acción de los molinos se levantaba en grandes nubarrones, y toda la pieza parecía envuelta de humo: allí todo estaba lleno de polvo, y los diez ó doce trabajadores que se ocupaban en rellenar con sus palas el molino tenían el aspecto de cadáveres; ¡tal era la facha miserable de los pobres! Yo estuve 3 ó 4 minutos y me parecía que había tragado arena y polvo toda mi vida: se me metía por las narices, por la boca, por los ojos . . . y pensar que aquellos infelices respiraban 12 horas carbón y polvo; yo creo que infaliblemente están condenados á muerte y que es un crimen el abandonar así á tan pobre gente.

Tomorrow is the opening of the Salon du Champ de Mars. It is the first time that I have two pictures on the *cimaise* [a small shelf used to prop up pictures] or on the socle. I can take some satisfaction from this (for the moment), since you know how I peddle my pictures, like potatoes in the market. To my painting of the burial I have given the title *Les Ignorés*, and as you will see [have seen?] I am busying myself now with the lowly and the disinherited. What book would you recommend me to read to inspire me in this plan? By someone who has written against such naked materialism and such infamous exploitation of the poor, and the war of the rich against the wretched! I am seeking a subject worthy of being developed into an eight-meter canvas. I am now reading *Le Socialisme contemporaire* by E. de Lavelaye, in which he has summarized the theories of Karl Marx, Lassalle, etc., Catholic socialism, conservative, evangelical, etc. The book interests me very much, but what I would like is a book that would highlight the miseries of our contemporary society, a kind of Divine Comedy, a Dante who would walk through workshops where one can hardly breathe, and where men, little kids, and women live in the most wretched conditions one could imagine. My dear fellow, I have myself gone to see an iron foundry. I spent five hours there, and believe me, no matter how hardhearted a person may be, the spectacle that I witnessed there made the deepest impression upon me. Despite all the evil that the friars commit over there, our compatriots are fortunate compared to this misery and death. There was a workshop there for grinding up sand and coal, which, converted into the finest dust by the action of the milling machine, swirled up in huge black clouds, and the whole room seemed swathed in smoke. Everything there was filled with dust, and the ten or twelve workers busy shoveling the coal and sand into the machine looked just like corpses. Such was the miserable sight of the poor! I stood there for three or four minutes, and it seemed as if I had swallowed sand and dust all my life; they penetrated me through the nostrils, the mouth and the eyes . . . And to think that those unfortunates breathe coal and dust twelve hours a day: I believe that they are inevitably condemned to death, and that it is a crime to abandon such poor people in this way.[75]

75. *Cartas entre Rizal y sus colegas,* p. 660. My thanks to Ambeth Ocampo for sending me the text. See also his comment on the Luna letter in his *Rizal without the Overcoat* (Pasig City, Manila: Anvil, 2000), pp. 62–3. Laveleye (1822–92) was a renowned Belgian polymath and bimetallic political economist.

Unfortunately we do not have Rizal's reply to this missive. But Luna refers to Marx and Lassalle without further explanation, meaning that he knew Rizal needed none. Furthermore, though he was older than the novelist, he was asking him to recommend some inspirational reading on the ravages of contemporary industrial capitalism.

A rather less instructive possible clue is an article published in Madrid in January 1890 by Vicente Barrantes, a former high official in Manila, and now a self-proclaimed expert on the Philippines. (Barrantes probably recognized himself in *Noli me tangere*'s portrait of a senior civil servant who throws well-off mestizos and *indios* into prison to extort money from them.) After describing Blumentritt as an agent of Bismarck's "reptile fund," he denounced Rizal as "anti-Catholic, Protestant, socialist, and Proudhonian."[76] "Proudhonian" was probably deployed simply to belittle Rizal as a mere acolyte of the admirable Catalan democrat and federalist republican Francisco Pi y Margall, who had published a translation of Proudhon's *Du principe fédératif* in 1868.[77] Rizal was amused by this tirade and in a letter to Blumentritt of March 6 he wrote sarcastically that if Barrantes died of rage at Rizal's scorching reply in *La Solidaridad*: "es wäre eine grosse Verlust in meiner Menagerie; er ist einer der schönsten Exemplaren meines Schlangen und Hippopotames" (it would be a great loss for my menagerie. He is one of the finest examples of my snakes and hippopotami).[78]

But probably the most telling evidence—which may indicate why no reply to Luna has been found—is *El Filibusterismo* itself. For while Del Pilar and *La solidaridad* continued to attack the Orders as the main enemy of Filipino aspirations, and sought support in the ranks of Sagasta's liberals (among others), Rizal's second novel lets the friars off rather lightly. One or two reasonable ones are allowed to appear, and the Fr Salví, the sinister lecherous schemer of *Noli me tangere*, is here a minor, even laughable presence. The figure who is most savagely pilloried this time around is the condescending, incompetent, utterly opportunist liberal Don Custodio, who betrays the students who look to him for support.

It is therefore difficult to avoid the conclusion that although *El Filibusterismo* was highly inflammatory and subversive at one level, at another it was narrow and lacking in any coherent political position. Most likely the main reason for this

---

76. The article appeared in the laughably titled *La España Moderna* on January 2.

77. Though Pi y Margall was almost forty years older than Rizal, he was a close friend, and one of the few prominent political figures in Spain who supported Filipino aspirations. See Sarkisyanz, *Rizal*, p. 112, and chapter 8 (devoted to the two men's relationship).

78. *The Rizal–Blumentritt Correspondence*, vol. 2 (1890–1896), third unnumbered page after p. 336.

strangeness is that Rizal was a novelist and a moralist, not a political thinker. He may indeed have read some of the writers so visibly absent from his library and correspondence, but they do not seem to have left much of an impression on him. And quite likely, too, his obsession, especially during his second sojourn in Europe, with his own country, and the calamities that had befallen his family and townspeople, left him largely oblivious or indifferent to the social misery in Europe itself. There is nothing in Rizal's voluminous writings like Luna's horrified description of the Parisian iron foundry; the painter's naïvely expressed, but telling remark that the Filipinos were fortunate compared with the industrial workers of Paris seems utterly outside the novelist's frame of reference.

INTERPRETING *EL FILIBUSTERISMO*:
TRANSCONTINENTALISM AND PROLEPSIS

In its early chapters, *El Filibusterismo* appears to be set firmly in the real time and place of Valeriano Weyler's rule in the Philippines (March 1888 to April 1891). The oafish, brutal and cynical Su Excelencia is clearly modelled on the future Butcher of Cuba,[79] while the unnamed, liberal-minded, pro-native High Official who opposes the Captain-General, and is dismissed for his pains, is a thinly veiled portrait of Manila civil governor Centeno. This temporal emplacement is sharply confirmed by one of the subplots, which opens in chapter IV, and introduces the reader to the melancholy story of the honest peasant Tales. This man clears and works a small piece of land on the wooded confines of Ibarra's home township San Diego (modelled after Rizal's hometown Calamba).[80] As he prospers, agents of the nearby hacienda of an unnamed Order inform him that the land falls within the hacienda's legal boundaries, but

---

79. In the final chapter of *El Filibusterismo* (at p. 281) Simoun describes how, as Ibarra, he fled secretly from the Philippines with ancestral valuables, and devoted himself to the trade in gems. Then: "Tomó parte en la guerra de Cuba, ayudando ya á un partido ya á otro, pero ganando siempre. Allí conoció al General, entonces comandante, cuya voluntad se captó primero por medio de adelantes de dinero y haciéndose su amigo despues gracias á crimenes cuyo secreto el joyero poseía . . ." [He took part in the Cuban war, aiding now this side, now that, but always making a profit. It was there that he got to know the General, then a major, whose will he first captured by financial advances, later making him a friend thanks to secret crimes to which the jeweler was privy]. Weyler became a major in Cuba in March 1863. What these "secret crimes" amount to is unclear—cruelties, corruption, or libertinage? A curious section of Martín's hagiography discusses the general's ruthless and voracious sexual appetites. Of a married woman with whom he had a secret affair while boss of Cuba, Weyler himself noted: "The woman pleased me so much that if a rebel battalion had tried to block our assignations, I would have tried to reach her even if a forest of bayonets stood in my way." *Valeriano Weyler*, pp. 256–7.

80. Chapters IV ("Cabesang Tales") and X ("Riqueza y Miseria" [Riches and Destitution]).

he may stay on if he pays a small rent. Each year thereafter the rents are steeply raised, till Tales cannot, and will not, pay any more; threatened with eviction, he refuses to budge, and arms himself to defend his land. Meantime he loses all his money in a vain attempt to win his rights in court. Finally he is captured by bandits and held for ransom. After the ransom is finally paid, he returns to find his property taken over by the hacienda and a new tenant in place. That night the new tenant, his wife, and the friar in charge of rents are brutally murdered, with the name Tales smeared in blood on their bodies.

At this point something quite extraordinary happens. The narrator suddenly cries out, as it were from Belgium:

> Tranquilizaos, pacíficos vecinos de Kalamba! ¡Ninguno de vosotros se llama Tales, ninguno de vosotros ha cometido el crímen! ¡Vosotros llamaís [a list of names follows ending with] Silvestre Ubaldo, Manuel Hidalgo, Paciano Mercado, os llamaís todo el pueblo de Kalamba!

> Be calm, peaceful inhabitants of Calamba! Not one of you is called Tales, not one of you has committed the crime! You are called . . . Silvestre Ubaldo, Manuel Hidalgo, Paciano Mercado, you are called the entire people of Calamba![81]

Ubaldo and Hidalgo were Rizal's brothers-in-law, while Paciano was his beloved elder brother. All were severely punished for resisting the Dominicans in 1888–90. And "San Diego" is calmly unmasked as "Kalamba."[82] Later in the novel, we learn that Tales joins the bandits, and after his daughter Julí's suicide to escape Father Camorra's lust, allies himself with Simoun, and finally becomes Matanglawin (Tagalog for *Hawk-eye*), the uncaught bandit chief who terrorizes the countryside around Manila. Historically, there seems to have been no figure like Matanglawin in the Philippines of that time, though there were plenty of small bandits in the hilly country to the south of the colonial capital. But were there perhaps one or two in the violent, hungry Andalusia of Rizal's student days?

TRANSPOSITIONS

The main subplot of *El Filibusterismo* is, as mentioned earlier, the ultimately unsuccessful campaign of the students to have the state establish an academy

81. This apostrophe is how Chapter X ends. It is reminiscent of the famous ending to Dekker's *Max Havelaar*, where the author explicitly casts aside his characters and his plot to launch a hairraising broadside in his own name at the Dutch colonial regime in the Indies and its backers in the Netherlands.

82. One of Rizal's political hobbies at this time was to insist on spelling Tagalog words, even when, or perhaps especially when, they derived from Spanish, with his own orthographic system. One of the provocations involved was to substitute the aggressively non-Castilian *k* for *c*. Hence *Kalamba* for *Calamba*.

for (lay) instruction in the Spanish language—the first step towards the hispanicization of the population. In historical fact, there was never any such student campaign in Manila, and in any case Weyler would not have tolerated it for a moment. But the subplot is visibly a microcosmic version of the tactical assimilation campaign conducted by Del Pilar in Spain from 1889 onward—in which Rizal had lost all faith. The detailed picture of the students seems completely unlike the one we can gain from other sources on the highschool and college world Rizal experienced in Manila in the late 1870s, virtually innocent of politics. Most of the students are depicted satirically as young opportunists, blowhards, cynics, rich do-nothings, or spongers. The only one who is painted as fully goodhearted and patriotic, the *indio* Isagani, is still a firm, naïve believer in the campaign, and without any serious political ideas. It is thus not easy to avoid the conclusion that almost the entire subplot is simply 1880s Madrid oceanically transferred to an imagined 1890s Manila.

But this is by no means all. In the crucial early chapter ("Simoun") in which the reader learns—because Basilio accidentally recognizes him—that Simoun is actually Ibarra, the naïve hero of *Noli me tangere*, the question of the campaign is introduced into their conversation. To the reader's probable surprise, the cynical nihilist conspirator Simoun sounds, as it were, a violently Basque note.[83]

¡Ah, la juventud siempre inexperta y soñadora, siempre corriendo trás las mariposas y las flores! Os ligaís para con vuestros esfuerzos unir vuestra patria á la España con guirnaldas de rosas cuando en realidad ligaís forjaís cadenas más duras que el diamante! Pedís igualdad de derechos, españolización de vuestras costumbres y no veís que lo que pedís es la muerte, la destrucción de vuestra nacionalidad, la aniquilación de vuestra patria, la consagración de la tiranía! ¿Qué seréis en la futuro? Pueblo sin caracter, nación sin libertad; todo en vosotros será prestado hasta los mismos defectos. Pedís españolización y no palidecéis de vergüenza cuando os la niegan! Y aunque os la concedieran, qué queréis? ¿Qué vaís á ganar? Cuando más feliz, país de pronunciamientos, país de guerras civiles,

---

83. The comparison is not idle. Zea quotes from Unamuno's "Elogio" (see note 19) the following: "El castellano es en Filipinas, como lo es en mi país vasco, un lenguaje advenedizo y de reciente implantación . . . Yo aprendía a balbucir en castellano, y castellano se hablaba en mi casa, pero castellano de Bilbao, es decir, un castellano pobre y tímido . . . nos vemos forzados a remodelarlo, a hacernos con esfuerzo una lengua. Y esto, que es en cierto respecto nuestro flanco [*sic*] como escritores, es a la vez nuestro fuerte" [In the Philippines, as in my own Basque country, Spanish is a foreign language and of recent implantation . . . I learned to stammer in Spanish, and we spoke Spanish at home, but it was the Spanish of Bilbao, i.e. a poverty-stricken and timid Spanish. [Hence] we have been forced to remodel it, to forge by our efforts a language of our own. So it is, that what in a certain respect is our weakness as writers is also our strength] (p. xxix).

república de rapaces y descontentos como algunas repúblicas de la América de Sur!
. . . El español nunca será lenguaje general en el país, el pueblo nunca lo hablará
porque para las concepciones de su cerebro y los sentimientos de su corazón no
tiene frases ese idioma: cada pueblo tiene el suyo, como tiene su manera de sentir.
Qué vais á conseguir con el castellano, los pocos que lo habéis de hablar? Matar
vuestra originalidad, subordinar vuestros pensamientos á otros cerebros y en vez
de haceros libres haceros verdaderamente esclavos! Nueve por diez de los que os
presumís de ilustrados, sois renegados de vuestra patria. El que de entre vosotros
habla ese idioma, descuida de tal manera el suyo que ni lo escribe ni lo entiende y,
cuántos he visto yo que afectan no saber de ello una sola palabra! Por fortuna
tenéis un gobierno imbécil. Mientras la Rusia para esclavizar á la Polonia le
impone el ruso, mientras la Alemania prohibe el francés en las provincias
conquistadas, vuestro gobierno pugna por conservaros el vuestro y vosotros en
cambio, pueblo maravilloso bajo un gobierno increíble, vosotros os esforzáis en
despojaros de vuestra nacionalidad! Uno y otro os olvidáis de que mientras un
pueblo conserve su idioma, conserva la prenda de su libertad, como el hombre su
independencia mientras conserva su manera de pensar. El idioma es el pensamiento de los pueblos.

Ah youth! Always naïve, always dreaming, always running after butterflies and flowers.
You unite so that by your efforts you can bind your motherland to Spain with garlands
of roses, when in fact you are forging chains harder than a diamond! You ask for
equality of rights, and the hispanization of your customs, without understanding that
what you ask for is death, the destruction of your nationality, the obliteration of your
motherland, and the consecration of tyranny! What will you become in the future? A
people without character, a nation without liberty; everything in you will be borrowed,
even your very defects. You ask for hispanization, and you do not blanch with shame
when it is denied you! And even should it be granted to you, what do you want with it?
What would you gain? If you are lucky, a country of pronunciamientos, a country of
civil wars, a republic of predators and malcontents like some of the republics of South
America! . . . Spanish will never be the common language in this country, the people will
never speak it, because that language does not have the words to express the ideas in their
minds and the sentiments in their hearts. Each people has its own, as it has its own way
of feeling. What will you gain from Spanish, the few of you who speak it? Kill your
originality, subordinate your thoughts to other minds, and instead of making yourselves
free, turn yourselves into veritable slaves! Nine out of ten of you who presume yourselves
ilustrados are renegades to your country. Those who speak Spanish forget their own
tongue, which they no longer write or understand. How many have I seen who pretend
not to know a single word of it! Luckily you have a government of imbeciles. While
Russia, in order to enslave Poland, compels her to speak Russian, while Germany
prohibits French in the conquered provinces, your government endeavors to have you
keep your own tongue, and you, in turn, an amazing people under an unbelievable
government, you insist on stripping yourselves of your own nation-ness. One and all, you
forget that so long as a people conserves its language, it also preserves the guarantee of its

liberty, as a man his independence while he preserves his way of thinking. Language is the very thought of a people.[84]

The tirade is powerful enough to let the reader forget that Ibarra–Simoun had an unscrupulous and cruel Basque grandfather, and that for the purposes of his disguise he affects a bad, heavily accented Tagalog; or that this denunciation of Hispanicization is expressed in excellent Spanish. She might also overlook a contradictory argument of Simoun a few lines earlier: "¿Queréis añadir un idioma más á los cuarenta y tantos que se hablan en las islas para entenderos cada vez menos?" (Do you want to add still one more language to the forty-odd already spoken in the islands so that you understand each other all the less?)[85] But the important thing is that while in Europe Rizal never wrote publicly in these vitriolically nativist terms—which would have appalled the comrades around *La Solidaridad*. In Spain he would have been speaking to the present, but transferred to Manila he is speaking to the future, with Poland and Alsace brought in as warnings.

Similar space–time shifts are visible as the novel moves towards its climax. After the campaign for a Spanish-language academy has failed, mysterious subversive posters (*pasquinades*) appear all over the university one night, leading the regime to indiscriminate arrests—a clear replication of Cánovas's raids on the Central University of Madrid at the start of Rizal's senior year. The mysterious posters quickly cause a general panic, fed by wild rumors of insurrection and invasions of ferocious bandits, which recall the Mano Negra panic in Andalusia in 1883, and foreshadow the so-called "revolutionary" peasant attack on Jerez early in 1892. It is interesting that Rizal works to anchor these plot developments in the Philippines by giving the relevant chapter the (untranslated) Tagalog title *Tatakut*, which means "panic."

DANSONS LA RAVACHOLE

Finally, we come to Simoun's bomb plot itself, which is to be accompanied by armed attacks by Tales's men and others outside the law, who have agreed to coordinate with the mysterious jeweler.

There are a number of curious features to this failed conspiracy. First, imagined in 1890–91, it precedes rather than follows the spectacular wave of

<hr>

84. *El Filibusterismo*, chapter VII ("Simoun"), pp. 47–8.
85. *Ibid.* p. 47. Logically, this implies that there are forty-odd peoples in the Philippines, not one. It also ignores the decisive role of Spanish as a lingua franca, the one communicative link between the other forty-plus. Rizal had taken Herder too seriously to heart. Even today, Tagalog spreads faster as a market lingua franca than as a national *idioma*.

bomb outrages that rocked Spain and France in 1892–94. From 1888 on, however, a growing number of explosions of bombs and petards had occurred, typically in industrial Barcelona, but also in Madrid, Valencia, and Cádiz. Most were planted in factories, few caused loss of life or serious injuries, and almost none resulted in the unmasking of the perpetrators. There is every reason to suppose that they were arranged by angry workers under the influence of anarchist ideas, though perhaps some were organized by police agents provocateurs. But the numbers of bombings and their gravity increased markedly after the "Jerez uprising" of January 8, 1892. That night, some fifty or sixty peasants entered the town to attack the prison where some of their comrades had earlier been incarcerated and tortured. It seems they expected, naïvely, that the local military garrison would support them. The police dispersed them, and it turned out that one peasant, and two townspeople had been killed. Near the end of his third period in power, Cánovas launched an indiscriminate wave of repression against peasants and workers, and on February 10, four of the supposed leaders of the "uprising" were publicly garroted.[86]

A month later, a series of serious explosions started in Paris, the work of the half-Dutch, half-Alsatian François-Claude Koenigstein, better known as Ravachol, a criminal with a record of murder and robbery. He was quickly caught and put on trial. Claiming that he had acted in revenge for earlier violent police

---

86. Núñez, *El terrorismo*, p. 49; Esenwein, *Anarchist Ideology*, pp. 175–80. Nineteenth-century Spain practised three kinds of capital punishment: by the gun, the noose, and the garrote. The first three were thought to cause almost instantaneous death; the garrote, as a medieval instrument of torture, took longer, and so was reserved for the "worst" (i.e. political) offenders. Incidentally, Esenwein's excellent research has turned up some strange things. From one angle, the chain of events began with the Haymarket "Riot" in Chicago at the beginning of May 1886. In an atmosphere of anti-"communist" and anti-immigrant hysteria, and after a travesty of a fair trial, four anarchists were hanged that November. The executions aroused indignation all over Europe (and of course also in the US), and on the initiative of French workers' organizations, May Day came to be celebrated annually (except in the US) in commemoration of the victims. The whole Spanish Left was a vigorous supporter of the new tradition, especially while Sagasta was still in power. Just after the May Day commemorations of 1891, two bombs exploded in Cádiz, killing one worker, and injuring several others. The local police arrested 157 people, but never found any provable perpetrator, so the possibility of agents provocateurs cannot be ruled out. It was some of these prisoners whom the men of Jerez intended to liberate. The odd thing is that just at this juncture none other than Malatesta, accompanied by the rising anarchist intellectual star Tarrida del Mármol, was on a lecture and organizing tour of Spain, and was due to speak in Jerez. On hearing the news of the violent events, Malatesta rather courageously decided to keep going towards Cádiz, but disguised as a prosperous Italian businessman. He doesn't seem to have accomplished anything. Esenwein thinks it significant that neither at the time nor later did the anarchists proclaim January 8 as "propaganda by the deed." On the contrary, they always insisted that they had nothing to do with it.

repression against a workers' demonstration in Clichy, followed by the trial of some workers at which the prosecutor demanded (but did not win) the death penalty, Ravachol told the court that he had acted on revolutionary anarchist principles. On July 11 he went to the guillotine shouting "Vive l'Anarchie!" and promising that his death would be avenged.[87] His was the first political execution in France since the massacres of the Communards.

In spite of his dubious past, Ravachol's death made him an instant hero of the *anarchisant* Left on both sides of the Pyrenees. Núñez quotes a well-known popular song of the time, "La Ravachole," as follows:

> Dansons la Ravachole!
> Vive le son, vive le son!
> Dansons la Ravachole!
> Vive le son
> De l'explosion!

Elisée Reclus, the famous theorist of anarchism, was quoted in the Spanish anarchist press as saying, "I am one of those who see in Ravachol a hero with a rare grandeur of spirit," while the writer Paul Adam, a member of Mallarmé's circle, wrote an "Éloge de Ravachol" in which he affirmed that "Ravachol saw the suffering and misery of the people around him, and sacrificed his life in a holocaust. His charity, his disinterestedness, the vigor of his actions, his courage in the face of ineluctable death, raised him to the splendour of legend. In these times of cynicism and irony, a saint has been born to us."[88] The Spanish anarchist press described Ravachol as a "violent Christ" and a "brave and dedicated revolutionary," and some anarchists put out two short-lived publications in his honour: *Ravachol* in late 1892 and *El Eco de Ravachol* early in 1893.

The autumn of 1893 saw major repercussions from the Ravachol affair. On September 24, Paulino Pallás threw two bombs at the Captain-General of Catalonia, General Arsenio Martínez Campos (signer of the Pact of Zanjón,

---

87. See Maitron, *Le mouvement*, pp. 213–24. In his prison cell Koenigstein told interviewers that he had lost his religious faith after reading Eugène Sue's *Le juif errant*! Maitron points out that French anarchism in this period was largely a matter of tiny, clandestine or semi-clandestine units without real organizational ties between them. This characteristic made it hard for the police to monitor them effectively, and also made it relatively easy for criminal elements to penetrate them. French anarchism did not become a real political force till the end of the 1890s with the abandonment of propaganda by the deed, and the onset of syndicalism in working-class political life. Spanish anarchism had a much stronger and wider social foundation. That Ravachol was partly Alsatian is my deduction from the testimony of Ramón Sempau in his *Los victimarios*, p. 15.

88. Núñez, *El terrorismo*, pp. 121–3. Without access to the French originals, there seems no special point in including here the words of the Spanish translation.

which brought Céspedes's ten-year insurrection in Cuba to a peaceful end).[89] This *attentat* resulted in one death, and several grave injuries, but Martínez Campos himself was only scratched. Pallás made no attempt to hide or escape, but throwing his cap into the air, shouted "Viva l'Anarquía!" He was executed by firing squad a month later at the soon-to-be notorious fortress of Mont-juich.[90] On November 7, the 32-year-old Santiago Salvador threw a huge bomb into the Barcelona Opera House during a performance of Rossini's opera

---

89. According to a contemporary newspaper report, Pallás did not use the standard "Orsini bomb" but rather one described as "Fenian." *Ibid.*, p. 53. Felice Orsini (b. 1819) was a veteran of the 1848 revolutions, a deputy in the ephemeral Roman Republic, and a committed Italian nationalist. Imprisoned by the Austrian regime in the fortress of Mantua in 1855, he made a spectacular escape, and headed for Palmerston's London, where Mazzini was plotting insurrection from seedy lodgings on the Fulham Road. Orsini's sensational 1856 memoir *The Austrian Dungeons in Italy: a narrative of fifteen months of imprisonment and final escape from the fortress of S. Giorgio* (London: G. Routledge, 1856) quickly sold 35,000 copies, and his Byronic good looks and fervent rhetoric made him wildly popular on the lecture circuit. Meantime, he was inventing a new type of bomb, made mainly from fulminate of mercury, which did not need a fuse but exploded on impact. He tested it in Putney, and in disused quarries in Devonshire and Sheffield. Then, believing that the assassination of Louis-Napoléon would spark a revolution in France which would cause Italy to follow Paris's example, he crossed the Channel, and tried out his invention on January 14, 1858. His target was barely scratched, but 156 people were injured, and eight eventually succumbed. Orsini was guillotined on March 13. Palmerston tried to pass a Conspiracy To Murder Bill, making plotting to murder foreign rulers a felony, but mishandled its passage, and was driven from office. See Jad Adam, "Striking a Blow for Freedom," *History Today*, 53:9 (September 2003), pp. 18–19.

90. For Spain, this was the first clear example of "propaganda by the deed." In October 1878 a young Catalan cooper called Juan Oliva had fired a gun at Alfonso XII but missed. A year later, the nineteen-year-old Francisco Otero tried to do the same, but proved an equally poor shot. Neither was clearly connected to anarchist circles, and both were promptly executed. (Núñez, *El terrorismo*, p. 38.)

Pallás was a poor young lithographer from Tarragon, who had emigrated to Argentina; he married there, and then moved to Brazil in search of a better livelihood to support his family. He had become a radical and anarchist while working as a typesetter in Santa Fé. On May Day 1892 he threw a petard into the Alcantara theatre in Rio shouting "Viva la anarquía!" No one was hurt, and the audience burst into cheers. The reason for this enthusiasm is that in the early days of Brazilian anarchism the comrades were too poor to buy a building for holding political meetings and putting on their own plays, so they rented local theatres instead. Pallas' Rio audience would have been Spanish and Portuguese anarchists, while Sao Paolo was the domain of their Italian immigrant opposite numbers. (See Edgar Rodrigues, *Os Anarquistas, Trabalhadores italianos no Brasil* [Sao Paolo: Global editora e distribuidora, 1984], pp. 66 and 73). When the Spanish police searched his house they found anarchist newspapers, a copy of Kropotkin's *The Conquest of Hunger*, and a lithograph of the Haymarket Martyrs. Most historians have argued that he acted partly out of indignation at the Jerez garrotings, but Núñez says there is no document in Pallás's hand to support this claim. Compare Esenwein, *Anarchist Ideology*, pp.184–5; Núñez, *El terrorismo*, pp. 49 and 53; and Maura, "Terrorism," p. 130 (he says two were killed, and twelve wounded).

Guillermo Tell, causing a large number of deaths and severe injuries among scores of the city's moneyed elite. Many innocent suspects were arrested and tortured before Salvador was caught in hiding.[91] After declaring he had acted to avenge Pallás, whom he knew and admired, he was garroted at Montjuich on the 24th.[92] Sagasta (in power again since 1892), proclaimed martial law in Barcelona, which lasted for a year. Its executor was none other than Weyler, just back from the Philippines. The anarchist press was forcibly shut down.

Then, on December 9, Auguste Vaillant hurled a large bomb into the French Parliament, which killed no one, but wounded several of the deputies. On February 5, 1894, he was guillotined, the first instance in French memory of the death penalty being used in a case where no victim had died.[93] (President Sadi Carnot, mediocre grandson of Lazare Carnot, the Revolution's great military chief, refused to commute the sentence, for which he was stabbed to death in Lyon, on June 24, 1894. His assassin, the young Italian anarchist Sante Jeronimo Caserio, was guillotined two months later.) The culmination of this wave of anarchist bombs (though not its end by any means) came with a series of deathdealing explosions in Paris immediately following Vaillant's execution, and clearly in part intended to avenge him. The perpetrator was found to be Émile Henry, a young intellectual born in Spain to fleeing Communard exiles.[94] He too was quickly caught, and

91. The opera selected may not have been random. At its first convention in 1879 the Narodnaya Volya produced a program that, *inter alia*, stated: "we will fight with the means employed by Wilhelm Tell;" the legendary Swiss archer was widely regarded as an ancestral hero by late-nineteenth-century European radicals. See Walter Laqueur, *A History of Terrorism* (New Brunswick, NJ: Transaction, 2002, revised edition), p. 22.

92. Salvador had started out as a Carlist and ardent Catholic, but poverty, petty crime (smuggling), and unpayable debts had aroused his interest in anarchism. Five other people were executed with him, though there is no convincing evidence that he did not, like Pallás, act on his own. See especially Esenwein, *Anarchist Ideology*, pp. 186–7, and Maura, "Terrorism," p. 130. According to Bécarud and Lapouge, *Anarchistes*, p. 44, when he was asked what would happen to his daughters after his execution, Santiago Salvador said: "If they are pretty, the bourgeois will take care of them." Anarchist *boutade*? Or myth?

93. Maitron says Vaillant came in handy for certain *dirigeants* of the Third Republic, who were reeling from public revelations about the Panama Canal Bubble scandal, and found him a wonderful way to shift public attention elsewhere—also to enact harsh laws against "revolutionary propaganda" of any kind. *Le mouvement*, p. 237.

94. Henry was a three-year-old baby when the family fled. In Spain, his father was forced to find work in a mine, and died an excruciating death from mercury poisoning. Returning to France after the amnesty of 1880, the boy proved a brilliant student, who got into the École Polytechnique. But he dropped out in 1891 (aged 23) for the sake of anarchism. See Joan Ungersma Halperin's riveting *Félix Fénéon: Aesthete and Anarchist in Fin-de-Siècle Paris* (New Haven: Yale University Press, 1988), p. 268.

guillotined on May 21.[95] (For this study the single most important bombing did not come till the "outrage" of Corpus Christi Day on June 7, 1896, in Barcelona, but this will be left for consideration in Chapter 4.)

None of these five famous bombers of 1892–94 fit Simoun's personal profile. All of them were quite young, poor, half-educated (except for Henry), and self-proclaimed anarchists. None of their bombs had anything Huysmanesque about them. But consider some of the words that Emile Henry spoke at his trial, as reported by Joll.[96] Asked why he had killed so many innocent people, Henry replied sardonically, "Il n'y a pas d'innocents" (There are no innocents). Then:

> I was convinced that the existing organization [of society] was bad; I wanted to struggle against it so as to hasten its disappearance. I brought to the struggle a profound hatred, intensified every day by the revolting spectacle of a society where all is base, all is cowardly, where everything is a barrier to the development of human passions, to generous tendencies of the heart, to the free flight of thought . . . I wanted to show the bourgeoisie that their pleasures would be disturbed, that their golden calf would tremble violently on its pedestal, until the final shock would cast it down in mud and blood.

He went on to declare that anarchists

> do not spare bourgeois women and children, because the wives and children of those they love are not spared either. Are not those children innocent victims, who, in the slums, die slowly of anaemia because bread is scarce at home; or those women who grow pale in your workshops and wear themselves out to earn forty sous a day, and yet are lucky when poverty does not turn them into prostitutes; those old people whom you have turned into machines for production all their lives, and whom you cast on the garbage dump and into the workhouse when their strength is exhausted. At least have the courage of your crimes, gentlemen of the bourgeoisie, and agree that our reprisals are fully legitimate.
>
> You have hanged men in Chicago, cut off their heads in Germany, strangled them in Jerez, shot them in Barcelona, guillotined them in Montbrisons and Paris, but what you will never destroy is anarchism. Its roots are too deep; it is born in the heart of a corrupt society which is falling to pieces; it is a violent reaction against

95. Clémenceau, deeply moved by Henry's execution, wrote: "Le forfait Henry est d'un sauvage. L'acte de la société m'apparaît comme une basse vengeance . . . Que les partisans de la peine de mort aillent, s'ils l'osent, renifler le sang de la Roquette. Nous causerons après." [Henry's crime was that of a savage. But society's act seems to me a base revenge . . . Let the partisans of the death penalty go, if they have the courage, to sniff the blood at La Roquette (after 1851, the prison where all death sentences in Paris were carried out). Then we shall talk.] Quoted in Maitron, *Le mouvement*, p. 246.

96. *Ibid.*, p. 115–19. Note Henry's references to Jerez and Chicago, as well as Pallás and Vaillant.

the established order. It represents egalitarian and libertarian aspirations which are battering down existing authority; it is everywhere, which makes it impossible to capture. It will end by killing you.

Henry's rhetoric uncannily reproduces that of Simoun: hastening the rush of a corrupt system to the abyss, violent revenge against the ruling class (including its "innocents") for its crimes against the wretched and the poor, and the vision of an egalitarian and free society in the future. Although Tagalog peasants had their own utopian and messianic traditions, embedded in folk-Catholicism,[97] Simoun's discourse does not reflect them, but rather a language of European social fury that went back at least to the French Revolution, if not before. But Simoun is imagined in a more complex, and also contradictory manner. There is in him a negative photograph of the aristocratic "socialist" Rodolphe, who practices his own vigilante justice on evildoers and exploiters, of Des Esseintes adding one more enemy to a hideous society, and perhaps even of Nechayev.[98] At the same time, however, Simoun is an anticolonial nationalist, with a revolution of sorts on his mind. But if one were to ask the illegitimate question "Supposing the bomb-plot had succeeded, what next?" the illegitimate answer would have to be, "Nihil." Simoun has no plans for the aftermath of his successful vengeance, and nothing in El Filibusterismo suggests that anyone else has either: only a dream of "liberty," formless and utopian. (This must be one reason why the conspiracy has to fail.) It is exactly here that Rizal marked

---

97. The locus classicus is Reynaldo Clemeña Ileto, Pasyón and Revolution: Popular Movements in the Philippines, 1840–1910 (Quezon City: Ateneo de Manila Press, 1989).

98. One should not rule Nechayev out. The Catechism of a Revolutionary that he coauthored with Bakunin in 1869 was widely read all over Europe. In the issues of La Solidaridad of January 15 and 31, 1893, there is a curious two-part article by Blumentritt, titled "Una Visita," describing an unexpected visitor in the form of Simoun, who explains that Rizal had him appear to die in the novel to conceal from the colonial authorities his survival and his massive political multiplication among the Filipino population. A long and heated debate develops between them on the future of the Philippines, and on the methods to be pursued in the political struggle. At one point, the indignant ethnologist says: "Señor Simoun, usted es no solo filibustero sino también nihilista" (Mr Simoun, you are not merely a subversive, you are also a Nihilist). To this, as he makes his mysterious departure, Simoun retorts sardonically: "Me marcho á Rusia para estudiar allí en la escuela de nihilistas" [I am leaving for Russia, to enrol there in the school of the Nihilists]! Nechayev had died before Rizal arrived in Europe. But Blumentritt was Rizal's closest friend, and I think it unlikely that he would have associated Simoun with Nihilism if the two had not discussed the latter seriously. Besides, Dostoievsky's The Possessed had come out in French translation in Paris in 1886, not long after Rizal had left the French capital for Germany. We know also, thanks to De Ocampo, that Rizal read (but when exactly?) Turgenev's Fathers and Sons in a German translation. (My thanks to Megan Thomas for bringing Blumentritt's articles to my attention.)

the crisscrossing of anticolonial nationalism and "propaganda by the deed," with its planless utopianism and its taste for self-immolation. From my deed and death something will come which will be better than the unlivable present.

The same thematic appears in the scene where Basilio, learning of the "infernal machine" inside the pomegranate, exclaims: "¿Qué dirá el mundo, á vista de tanta carnicería?" (But what will the world say at the sight of such carnage?) Simoun sardonically replies thus:

¡El mundo aplaudirá como siempre, dando la razón al más fuerte, al más violento! Europa ha aplaudido cuando las naciones del occidente sacrificaron en América millones de indios y no por cierto para fundar naciones mucho más morales ni más pacíficas; allí está el Norte con su libertad egoista, su ley de Lynch, sus engaños políticos; allí está el Sur con sus repúblicas intranquilas, sus revoluciones bárbaras, guerras civiles, pronunciamientos, como en su madre España! Europa ha aplaudido cuando la poderosa Portugal despojó á las islas Molucas, aplaude cuando Inglaterra destruye en el Pacífico las razas primitivas para implantar la de sus emigrados. Europa aplaudirá como se aplaude al fine de un drama, al fin du una tragedia; el vulgo se fija poco en el fondo, ¡sólo mira el efecto!

The world will applaud, as always, legitimizing the more powerful and the more violent. Europe applauded when the nations of the West sacrificed the lives of millions of *indios* in America, and definitely not in order to found other nations far more moral or peace-loving. Yonder stands the North, with its egoistic liberty, its lynch law, its political manipulations; yonder stands the South with its turbulent republics, its barbarous revolutions, its civil wars, and its pronunciamientos, like its mother Spain! Europe applauded when a powerful Portugal plundered the Moluccas, and [now] applauds as England destroys in the Pacific region the local primitive races in order to implant that of its own emigrants. Europe will applaud [us], as it applauds the end of a drama, the denouement of a tragedy. The common people barely notice the bases of what is happening, they simply observe its effects![99]

The examples Simoun gives are English, Portuguese, and American, but his logic applies just as certainly to Argentina, Colombia, Venezuela, and Peru, representing those caudillo-ridden post-revolutionary Latin American republics of which Simoun has earlier spoken so contemptuously. At the same time, however, the examples, stated and unstated, are all of violent "successes." Seen in the light of this rhetoric, a "success" of this type was becoming imaginable in the Philippines. Five years after the publication of *El Filibusterismo* Andrés Bonifacio would begin an armed insurrection on the outskirts of Manila—a bare eighteen months after Martí led the way in Cuba.

---

99. *El Filibusterismo*, chapter XXXIII ("La última razón" [The final argument]), p. 250.

AN ENIGMATIC SMILE

This brings us to one last political aspect of *El Filibusterismo*. The novel's final pages are filled with a lengthy dialogue between the dying Simoun and the gentle native priest, Father Florentino, with whom he has found temporary refuge. Simoun poses to the priest the question of Ivan Karamazov: If *vuestro Dios* demands such inhuman sacrifices, such humiliations, tortures, expropriations, misery and exploitation of the good and innocent, telling them simply to suffer and to work, *Qué Dios es ése*? (What kind of God is this?)[100] Florentino replies with a lengthy homily justifying the divinity's ways to man. He tells Simoun that God understands all his sufferings and will forgive him, but that he has chosen evil methods to achieve worthy ends, and this is inadmissible. Most commentators have assumed that the old priest represents Rizal's last word on the politico-moral drama of the novel. But to make this judgment so easily requires overlooking two things. First, Simoun says nothing during or after the homily, and he may not even be listening. He makes no proper confession and nor does he ask for forgiveness. Moments later he is dead. Second is the strange brief chapter near the end, called "El misterio," of whose seven pages in the original manuscript three were blacked out by the author.

We are in the house of the rich Orenda family, at which three callers have arrived in the chaotic aftermath of the failed explosion and armed incursions. One of the visitors is the young blade Momoy (suitor of the eldest Orenda daughter Sensia), who attended the fateful wedding party of Paulita Gomez and was a befuddled witness to what happened. Another is the student Isagani who, to save Paulita's life, had seized the lethal lamp and plunged into the Pasig river with it. Momoy tells the family that an unknown robber ran off with the lamp, before diving into the water. Sensia breaks in to say, remarkably: "Un ladrón? Uno de la Mano Negra?" (A robber? A member of the Black Hand?) "No one knows," Momoy continues, "whether he was a Spaniard, a Chinese, or an *indio*." The third visitor, a silversmith who helped do the wedding decorations, adds that the rumor is that the lamp was on the verge of exploding and the house of the bride was also mined with gunpowder. Momoy is stunned and panic-stricken at this, and by his expression shows his fear. Then, seeing that Sensia has noticed, and mortified in his masculinity, he says: "¡Qué lastima!" exclamó haciendo un esfuerzo; "qué mal ha hecho el ladrón! Hubieran muerto todos" ("What a shame!" he exclaimed with an effort. "How the robber bungled it! All would have been killed . . ."). The women are completely petrified. Then:

---

100. *Ibid.*, chapter XXXIX (untitled), p. 283.

"Siempre es malo apoderarse de lo que no es suyo," contestó Isagani con
enigmática sonrisa; "si ese ladrón hubiese sabido de qué se trataba y hubiese
podido reflexionar, de seguro que no lo habría hecho." Y añadió despues de una
pausa: "Por nada del mundo quiseira estar en su lugar"

"It is always wrong to seize something which does not belong to one," said Isagani
with an enigmatic smile. "If the robber had known what it was all about, and if he
had been able to reflect upon it, he certainly would not have done what he did." And,
after a pause, he added: "I would not be in his place for anything in the world."

An hour later, Isagani takes his leave to "retire permanently" in the household
of his uncle (Father Florentino), and disappears from the novel.[101] The
goodhearted, patriotic student, who has never smiled enigmatically before
(it is the specialty of saturnine Simoun), regrets that he wrecked the jeweler's
scheme. The Spanish makes it clear that to retire "permanently" (*por siempre*)
is merely his intention at the moment of departure. In whose footsteps will he
follow? It is as if the reader is invited to await a sequel to *El Filibusterismo*.

We are now perhaps in a better position to understand both the proleptic
character of the book, and the significance of Rizal's terming it a Filipino
novel. The prolepsis is mostly engineered by a massive, ingenious transfer of
real events, experiences, and sentiments from Spain to the Philippines, which
then appear as shadows of an imminent future; their imminence is in turn
guaranteed by a firm embedment in the time of Captain-General Weyler,
who was still in power when the book came out. But Simoun is another
matter altogether. He has his origins in previous fictions, including *Noli me
tangere*, and enters the novel not from Spain, but from an imagined Cuba,
and from wanderings across the earth. He is a sort of *espectro mundial* come
to haunt the Philippines, mirroring what Izquierdo had once fantasized as the
invisible machiavellian network of the International. Not there yet in reality,
but, since already imagined, just like his nation, on the way.

The Spanish empire had always been primarily American, and its virtual
evaporation between 1810 and 1830 promised a final liquidation to the
residues, while also proffering warnings of the consequences of prematurity.
Europe itself, Rizal thought, was menaced by a vast conflagration among its
warring powers, but also by violent movement from below. *El Filibusterismo*
was written from the wings of a global proscenium on which Bismarck and
Vera Zasulich, Yankee manipulations and Cuban insurrections, Meiji Japan
and the British Museum, Huysmans and the Commune, Catalonia and the
Carolines, Nihilists and anarchists, all had their places. *Cochers* and "ho-
meopathists" too.

---

101. *Ibid.*, pp. 271–2.

In late 1945, a bare two months after the Japanese occupation of his country had collapsed, but at a moment when Dutch colonialism had yet to return in force, Indonesia's young first prime minister, Sutan Sjahrir, described the condition of his revolution-starting countrymen as *gelisah*. This is not a word that is easily translated into English: one has to imagine a semantic range covering "anxious," "trembling," "unmoored," and "expectant." This is the feel of *El Filibusterismo*. Something is coming.

4

Trials of a Novelist

CHERNYCHEVSKY'S QUESTION

Having packed off virtually the entire edition of *El Filibusterismo* to his trusted older friend José Basa in Hong Kong, and having wound up his remaining affairs, Rizal left Europe on October 19, 1891. Except for a single somber day, he would never set foot on it again. The timing was well chosen. Valeriano Weyler's four-year term as Captain-General of the Philippines would end within a month. His successor, General Eulogio Despujol, who had made his career largely as a capable staff officer, was thought to be much less ferocious. (Indeed, he soon made himself highly popular with his colonized subjects by publicly sacking many corrupt officials and packing them off home, as well as taking his distance from the powerful religious Orders).[1]

Rizal's family had repeatedly warned him not to come back, urging him rather to settle in the placid security of Hong Kong, only 800 miles from Manila, where they would try to visit him. Within days of his arrival in the Crown Colony, his aged father, his brother Paciano, and one of his brothers-in-law arrived, the last two having "escaped" from internal exile on the island of Mindoro.[2] Before the end of the year, his almost completely blind mother and two of his sisters followed. The young novelist opened a successful ophthalmological practice, and his happily reunited family appeared to welcome the idea of settling down under British rule. But his reputation

---

1. See Schumacher, *The Propaganda Movement*, pp. 274–5, for details on Despujol's policies and personality.

2. It seems unlikely that all these people could leave the Philippines as regular steamship passengers without the knowledge of the colonial authorities. Perhaps it was easier to close their eyes than formally to rescind Weyler's sequestration decrees.

as his country's foremost intellectual leader, and the terms on which he had left Europe, made it difficult for him long to accede to his family's wishes. He was besieged with letters from his more radical comrades, still in Europe, asking him what he would do "next," and promising their full support, whatever "next" turned out to be. Having told Del Pilar and his associates that they were wasting their time in Europe, Rizal knew how devastatingly being seen to waste time in Hong Kong could be turned against him.

Chto dyelat? We can see in photographic negative one central alternative from an alarmed, trenchant letter from Ferdinand Blumentritt, dated January 30, 1892.

> Vor allen bitte ich Dich, lass Dich in keine revolutionären Agitationen ein! Denn, wer eine Revolution inszeniert, muss wenigstens die Wahrscheinlichkeit eines Erfolges für sich haben, wenn er sein Gewissen nicht mit dem unnütz vergossenen Blute belasten will. So oft ein Volk gegen ein anderes herrschendes, eine Kolonie gegen das Mutterland sich empörten, hat die Revolution nie durch eigene Kraft gesiegt. Die amerikanische Union wurde frei, weil Frankreich, Spanien und Holland sich mit ihr allierten. Die spanischen Republiken wurden frei, weil im Mutterlande Bürgerkrieg herrschte u. England u. Nordamerika sie mit Geld und Waffen versorgten. Die Griechen wurden frei, weil England, Frankreich u. Russland sie unterstützten, Rumänen, Serben, Bulgaren wurden durch Russland frei. Italien wurde frei durch Frankreich u. Preussen, Belgien durch England und Frankreich. Überall, wo die Volker auf die eigene Kraft vertrauten, erlagen sie der Soldatesca der Legitimen Gewalt: so die Italiener 1830, 1848 u. 1848, die Polen 1831, 1845 und 1863, die Ungara 1848 u. 1849, die Kider 1868.

> Above all, I beg you not to get involved in revolutionary agitation! For he who stages a revolution should at the least have before him the likelihood of success, if he does not wish to have his conscience burdened with useless bloodshed. Whenever a people has rebelled against another people dominating it, [or] a colony against the Motherland, the revolution has never succeeded solely on the basis of its own strength. The American Union became free because France, Spain and the Netherlands allied with it. The Spanish republics became free because civil war raged in the Motherland, and England and North America provided money and guns. The Greeks became free because England, France and Russia offered their support. The Rumanians, Serbs and Bulgarians were liberated by Russia. The Italians were liberated thanks to France and Prussia, and the Belgians thanks to England and France. Everywhere, those peoples who relied solely on their own strength were crushed by the soldiery of Legitimacy: the Italians in 1830, 1848, and 1849; the Poles in 1831, 1845, and 1863, the Hungarians in 1848 and 1849, and the Cretans in 1868.[3]

---

3. *Cartas entre Rizal y El Profesor Fernando Blumentritt, 1890–1896*, pp. 783–4. The transcribed text is corrupt. *Ungara* should be *Ungarn*. *Kider* was certainly originally *Kreter*. The Christian Cretans' uprising against Turkish cont'd over/

Blumentritt went on to say that no revolution of this kind has any chance of success unless: (1) part of the enemy's army and navy mutiny; (2) the Motherland is at war with another nation; (3) money and weapons have been prepared well beforehand; (4) a foreign power officially or secretly supports the insurrection. He added, "Not one of these conditions is met in the Philippines [today]."[4] Teaching at Leitmeritz, in the heart of a Habsburg empire which never helped any people to be free, but around which Poles, Hungarians, Italians, Serbs, Bulgarians, Rumanians, Greeks, and even Cretans orbited, Blumentritt appeared to have recent history and the rules of strategy firmly on his side. He was also right that in 1891 none of his four preconditions for Philippine success was present. But would this situation long persist?

On the other hand, Rizal's energetic younger friend Edilberto Evangelista (later a slain hero of the 1896–98 armed insurrection against Spain) wrote to Rizal thus on April 29, 1892 from (then) French-speaking Ghent:[5]

Pourquoi ne tentez-vous pas un effort pour savoir au moins le nombre de ceux qui suivrent vos idées et qui sont allumés du même élan; je veux dire qu'il faut donner une forme à vos pensées, en organisant en dépit du Gouvernement un Club Revolutionnaire dont la direction vous en auriez à Hongkong ou à autre part n'importe quoi. Ne l'ont-ils pas les Séparatistes de Cuba? N'ont-ils pas les Progresistes [*sic*] d'Espagne?

Why don't you try at least to find out the number of those who accept your ideas and are on fire with the same élan; what I mean is that it is essential to give

3 *cont'd*   rule in 1868 was indeed bloodily crushed. It is curious that the many biographies of Rizal that feature quotations from this famous letter always offer the reader the incomprehensible "the Kider," or "los Kider," seemingly unaware of any oddity. Even more weirdly, the National Historical Institute's *The Rizal–Blumentritt Correspondence, 1890–1896* (Manila: 1992), p. 430, offers "the Irish" as a translation. What must have happened is that the bemused transcriber read the close-set *et* as a *d*, leaving an impenetrable *Krder*. A vowel was then needed which could be read from Kreter's first *r*, and only *i* had the necessary vertical shape.

4. Note the phrasing of "lass Dich nicht in keine revolutionären Agitationen ein" in the quoted extract, which implies not leadership but entanglement. In his earlier-cited letter to Rizal of July 4, 1892, the Austrian wrote: "They were not Pilaristas but Rizalistas who have written to me that Rizal should found a revolutionary newspaper or start a revolutionary movement. I admonished them not to advise you to do such a thing, and so I wrote to you at once." These letters of Blumentritt appear not to have survived.

5. Evangelista, along with José Abreu and José Alejandrino, had been persuaded by Rizal to leave "backward" Spain and study engineering (on Blumentritt's advice) in Ghent. Alejandrino, later to become a general in the Revolution, lived with Rizal in Brussels while *El Filibusterismo* was being written, found him a publisher in Ghent, and helped with proofreading. Evangelista, Alejandrino, and Antonio Luna were all strong Rizal partisans against what Alejandrino called "the lamentable policy" of Del Pilar. See Schumacher, *The Propaganda Movement*, pp. 236, 271–2.

form to your ideas by organizing, in defiance of the government, a Revolutionary Club, which you could direct from Hong Kong or any other place. Isn't this what the Cuban separatists have (done)? And Spain's Progressives?[6]

CONRAD COUNTRY

Rizal's first plan for resolving, or evading, these contradictory pressures was to form a settlement for his family and like-minded friends on the bay of Sandakan in what is today the east Malaysian federal state of Sabah. Geographically, it was as close to the Philippines as one could get—250 miles from Jolo, seat of the once-powerful Muslim sultanate of Sulu, still restive under loose Spanish overlordship, and a little over 600 miles from Manila. The same distances separated Havana from Miami, and from Tampa, where Martí was recruiting revolutionaries among the Cuban tobacco-worker communities. Politically, too, it could seem promising. The northern littoral of Borneo was, in the 1890s, a very peculiar Conradian place. On the western portion lay the kingdom of the so-called White Rajahs, founded by the English adventurer James Brooke in the 1840s, and under London's hands-off protection from the 1880s. The residues of the once-powerful sultanate of Brunei occupied a small niche in the middle, while the eastern portion, including Sandakan, was governed after 1882 by a private business, the British North Borneo Chartered Company. Better still, in 1885 the Spanish had been induced to abandon any quasi-legal claims to the territory deriving from the shifting suzerainty of Jolo. Hence, while Hong Kong was under the suspicious eyes of the Spanish consul and the Catholic Orders' local branches, Sandakan was free of both. It is not surprising, therefore, that some of Rizal's more fiery comrades in Europe, such as Evangelista and Antonio Luna, dreaming of Martí's Florida, were enthusiastic about the planned settlement. Some time in January 1892, Luna wrote to Rizal in Hong Kong that "Borneo será un Cayo Hueso para nosotros, y muy probable sea yo también uno de sus habitantes, si las circunstancias me obligan" (Borneo will be for us a Cayo Hueso [Bone Reef, phonetically garbled by the Americans into Key West], and it is very probable that I

---

6. *Cartas entre Rizal y sus colegas de la Propaganda*, p. 800. Martí had formed his Cuban Revolutionary Party in the United States the previous January. The Spanish reference is certainly to the radical republican followers of Manuel Ruiz Zorrilla, who spent much of his political life plotting revolution in Parisian exile. A number of Rizal's friends contributed to the Zorrillista newspapers *El Porvenir* and *El Progreso*, which were generally friendly to the Filipino cause. See Schumacher, *The Propaganda Movement*, pp. 46, 55 and 202.

will become one of its denizens, if circumstances make it necessary).[7] On the other hand, Sandakan also promised an unbadgered life for Rizal's family, and for the novelist himself, his library and his writing.[8] He also

---

7. *Cartas entre Rizal y sus colegas*, pp. 771–2. The whole letter is of great interest, since Luna was highly intelligent. He told Rizal he was heading back to Manila to work for independence. "Para todo eso será preciso mucho estudio, mucho tacto, prudencia y nada de alardes de ser fuertes . . . Con constancia y silencio seremos unos jesuitas para plantar una casa donde pongamos un clavo. Ofrezco, pues, en este sentido mi concurso, pero con la sola condición de que podré desligarme de la campaña activa si viera que será sólo un motín. . . . Creo que me comprendes bien, si nos vencen que cueste mucha sangre. Iré, pues, á Manila y en todos mis actos tendré siempre presente mi deber de separatista. Nada de desconfianzas, si las circunstancias me colocan al lado de los españoles en Manila, peor para ellos: me ganaré la vida e iré minando el suelo á costa de ellos hasta que la fruta esté madura, Tenéis ya, pues (si son vuestras ideas éstas), un satélite por aquí que trabajará con constancia." [But this will require much study, much tact, prudence, and no empty boasting about our strength. . . . With constancy and silence we will be like Jesuits, setting up a house for which we have a key. So, in this sense, I am offering you my assistance, but with the single condition that I can disengage from the active campaign if I see that it will be nothing more than a mutiny . . . I believe you understand me well, that if they win, it will cost much bloodshed. In any case, I am leaving for Manila, and in all my actions my duty as a separatist will always be before my eyes. No suspicions: if circumstances place me at the side of the Spaniards in Manila, so much the worse for them. I will earn my living and continue mining the land to their cost, until the fruit is ripe. You will have, then (if these ideas are also yours), a satellite on the spot who will work with constancy.]
8. Touchingly, Rizal wrote thus to Blumentritt on January 31, 1892: "Während ich aus meine Amtspflichten ausruhe, schreibe ich den dritten Theil meines Buches auch in Tagalisch. Es wird sich nur um Heimlich tagalischen Sitten die Rede sein, nur um tagalischen Übungen, Tubungen, und Fehler. Leider dass ich es nicht auf Spanisch schreiben darf, denn ich habe einen sehr schönen Gegenstand im kopfe gefunden; ich will einen Roman nach den modernen Sinne des Wortes erdichten, künstlich und litterarisch. Diesmal will ich die Politik und alles den Kunst aufopfern; schriebe ich es auf Spanisch, so warden die armen Tagalen, denen es gewidmet, nichts davon wissen und doch die haben es am meisten nöthig . . . Doch es kostet mir viele Mühe, denn viele von meinen Gedenken konnen sich nicht frei ausdrucken, sonst muss ich neologismes einführen; ausserdem mir fe[h]lt die Übung in Tagalisch zu schreiben." [While resting from my professional labors (as a doctor), I am writing the third part of my book in Tagalog. It will deal solely with Tagalog customs, [i.e.] exclusively with the habits, virtues and defects of the Tagalogs. I feel I cannot write the book in Spanish now that I have found a beautiful theme; I want to write a novel in the modern sense of the word, an artistic and literary novel. This time I would like to sacrifice politics and the rest for the sake of art; if I write in Spanish, then the poor Tagalogs, to whom the work is dedicated, will not understand it, even though it is they who most need to do so . . . The book is giving me a lot of trouble, as many of my thoughts cannot be freely expressed without the need to introduce neologisms. Besides, I lack practice in writing in Tagalog.] *The Rizal – Blumentritt Correspondence, 1890–1896*, unnumbered pages from p. 431. This third novel was never finished. What little there is of it has been carefully reconstructed by Ambeth Ocampo in his *The Search for Rizal's Third Novel, Makamisa* (Manila: Anvil, 1993). Rizal gave up writing it in Tagalog cont'd over/

hoped that many of the dispossessed people in his hometown Calamba would also join him in this Bornean sanctuary.[9]

At the end of March, Rizal made the first of several visits to North Borneo after preliminary negotiations with the British North Borneo Charter Company's representative in Hong Kong. Initially, the prospects seemed quite rosy. Rizal was offered 5,000 acres of uncultivated land rent-free for three years, with the possibility of eventual purchase at a low price. The British North Borneo Charter Company, eager for settlement in a very sparsely populated region, further accepted that the Filipino community would be run by its own members according to their own customs, and be subject neither to corvée nor to unreasonable taxes. But within a few months the whole project started to collapse. Rizal began to realize that he could not raise anything close to the money needed to get the little colony going. Furthermore, populating it would require the agreement of the Spanish to a substantial migration. Rizal wrote to the new Captain-General explaining that he wished to settle down quietly with family and townspeople, but Despujol was not persuaded. An emigration on this scale would put his government in a bad light; besides, the conservative press in Spain would be likely to view it as the start of a Bornean Tampa just out of Manila's political and military reach.[10]

Rizal's alternative, more alarming for his family, was to create the first legal political organization for Filipinos in the Philippines itself. What this plan amounted to is difficult to determine. No document in Rizal's own hand survives. Virtually all the written evidence, often contradictory, comes from testimony given to, or extracted by, police interrogators and torturers four

8 cont'd after twenty manuscript pages, and reverted to Spanish. *Makamisa* means "After Mass," and the text, focused on the townspeople of Pili and their Peninsular parish priest, returns to the satirical *costumbrista* style of *Noli me tangere*. Perhaps this is why he gave up on it, or maybe he concluded that he could not go beyond *El Filibusterismo*. In any event, after mid-1892 he seems to have abandoned any idea of further novel-writing.

9. It will be recalled that it was Rizal who had strongly urged the tenants and townspeople of Calamba to take the Dominicans to court, and pushed the case right up to the Supreme Court in Madrid. As already noted, when the vengeful Order won the case, and Weyler, in addition to burning houses, forbade the recalcitrants to reside anywhere near Calamba, Rizal was devastated and felt enormously guilty for the suffering he had brought on his hometown.

10. The comparison between Sandakan and Tampa is, in one sense, unwarranted. The British had no designs on the Philippines, whereas powerful groups in the United States had had their avaricious eyes on Cuba for some time. But the contrast may have seemed less obvious in the 1890s than it does today. It is hard to imagine Antonio Luna and Edilberto Evangelista promising from Europe to join Rizal in Sandakan if they expected no more from it than a chance to grow vegetables and read some books.

years later, after the outbreak of the Revolution.[11] (Rizal himself was not interrogated in 1892 though, as we shall soon see, he was arrested within ten days of returning to Manila, and just after a private banquet held to proclaim the founding of what he called the Liga Filipina.)

LA LIGA FILIPINA

The five stated aims of the Liga Filipina appear to have been compatible with the thinking evident in Rizal's writings and correspondence after 1890: (1) union of the entire archipelago into a compact, vigorous, and homogeneous body; (2) mutual protection in every exigency and need; (3) defence against all violence and injustice; (4) development of education, agriculture and commerce; and (5) the study and application of reforms.[12] The first point clearly implied that colonial law would have to be radically changed to eliminate the tiered privileges of Peninsulars, creoles, and mestizos. The remaining points suggested that the colonial state was often lawless, and doing very little to create a modern society. As a whole, however, the program, and the polite language it employed, was within the bounds of existing colonial Philippine legality. Beyond that there was the unstated example of 1880s Cuba where, as we shall shortly see, slavery had been abolished, political parties, to say nothing of civic and even leftwing associations, had been been legalized (within definite limits), and, within comparable limits, a various and lively press had developed. If all this was possible in Cuba, why not also in the Philippines? It seemed a reasonable try.

But the Liga's internal organization, as far as the confessions of 1896 outlined it, was clearly designed for partial clandestinity. Formally, it was to be based on local councils, whose heads would form higher councils at the provincial level; the heads of the provincial councils would then create a supreme council with power of command over the entire Liga. Yet each member was bound to

---

11. See Guerrero, *The First Filipino*, pp. 315–16. Guerrero refers to W.E. Retana's 1907 work *Vida y escritos del Dr José Rizal* as his main source, and Retana relied almost entirely on the police reports. A very important exception is the *Memoria* of Isabelo de los Reyes, composed while he was held in Manila's Bilibid prison, suspected (unjustly) of complicity in Bonifacio's insurrection of August 1896. He interviewed many of his *insurrecto* fellow-prisoners. It was soon published, with the addition of other material, as *La sensacional memoria de Isabelo de los Reyes sobre la Revolución Filipina de 1896–97* (Madrid: Tip. Lit. de J. Corrales, 1899).

12. Guerrero, *The First Filipino*, p. 295, citing Retana's book (pp. 236ff.), where the source is said to be an unidentified document given to the author by Epifanio de los Santos.

sacrifice all personal interests and obey blindly and to the letter all commands and all verbal or written instructions of his own councils or the head of the next higher council; and immediately and without losing time inform the authorities of his council of anything he might see, observe, or hear constituting a danger to the tranquillity of the Liga . . .; and keep the deeds, acts, and decisions of his council and of the Liga . . . absolutely secret from outsiders, even though these are his own parents, brothers, children, etc., and even at the cost of his own life.

He should also "submit to no humiliation," "go to the rescue of any fellow member in danger, and also recruit new members." (Characteristically, perhaps, wives and sisters were evidently not worth the mentioning.)[13]

It is not easy to believe that this authoritarian structure, evidently adapted from Masonry's ancestral lore, was Rizal's brainchild.[14] The novelist seems to have become a Mason some time after his return to Europe in 1888, but the lodge was in Madrid, where he stayed only briefly. Nothing suggests that he was active after moving back to northern Europe. So far as is known, no natives in the colony became Masons until 1891, though their numbers increased rapidly thereafter.[15] It is much more likely that the structure was the brainchild of Andrés Bonifacio, who formed the underground revolutionary Katipunan not long after Rizal's deportation to Mindanao and the Liga's abrupt disintegration.[16] For *katipuneros* interrogated under torture in

13. Guerrero was inclined to trust the interrogations, but only up to a point. A generation earlier, Rafael Palma had used them unsuspiciously in his *Biografía de Rizal* (Manila: Bureau of Printing, 1949). The shift is instructive. In the 1940s, Rizal was still an uncontroversial revolutionary hero. By the 1960s, he had come under attack for bourgeois shilly-shallying, if not worse, and Guerrero's work was in part a nuanced response.

14. In December 1896, Rizal told his interrogators that on arriving in Hong Kong he had been asked by José Basa, an active Mason, to draw up statutes for a Liga Filipina on the basis of Masonic practices, but had no idea what Basa did with them. This seems a bit too casual, but no such statutes in his hand have ever come to light. See Horacio de la Costa, SJ, ed. and trans., *The Trial of Rizal: W.E. Retana's Transcription of the Official Spanish Documents* (Quezon City: Ateneo de Manila University Press, 1961), p. 6: "excitado por D. José Basa . . . redactó los estatutos y reglamentos de una Sociedad denominada 'Liga Filipina,' bajo las bases de las prácticas masónicas . . . que en este momento no recuerda el declarante haber indicado ningún fin político en los estatutos, que se los entregó á José Basa, no recordando á la persona que se los remitió." It should be mentioned that in Spain Del Pilar was also thinking about a Liga Filipina—it was in the air, so to speak.

15. Schumacher, *The Propaganda Movement*, pp. 174–5.

16. Here Isabelo's recollections are very interesting, though many historians have found him an unreliable witness. "No es extraño, pues, que Rizal dejara encargo de invitarme á figurar en la Liga filipina, cuando él fué deportado á Dapitan. El inspirado compositor musical, D. Julio Nakpil, fué el encargado de llevarme un ejemplar de los Estatutos de la Liga, diciéndome que Rizal en persona había estado en mi casa, antes de ser deportado, pero que no me encontró.   cont'd over/

late 1896 it would have been easy to attribute their organization's shape to the Liga, both because this was what the interrogator wanted to hear, and because Bonifacio always claimed that the two associations were continuous.

And then? Here the comparison with Martí is illuminating.[17] Martí was a first-generation creole, whose native language was Spanish, and who married, not very happily, into the Cuban plantocracy (he may have been gay). Most of his adult life had been spent in Mexico and the United States which, in 1892, for all its voracious intracontinental expansionism, was not yet a colonial power; in the broad, old sense of the word, he was an *americano*. He had extensive contacts throughout Latin America, even serving as honorary Uruguayan consul in the United States. He made his reputation as an orator, poet, and brilliant publicist over many years. Furthermore, he had extensive experience of political organizing, and could build on Cuba's internal insurrections in previous decades, as well as armed incursions launched, with various degrees of participation by interested American lobbies, from the United States. He had no illusions about what would happen to him if he returned legally to Cuba, and had a number of alternatives before him. And: as a result of the ten-year-long Céspedes-initiated rebellion of 1868–78, and its short aftermath, the Guerra Chiquita of 1879–80, there were thousands of

---

16 cont'd   Cuando lei en los Estatutos 'obediencia ciega y pena de muerte al que descubriese algún secreto de la Liga,' . . . soy de carácter y de opinión muy independiente, y acaso serviría yo sólo para perturbar la disciplina que es muy necesaria en toda sociedad" [It is not surprising that when Rizal was deported to Dapitan, he left instructions to have me invited to become a member of the League. The inspired composer Don Julio Nakpil was the one charged with bringing me a copy of the League's statutes, telling me that Rizal had personally gone to my house, but had not found me at home. When I read in these statutes about "blind obedience and the penalty of death for anyone revealing any League secret," (I refused tactfully to join, offering various reasons.) My character and opinions are very independent, and maybe my joining would serve only to disturb the discipline that is very necessary for any association.] *La sensacional memoria*, p. 105. There is no obvious reason to doubt Isabelo's veracity, but it is inconceivable that Rizal would have written up any statutes demanding "blind obedience" and imposing the death penalty for disclosing the Liga's secrets. While it is true that Rizal went to Isabelo's home to talk to him but found him out, it is implausible that he would have sent Nakpil to convey the invitation. Isabelo was the most important Filipino journalist in Manila, and a regular contributor (under noms de plume) for *La Solidaridad*. Nakpil at that time was a member of Manila's artisanate—not at all Rizal's milieu— the son of a silversmith, and an autodidact teacher, performer, and repairer of pianos. (His career as a patriotic composer began only after Rizal's death.) He was active in Bonifacio's Katipunan, and after the Supremo's execution, married his widow. See the entry for him in *Filipinos in History*, vol. II, pp. 49–52. There are thus strong grounds for suspecting that he was sent to see Isabelo, not by Rizal, but by Bonifacio.

17. On Martí's origins and career, I have relied mainly on Thomas, *Cuba*, chapter xxv. Martí's father came from Valencia and his mother from Tenerife.

battle-hardened veterans, with long experience in guerrilla warfare, available for renewed armed struggle.

Rizal was a mestizo, partly *indio*, partly Chinese, and partly Spanish, whose native language was not Castilian, and most likely he was never legally married.[18] His adult formation took place all across western Europe, not in the Americas. (He was furious to be taken for an *americano* on first arriving in Marseilles.) He was a skilled publicist, if not an orator, but he was above all an astonishing novelist. His early move to northern Europe, beneficial as it was in so many ways, cost him what Martí had in abundance—practical political experience. The region in which his country was located was almost entirely, and variously, colonial: the British in India–Burma, Malaya, Singapore, and to a shady degree in northern Borneo, the French in Vietnam, Cambodia, and Laos, the Dutch in the vast Indies, and only Siam formally independent. Though Rizal read intensively about many of these places, especially those using Austronesian languages related to his own, he had visited none, except Singapore, and north Borneo for a few days. Manchu China was approaching its final agony. For him there was no close-by *point d'appui*, unlike Martí's vast republican New World. The Philippines had its

---

18. During the last part of his internal exile (for which, see below) he lived contentedly with a woman called Josephine Bracken. Her background is a bit murky. In the brief description of her life that she is said to have penned in February 1897, after Rizal's death, she wrote that she was the daughter of two Belfast Catholics, and was born on August 9, 1876 in Hong Kong's Victoria Barracks, where her father served as a corporal. Her mother, Elizabeth MacBride, died giving birth to her and her father felt he had no choice but to have her adopted by the Taufers, a childless couple he knew. Mr Taufer ran through three hostile wives till, nearly blind, he came with Josephine to seek Rizal's medical services in his place of internal exile on Mindanao island—some time in January or February 1895. After a week of treatment, he seemed better, and the pair returned to Manila. But Josephine deserted the old man there and returned to Mindanao to be with the eye-doctor. There was no possibility of getting married, as the Church insisted that Rizal recant his beliefs beforehand and there was no civil marriage in the colony. The military commandant in charge of him obviously shrugged at the presence of a standard Iberian-style *querida*. Five feet tall, Josephine was four inches smaller than Rizal. Guerrero, *The First Filipino*, pp. 360–67. Alas, Ambeth Ocampo has shown conclusively from internal evidence that this document is a forgery, though he does not identify the forger or his/her motives. While the parts about the Taufers and the medical visit to Dapitan are factual, he also cites research by Rizal biographer Austin Coates in various Hong Kong archives showing that Josephine's birth certificate contains the note "father unknown," and Coates's surmise that her mother was probably a Chinese laundress. The Jesuit father Vicente Balaguer claimed that he married Rizal and Josephine an hour or so before the former was executed, but no marriage certificate has been found, and it is by no means certain that Josephine ever visited Rizal in his death cell. See Ocampo, *Rizal without the Overcoat*, pp. 160–6. For the earlier, standard version, see Guerrero, *The First Filipino*, pp. 472–86. (Josephine stayed with one of Rizal's sisters after arriving with him from Dapitan.)

own tradition of local rural insurrections and creole mutinies, but they were mostly long gone, leaving little for him to work with except Cavite (1872) and its grisly garroting aftermath. In the early 1890s, there were no Catholic Filipinos with any experience of guerrilla warfare.

In the late spring of 1892, Rizal's choices were limited. He had left Europe for good. Sandakan felt more and more like an illusion. Hong Kong was a haven only so long as the British tolerated him—and they had absolutely no interest in upsetting colonial Manila. To remain faithful to his commitments and to all those who regarded him as national leader, he had, it appeared, only one road to travel—back home and above board.

THE SECOND HOMECOMING

On June 19, 1892 Rizal turned thirty-one. The following day he finished two letters, which he entrusted to his Portuguese friend Dr P.L. Márquez, Hong Kong's director of prisons. They were sealed, with instructions that they be opened and published in the event of his death.[19] On the 21st he wrote a personal letter to Captain-General Despujol carried on the same boat that was to take him to Manila.

Of the two sealed letters, one was addressed to his family and the other to "the Filipinos." Both were intended to explain why he had decided to make the perilous journey back to the Philippines. He wrote that by his actions he had brought much suffering to the innocent, members of his family and fellow townspeople above all, who had been harshly persecuted on his account. He would not change the course he had taken, but wished to take responsibility for it by facing the authorities in person, in the hope that they would henceforth spare all their other victims. The second letter provides a wider vision of his purpose:

Quiero, además, hacer ver á los que nos niegan el patriotismo, que nosotros sabemos morir por nuestras deber y por nuestros convicciones. Qué importa la muerte, si se muere por lo que se ama, por la patria y por los seres que se adoran? Si yo supiera que era el único punto de apoyo de la política de Filipinas, y si estuviese convencido de que mis paisanos iban á utilizar mis servicios, acaso dudara de dar este paso; pero hay otros aun que me pueden sustituir, que me sustituyen con ventaja; mas todavía: hay quienes acaso me hallan de sobra, y mis servicios no se han de utilizar, puesto que me reducen á la inacción. He amado siempre á mi pobre patria y estoy seguro de que la amaré hasta el último momento, si acaso los hombres me son injustos; y mi porvenir, mi vida, mis alegrías, todo lo he

---

19. On the admirable Márquez, see Palma, *Biografía*, p. 220. One could guess that the letters were not entrusted to his parents or sisters because, as so often happens in families, they could not be trusted not to sneak a peek.

sacrificado por amor á ella. Sea cual fuere mi suerte, moriré bendiciéndola y deseándole la aurora de su redención.

I also want to show those who deny [our capacity for] patriotism that we know how to die for our duty and for our convictions. What does death matter if one dies for what one loves, for one's country and those beings whom one reveres? If I thought I were the sole *point d'appui* for the politics of the Philippines, and if I were convinced that my countrymen would make use of my services, perhaps I would hesitate to take this step; but there remain others who can take my place, who are taking my place to advantage; furthermore, there are perhaps some who regard me as superfluous and see no need for my services, since they reduce me to inactivity. I have always loved my poor country and I am sure I shall love her to the last moment, [even] if men should prove unjust to me; my future, my life, my joys, I have sacrificed all for love of her. Be my fate be what it may, I shall die blessing her and yearning for the dawn of her redemption.[20]

This strange mixture of patriotic pathos and personal bitterness needs its own explication. Two months earlier, *La Solidaridad* had published what he regarded as a vicious personal attack on him and his politics. The attack came in the form of a crude lampoon entitled "Redentores de Perro Chico" (Tuppenny Redeemers). Here, Rizal was sure, he was mocked as "Iluso The First," a vain demagogue who poses in the style of Napoléon, and regards himself as God's emissary for the liberation of the City of Illusion (that is, the Philippines). He gathers around him a following of imbeciles, innocents, and fanatics and calls on them to take up arms against their oppressors. When a voice in his audience wonders how this is possible without arms, ships, and money, the mountebank replies:

¿Qué dices, desdichado? ¿Qué objetas? ¿Dinero? No es preciso. Un corazón y una espada; he ahí el secreto. ¡Buenos patriotas os hizo Dios! ¿La prensa? Hemos escrito ya bastante; no debemos esperar nada del gobernador, ni del alcalde, ni aun del señor cura. ¿Lo habeís oído? ¿Juzgaís que hago yo poco con vociferar? ¿Con enseñaros el camino? ¿Con impeliros á la lucha? Yo no debo combatir; mi vida es sagrada; ¡mi misión es más alta! . . . ¿Necesitáis vituallas? Ya lloverán del cielo, que ampara las causas justas, y si no, pasaos sin comer. ¿Armas? Compradlas. ¿Organización guerrera? Dáosla vosotros mismos. ¿Barcos? Id á nado. ¿Transportes? Llevad sobre vuestros hombros la impedimenta. ¿Equipo? Id en cueros. ¿Alojamientos? Dormid al raso. ¿Médicos? Moríos, que á todo obliga el patriotismo.

Wretch, what are you saying? What are your objections? Money? You don't need it. A sword and a stout heart—that is the secret. God has made you good patriots. The press? We have written enough. We should expect nothing from the

---

20. *Cartas entre Rizal y sus colegas*, pp. 831–2.

governor, the mayor, nor even the parish priest. Have you not heard me? Do you think I am not doing enough by vociferating? By showing you the path? By impelling you into battle? I myself should not fight. My life is consecrated. My mission is higher . . . Do you need supplies? They will rain down from Heaven, which aids good causes; and if they don't, then fast! Arms? Buy them! Military organization? Do it yourselves! Ships? Swim! Transportation? Carry your baggage on your own shoulders! Clothing? Go naked. Quarters? Sleep on the ground. Doctors? Die, as is the duty of all patriots.

The ragged, unarmed crowds head off to attack the oppressors but are immediately arrested, to universal laughter, and are either sent to the gallows or into exile. Iluso the First is not among them. "¡Se había ido á llorar las desdichas de la patria! ¡El ya demostró su patriotismo perorando!" (He had gone off to bewail the misfortunes of the fatherland. He had already proved his patriotism by his perorations.) He would say to himself; "seated on the Olympus of his grandiosities": "¡Yo esto reservado para mayores empresas! Y soy el único profeta; ¡el único que ama á su país como se debe, soy yo!" (I am reserved for higher things. I am the Only Prophet; the only one who loves his country as she deserves is I.) He ends up in a madhouse.[21]

It remains unclear what had happened in Madrid. Del Pilar was certainly upset by the rift between his supporters and the Rizalistas, irritated by the language of people like Luna, Alejandrino, and Evangelista, and perhaps alarmed by distorted rumors of the intentions behind the Sandakan settlement. He was fully aware that any hopeless armed revolutionary outbreak would be disastrous for his own assimilationist political campaign. It would be difficult to avoid denouncing it after the event, with unforeseeable consequences in the Philippines. It therefore makes sense that he wished to head off the possibility, and believed that a satirical piece against "hotheads" would work better than a straightforward article which would have to be taken as policy, and carefully justified. The lampoon's plural target—

---

21. *La Solidaridad*, April 15, 1892, pp. 685–7. A lively, though incomplete and not always accurate English translation of the whole piece can be found in Guerrero, *The First Filipino*, pp. 289–92. Though the lampoon was published under a pen name, it was plain that the author was Lete, whom Rizal had for some time regarded as an unprincipled intriguer. On receiving the April 15 issue, Rizal wrote to Del Pilar demanding an explanation, not only for the personal attack, but for the article's implying in public that a (foolish) armed assault on the Spanish was being planned. On July 20, Del Pilar answered calmly that the satire was not at all aimed at Rizal personally, but rather at all those foolish hotheads who wanted immediate rebellion without thinking seriously about the probably devastating consequences. It is almost certain that Rizal never received this letter since, as we shall shortly see, he was sent into internal exile in Mindanao on July 7. The texts of the two letters can be found in *Cartas entre Rizal y sus colegas*, pp. 809–11, 841–3.

"Tuppenny Redeemers"—is good evidence of Del Pilar's intentions. At the same time, he was a calm man, a practiced conciliator and shrewd strategist too, and he had no interest in driving Rizal into a corner. All his letters to the novelist are cordial and reasonable, which was not always true of the letters he received in reply. At the same time, the lampoon itself was clearly aimed at a single Redeemer—Rizal—("they call me 'Idol,' and say I am a despot"), not against hotheads in general. The most likely explanation is that Del Pilar and Lete agreed on the idea of a lampoon, but its execution was left to the latter, who was the principal editor of *La Solidaridad*; Lete then took the boorish opportunity to settle personal scores with Rizal. We do not know what transpired between Del Pilar and Lete after the article appeared, but Del Pilar cannot have been pleased. One would then read his long letter to Rizal as an awkward equivocation, accepting responsibility for a decision to satirize "hotheads," but pretending that what Lete actually wrote was no more than that. The only alternative would have been a written apology, which would certainly circulate, and which would have forced a break with Lete.

For the always-touchy Rizal, the lampoon was the last straw. To be mocked as a megalomaniac, self-appointed Redeemer was one thing, but to be pilloried as a coward who would send his countrymen to their deaths while seeking his own safety was quite another. Although the prime reason for going back to the Philippines was the situation of his kinsmen and towns-people, it is more than probable that the lampoon steeled his will. He would give the lie to it by coming to the colonial capital publicly, unarmed, and with no companions other than his immediate family.[22]

---

22. In his *Biografía*, p. 199, Palma cited a passage from the second page of José Alejandrino's memoir of 1933, *La senda del sacrificio [The Path of Sacrifice]*, as follows: "Uno del los asuntos que con frecuencia discutía con nosotros eran los medios de que podríamos valernos para promover una revolución en Filipinas, y sus ideas sobre este particular las expresaba en éstas ó parecidas palabras: 'Yo nunca encabezaré una revolución descabellada y que no tenga probabilidad de éxito, pues no quiero cargar sobre mi consciencia un imprudente e inútil derramamiento de sangre; pero quien quiera que encabece en Filipinas una revolución, me tendrá á su lado" [One of the subjects he frequently discussed with us was the means that could be available to us for promoting a revolution in the Philippines; and he expressed his ideas on the matter in the following or similar language. "I will never head a woolly-minded revolution with no probability of success, since I do not wish to burden my conscience with reckless and fruitless bloodshed. But if anyone else undertakes to head a revolution in the Philippines, he will find me at his side"]. It is possible that this recollection is correct, but it comes from forty years after the discussions took place, from one of the best-known generals of the Revolution fighting the Spanish and later the Americans, and at a time when the nationalist elite was united in wishing to have Rizal remembered as a revolutionary, as well as a martyr. In 1892, Alejandrino, who came from a wealthy landowning family in Pampanga, just north of Manila, was definitely among the Rizalista "hotheads" who annoyed and alarmed Del Pilar.

Rizal's third letter, written on June 21 as he embarked for Manila, was addressed to the Captain-General, saying that he was returning to settle some personal affairs, and appealing to Despujol to put an end to Weyler's persecution of his family. He was fully prepared to answer any charges on his own, and sole, responsibility. He landed in Manila on Sunday the 26th, took a room at a fine, brand-new hotel in the Chinatown of Binondo, and was granted a short interview with his correspondent that very evening.[23] The general—twice Rizal's age—immediately "pardoned" Rizal's father, and told the writer to call again in three days' time.

There is something remarkable about this, at least seen in comparative perspective. Here was a young colonial subject who nine months earlier had published a novel in which the unnamed Captain-General, along with the top colonial elite, had come within a hair of being Nobeled to smithereens. Furthermore, the colonial regime had come into possession of the book six months previously. (José Basa had tried to smuggle copies into the country using its smaller ports of entry, and one large consignment had been discovered in the central Philippine port of Ilo-Ilo.)[24] It is impossible to imagine a comparable encounter anywhere in the British, French, Dutch, or Portuguese empires—or even in Spanish Cuba. A guess or two: the first, Despujol was too busy to read the novel, or was not a novel-reader; the second, warmer: he knew a novel when he saw it.

Events moved with great speed. The next day, Monday, Rizal took a train on the newly opened railway line north of Manila, stopping at various towns, and discovering that, though no one recognized him, his name was on everyone's lips, and his arrival in Manila already known. Despujol received him again on Wednesday and Thursday, granting Rizal's sisters permission to return home from Hong Kong. The discussions were mainly about the Sandakan project, which Rizal insisted was still in the works, and which the general strongly opposed. A further interview was scheduled for Sunday, July 3. Meantime, agents of the police had been shadowing Rizal, and were on stand-by to search all the houses he had visited. That same day, Rizal formally launched the Liga Filipina in the private home of a wealthy political supporter. Among the many in attendance was Andrés Bonifacio, the young

23. As Rizal's ship left Hong Kong harbor, the local Spanish consul cabled Despujol to give him the news, adding "the rat is in the trap." Austin Coates, *Rizal—Philippine Nationalist and Patriot* (Manila: Solidaridad 1992), p. 230. This language could be taken as evidence of an elaborately prepared conspiracy, but is more likely to be a typical intelligence cliché. Had such a trap existed, it is not likely that Despujol would have bothered to meet Rizal six times in the following week. (Besides, a trap has to have a bait, and here there was none.) As we shall soon see, the decision to deport Rizal to Dapitan shows every sign of improvization.

24. *Ibid.*, p. 217. Most were immediately burned.

artisan and commercial agent who would launch the Revolution four years later. Rizal himself seems to have done no more than outline the Liga's objectives, explain why the focus of political struggle had to move from Spain to the Philippines, and ask for various kinds of support. On Tuesday morning, the planned mass police raids took place, which did not turn up much beyond copies of the novels, Masonic tracts, anti-friar pamphlets and so on—nothing that would have been punishable in Spain itself. There were no mass arrests.

A TROPICAL SIBERIA

On Wednesday Rizal saw Despujol for the fifth time in a week, to assure him that he was ready to return to Hong Kong. But the general now asked him to explain the hidden presence of anti-friar handbills—including a lampoon of Pope Leo XIII—in his luggage. Rizal replied that this was impossible. His sisters had packed for him, and would never have done anything so stupid, especially without his knowledge. Despujol then put him under arrest and confined him to Fort Santiago. But he was taken there in the Captain-General's own carriage and escorted by Despujol's own son and his personal aide-de-camp. The next day he was handed an order for internal exile at Dapitan, a tiny settlement on the northwest shore of the remote southern island of Mindanao.[25] There he would remain for most of the remaining four years of his life. It was not all bad. He had been treated with astonishing courtesy, and he had shown that he was anything but Iluso the First. But what had happened?

One can start with the contraband handbills, which Despujol told Rizal had been discovered at the time of his arrival from Hong Kong, ten days before the deportation order. If this really happened, it would have been reported immediately to the Captain-General; if he had found them subversive of Spanish rule, he would not have had so many cordial meetings with the smuggler, nor treated him with such demonstrative courtesy after his arrest. In his early biography (1907) of Rizal, Wenceslao Retana observed that the customs officer said to have discovered the printed slander was the nephew of Bernardino Nozaleda, the arch-reactionary Dominican arch-

---

25. It is instructive that the reasons given for Rizal's internal exile made no mention of the Liga Filipina or the banquet at which it was launched. This absence suggests that either Despujol did not take the Liga too seriously, or that he was not eager to open Rizal to charges of sedition against the state. In any event, this placid silence offers further support for the conclusion that the 1896 confessions about the founding of the Liga belonged to the Spanish panic of that year, not the calm induced by Weyler's relaxed successor in 1892.

bishop of Manila. He also pointed out that a Spanish judge, Miguel Rodríguez Berriz, had discovered, shortly before Rizal's arrival, that a number of anti-friar leaflets were being secretly printed in an orphanage run by the Augustinians.[26] Besides, Rizal did not give a fig for Leo XIII. It is thus virtually certain both that the handbills were forgeries, designed to compel the colonial regime to deal decisively with the *filibustero* who had, in the Calamba affair, dragged the domineering Dominicans up to the highest court in Spain. It is also most likely that Despujol knew or suspected that this was the case. Still, the handbills came in handy.

What really worried Despujol was something else. In the first place, Cayo Hueso East. Rizal had repeatedly assured him that he was serious about the Sandakan settlement, and that, if allowed to return to Hong Kong, he would continue working on it. Could one be certain that at some later point the novelist would not find some backers? In any case, in Borneo he was both outside the Spanish empire, and very close by. On the other hand, if the youngster were allowed to move freely in and around Manila, the enthusiasm his reputation aroused could result in disturbances among the colonized or Rizal's assassination at the hand of his *colon* and/or clerical enemies. Either, from Despujol's angle of vision, would be a political disaster. The logic of the situation said clearly: keep the fellow inside the Philippines, but out of harm's way; and also treat him in such a manner that he will not become a martyr, especially in the metropolitan press. Besides, the general, although a conventional Catholic, was an old-school gentleman, and, in the peculiar nineteenth-century Spanish sense of the word, a kind of liberal.[27] It is even possible that he actually liked Rizal, who had plenty of charm.

Rizal's destination and how it was chosen confirm this supposition. Dapitan was the site of a Jesuit missionary outpost, and the decision to exile Rizal there was, before its announcement, a secret known only to Despujol and the Catalan Jesuit Provincial, Pablo Pastells. When the enlightened absolutist Carlos III had expelled the Jesuits from his empire,

---

26. As quoted in Guerrero, *The First Filipino*, p. 337. Retana was an odd duck. In the 1880s and 1890s he had been a passionate publicist for the friars, the benefits of colonial rule, and of *hispanidad*—and a vitriolic propagandist against Rizal and his comrades. But the savagery of Rizal's execution in 1896 and the collapse of the Spanish empire in 1898 caused a weird sort of conversion. He became a devoted Rizalophile, claiming him as an example of all that was best in Spanish culture. A long-time resident in the Philippines and an ally of the Church, he was in an excellent position to know about friar machinations. But exactly the same story had already appeared eight years earlier in Isabelo's *Sensacional memoria*, pp. 64–5.

27. Ambeth Ocampo has suggested to me that the unusually courteous treatment Rizal received may have been the result of Masonic brotherhood. Many senior Spanish generals of Despujol's post-Isabel generation were Freemasons.

the parishes, properties, and benefices the Society of Jesus had controlled were swiftly grabbed by their rivals, especially the Dominicans and Augustinians. When the Jesuits were allowed back in 1859, just before Rizal's birth, it was only on condition that they would accept the expropriations by their clerical comrades, and confine themselves primarily to missionary work on the uncertain periphery between the colonial realm and the Muslim domains in the far south (Sulu and Mindanao). When they attempted to set up their own elite secondary school in Manila, the Ateneo we have often mentioned, they prevailed against venomous Dominican opposition thanks only to the secular governor of Manila. If, in nineteenth-century Europe, they were often regarded as the Church's sly, politicking intellectual vanguard, in the colonial Philippines, without valuable property interests to protect, they appeared as liberals. In 1892, the Ateneo still had teachers, including Pastells, who were fond of their former student, recognized that *Noli me tangere* mainly pilloried Dominicans and Franciscans, and in any case were delighted at the chance to dish the enemy. As for the Provincial himself, there seems to have been still another motive for his collusion with Despujol: a confidence that, isolated in Jesuit Dapitan, Rizal would be brought to his Catholic senses by the persuasions of the Society of Jesus. What a triumph to fling in the teeth of the other Orders![28] For the gentlemanly-machiavellian Despujol, what could be more enjoyable than to play the Jesuit queen of hearts against the Dominican knave of clubs?[29]

MARTÍ'S INSURRECTION

It was just at this conjuncture that, on the other side of the globe, Martí formed his revolutionary party-in-exile and made systematic efforts to prepare for a final revolutionary war. Towards the end of 1894, he felt the hour had come, and decided to open hostilities the following February. Cuba had changed dramatically over the preceding two decades, in a manner

---

28. In the above analysis, my interpretation relies in part on Guerrero's discussion in *The First Filipino*, pp. 333–5, as well as Coates, *Rizal*, pp. 236–7 (alas unsourced). During his years in Dapitan, Rizal was pushed into a lengthy theologico-political correspondence with Pastells, which, fortunately for posterity, has been published—Raul K. Bonoan, SJ, ed., *The Rizal–Pastells Correspondence* (Quezon City: Ateneo de Manila Press, 1994). Needless to say, though always extremely polite, Rizal had no difficulty in running rings around the hilariously provincial Provincial, who managed, the year after Rizal's judicial murder, to publish in his native Barcelona an enraged *La masonización de Filipinas: Rizal y su obra*.

29. One has to hand it to the general. This was the only genuinely intelligent, well-meaning, machiavellian decision taken by any nineteenth-century ruler of the Philippines.

José Martí

that seemed propitious to his aims. (Nothing comparable happened in the Philippines between Cavite in 1872 and Bonifacio's insurrection in 1896.) The Ten Years' War was the primary cause of this transformation. As noted earlier, it ended not with a devastating victory for Madrid, but with a political compromise. For years, Céspedes (who had freed his own slaves on the day he proclaimed his republic) had largely controlled the broken country of eastern Cuba, where slaves were relatively few, and the economy was based as much on cattle-ranching as anything else. But he had been unable to make a decisive onslaught on western Cuba, where the colonial capital was situated, and where the wealthy sugar plantations, with huge slave populations controlled by what some irony-free historians used to describe as the "colonial aristocracy," were dominant. During the war, the colonial regime, with Madrid behind it, had ceaselessly exploited the sanguinary phantom of Haiti to mobilize support among the Peninsular and creole elites on the island: in effect, if the rebellion prevailed, the "whites" would be massacred, and the prosperity of the island, built on the "ruins of Saint-Domingue," would vanish into the abyss. The fact that some of Céspedes's most successful

The legendary Antonio Maceo, second-in-command of the Cuban army of independence, and one of the outstanding guerrilla commanders of the nineteenth century.

guerrilla commanders were *negros*, such as the legendary Antonio Maceo, was manipulated by the Spaniards, not merely to solidify support in the West, but to undermine the solidarity of the rebel East.

Nonetheless, in the 1880s, Madrid recognized that the age of slavery was over. The crushing of the Confederacy by Grant and Sherman and the success of abolitionism in the British, French, and Dutch empires, meant that by 1878, only Brazil and Cuba were left as serious slave states.[30] Hence, after the Zanjón compromise, whereby the rebels laid down their arms in exchange for amnesty and reform, Madrid moved quickly and adroitly to bring Cuban slavery to a peaceful end. This peaceful end turned out be a mixed blessing, however, since it showed that the Haitian spectre was simply a hobgoblin. Furthermore, Madrid's

---

30. One might have expected Puerto Rico to be arrayed with Brazil and Cuba. But at the time of Isabel's fall and the start of Céspedes's uprising, the island had only 41,738 slaves, i.e. a mere 7 percent of the population. (There were ten times as many in Cuba.) This is why slavery was abolished there as early as 1873. Predictably, slave-owners were compensated, but not slaves. Ojeda, *El desterrado*, pp. 123 and 227.

Disraeli and Gladstone recognized that political reforms were unavoidable, and that serious measures had to be taken to revive the economy. The East had been physically devastated by the long war, and the West was reeling in the 1880s from the world depression and the superior efficiency of beet and cane sugar agribusiness in the United States and Europe. The political reforms, which for the first time permitted political parties in Cuba, a relatively free press, as well as administrative reform and rationalization, did not, however, engender the hoped-for consolidation of support for the decrepit empire. On the other hand, the opening to corporate metropolitan agribusiness finished off much of the inefficient plantocracy, while the encouragement of massive emigration from Spain had completely unforeseen consequences. Between 1882 and 1894 (the available figures exclude only 1888), no less than 224,000 Peninsulars emigrated to Cuba, whose population was then less than 2 million. Of these only 140,000 ever returned.[31] Ada Ferrer remarks that according to the census of 1887, only 35 percent of those described as "white" could read or write, while the figure for "colored" was 12 percent. (The percentages for both groups were significantly higher only in Havana).[32] That two-thirds of the "whites" in Cuba were then illiterate is sufficient evidence that most of the new immigrants were ex-peasants and proletarians from the metropole, especially Catalonia. This was how Marxism and anarchism came to Cuba. The impressive founder of Cuban anarchism, the Catalan émigré Enrique Roig, mentioned in Chapter 3, was a key element of this tide of impoverished, sometimes radical emigrants, and till his premature death in 1889 he was a strong supporter of Martí's enterprise.[33]

This demographic transformation, combined with the unalarming, gradual end of slavery, made it possible for Martí to recast the revolutionary enterprise in a nationalist style which transcended, or appeared to transcend, the discourse of race. So to speak, white and black Cuban males would (metaphorically, or on the battlefield) embrace each other as equals in the fight against imperial rule.[34] The gradual disappearance of "Haiti" and the collapse of the sugar "aris-

---

31. Thomas, *Cuba*, p. 276.

32. See her sharp *Insurgent Cuba: Race, Nation and Revolution, 1868–1898* (Chapel Hill: University of North Carolina Press, 1999), p. 116.

33. Thomas devotes one paragraph (p. 291) to Roig in his almost 1,700-page volume. Ferrer does not mention him at all.

34. Ferrer's attractive book, which is basically a convincing study of the race/nation question in nineteenth-century Cuba, does not flinch at inspecting the elements of racism and opportunism, often unconscious, thereby involved. The whole subject escapes Thomas's gargantuan optic.

Santiago de Cuba, 1856.

tocracy" left Madrid with fewer and fewer fanatical supporters. Rizal-style general nationalism thus spread rapidly after 1888 in almost all sectors.[35] These changes in turn made it possible for the revolutionaries of 1895 to break successfully through the East–West line. Maceo, the commanding mulatto hero of the Ten Years' War, proved able to march across the entire island from east to west, winning admiration and support as he advanced.

The war was seriously engaged in April, when Martí, Maceo, and the other five-star hero of 1868–78, Máximo Gómez, slipped into the island. In March in Madrid, the liberal prime minister Sagasta had solemnly proclaimed to the Senate that Spain was prepared "to spend the last peseta, and offer up the last drop of blood of her sons," to crush the rebellion, but he was not cut out to lead in time of war; his government

---

35. The increasingly open hostility to the colonial regime encouraged the remains of the plantocracy to think that they could not expect much in the long run from Madrid, and to ponder how they could stay influential in whatever was coming after it—maybe with the right kind of American support.

fell less than eight weeks later.[36] Back in power for the sixth and last time, Cánovas quickly persuaded the capable political general Arsenio Martínez Campos, architect of the negotiated end of the Ten Years' War, to return to Cuba as Captain-General and commander-in chief. We will remember Martínez Campos as the target of Paulino Pallás's anarchist bomb-attack of September 24, 1893, when he was functioning as Captain-General of Barcelona. Unscathed, he had then been sent to crush a rebellion in Spanish Morocco. He was the only figure with the experience and the prestige to achieve what was aimed for, a military–political settlement within the empire. Eight months later he was gone from Cuban soil.

As early as June 1895, despite the fact that Martí had been killed in action the previous month, the new Captain-General described without illusions the new realities. He wrote to Cánovas thus:

The few Spaniards in the island alone proclaim themselves as such . . . the rest . . . hate Spain . . . I cannot, as a representative of a civilized country, be the first to give an example of . . . intransigence, I must hope that they begin it. We could concentrate the families of the countryside in the towns, but much force would be needed to compel them, since already there are very few in the interior who want to be [Spanish] volunteers . . . the misery and hunger would be terrible. I would then have to give rations, which reached 40,000 a day in the last war. It would isolate the country from the towns, but it would not prevent espionage, which would be done by women and children. Perhaps we will come to this, but only as a last resort, and I think I lack the qualities to carry through such a policy. Among the present generals only Weyler has the necessary capacity for such a policy, since only he combines the requisite intelligence, courage, and knowledge of war. Reflect, my dear friend, and if after discussion you approve the policy I have described, do not delay in recalling me. We are gambling with the destiny of Spain; but I retain certain beliefs and they are superior to everything. They forbid me to carry out summary executions and similar acts . . . Even if we win in the field and suppress the rebels, since the country wishes neither to have an amnesty for our enemies nor an extermination of them, my loyal and sincere opinion is that, *with reforms or without reforms*, before twelve years we shall have another war.[37]

---

36. Fernández, *La sangre de Santa Águeda* p. 125, quoting from Carlos Serrano, *Final del imperio. España 1895–1898* (Madrid: Siglo Veintiuno de España, Edit. SA, 1984), p. 19. Fernández takes the occasion to remark that the famous phrase is often erroneously attributed to Cánovas. A case of liberals' cognitive dissonance?

37. Quoted in Thomas, *Cuba*, pp. 320–21. My italics.

The seasoned Captain-General, thinking long term, recognized that the imperial cause was lost (and hastened to get out). Reforms would be useless against the nationalist tide; military victory would mean colossal suffering, and would not prevent a further war within twelve years. It is probable that Cánovas understood the message, but he was also convinced that the fall of Cuba would not merely drive him from power and almost certainly destroy the cacique democracy that he and Sagasta had constructed in Spain over the past generation; it would also, by reducing Spain to a minor European state, be a devastating blow to Spanish national pride and self-confidence. Accordingly, he dispatched Weyler to Havana with plenary powers.[38] The general arrived in Cuba on February 10, 1896, and remained there for the next eighteen months. Cánovas was as good as his word. In support of Weyler, he ensured that in short order approximately 200,000 Spanish troops were shipped to the Caribbean island, at that time the largest military force ever conveyed across the Atlantic.[39]

Weyler fully lived up to Cánovas's expectations. With his steely Prussian efficiency he turned the military tide in the course of 1896. In December, Maceo and Máximo Gómez's son "Pancho" were killed in battle, and the bereaved father was largely on the run. But the costs were enormous. Hugh Thomas, on the whole sympathetic to Cánovas and Weyler (mainly out of contempt for what the hypocritical Americans were up to before, during, and after the war), comments that "the whole island had been turned into an immense concentration camp." Between 1895 and 1899, Cuba's population declined from about 1,800,000 to 1,500,000. Most of the casualties of the islandwide concentration camp were children who died of malnutrition and diseases parasitic thereupon. In 1899, Cuba had, so Thomas claims, the smallest proportion of children under five years of age in the censused parts of the world; no other country in the nineteenth century suffered the loss of one sixth of its population.[40] The economy was left ruined, a process in which

38. Weyler had been Captain-General of Catalonia since November 29, 1893, just two months too late for the execution of Paulino Pallás, but in time to oversee that of Santiago Salvador.

39. Thomas, *Cuba*, p. 349. By the time Madrid surrendered (to the Americans) in June 1898, the war had cost Spain over one and a half billion pesetas, plus over 40,000 casualties, mostly the victims of yellow fever and other diseases (p. 414).

40. *Ibid.*, pp. 328 and 423. Thomas's comparative claim is unwarranted in one case at least. On the eve of the war it declared against Brazil, Argentina, and Uruguay in 1865 Paraguay had a population of 1,337,439, mostly Guaraní, souls. When the war ended five years later this had been reduced to 28,746 adult males, 106,254 women over the age of fifteen, and 86,079 children, a total of 221,079. The losses amounted to 1,115,320 or 83 percent of the population. Paraguay's three enemies also lost a million lives. See Byron Farwell, ed., *Encyclopedia of Nineteenth Century Land Warfare* (New York: Norton, 2001).

THE GREAT WEYLER APE
PRESENTED BY SENOR SAGASTA

The Spanish military governor of Cuba, Valeriano "the Butcher" Weyler.

Gómez's ruthless scorched-earth campaign against the haciendas of the plantocracy played its own role.[41] But the deeper problem was that neither Cánovas nor Weyler had any plausible political, as opposed to military, solution to hand. As we shall see, this impasse was to be resolved by a wandering Italian lad, only a few years out of his teens.

RIZAL TO CUBA?

Recognizing that he was likely to be exiled in tiny Dapitan for a long time, Rizal had settled in soon after his arrival. He built himself a simple thatched

---

41. Ojeda, *El desterrado*, p. 340, quotes the justification provided by the Dominican chief of the Cuban military forces as follows: "When I put my hand on the suffering heart of the working people, and I felt it wounded with grief; when I touched, next to all that opulence, around all that astounding wealth, such misery and such moral poverty; when I saw all this in the house of the tenant, and found him brutalized by the cheating he endures, with his wife and children dressed in rags, living in a wretched hut erected on another's land, when I asked about schools and was told that there had never been any . . . then I felt enraged and profoundly disposed against the upper classes of the country, and in a moment of fury at the sight of such utterly melancholy and painful inequality, I cried out: 'Blessed be the torch.'" The quotation is taken from Juan Bosch, *El Napoleón de las guerrillas* (Santo Domingo: Editorial Alfa y Omega, 1982), p. 13.

house on stilts by the shore of the today still beautiful, serene bay; then he opened a medical practice and a little school for local boys, interested himself in agriculture and botany, and read whatever his relatives and friends were permitted to send in. His correspondence was, of course, censored, and his letters that have survived are calm but guarded. He had freedom to move around as he pleased within the settlement and was mostly treated courteously by the commandant. In the summer of 1893 a new Captain-General, Ramón Blanco, arrived in Manila to replace early a Despujol ever more disliked by the Peninsular community in Manila and the Orders. Though a veteran of the Carlist wars and of the Ten Years' War in Cuba, Blanco had the reputation of being a flexible man. Meantime various of Rizal's friends cooked up abortive schemes to come to his rescue: plans to hire a ship to free him and take him to Hong Kong, and others to have him pardoned by prime minister Sagasta, and then run for a Spanish seat in the Cortes. In November 1894, Blanco himself dropped by Dapitan on the way back from a successful little war against the Muslim Maranao in the central-northern part of Mindanao. He is said first to have proposed that Rizal return to Spain (Rizal rejected this idea) and then to have offered to have him moved back to Luzon, to one of the Ilocano provinces in the far north. But in the end nothing came of this.[42]

By 1895, however, the insurrection in Cuba was changing the whole context of politics in the Philippines. Blumentritt's "preconditions" were starting to be realized. Rizal's older friend Regidor, who had grown rich in London as legal adviser to English businessmen trading and investing in Spain, and who had many friends in high places in Madrid, learned that there was a severe shortage of doctors attached to the military in yellow-fever-ravaged Cuba. He therefore lobbied Blumentritt and Basa to persuade Rizal to volunteer. Finally, after much hesitation, Rizal yielded, and in November, while Martínez Campos still ruled in Havana, sent a letter to Blanco asking permission to offer his medical services to casualties in Cuba. Basa's belief was that this offer would be taken as evidence of Rizal's basic loyalty to the empire. In any case, the main thing was to get the exile out of the Philippines. The route to Havana lay through Spain; once there, Rizal could stay on safely under the protection of influential friends and political allies. The novelist's own motives are much less clear. He was a man with a prickly sense of honor, and would have recoiled from the idea of flatly lying to Blanco— who, after all, had earlier offered to let him go honorably to Spain. He had long been sure that nothing could be achieved in the metropole. The chances are good that in November 1895 he was fairly serious about Cuba.

42. Guerrero, *The First Filipino*, p. 342.

But for what reasons? Here one can only speculate. He knew Martínez Campos as the unsanguinary architect of the Pact of Zanjón which had ended the Ten Years' War. A doctor himself, he took seriously the Hippocratic duty to tend to the wounded, no matter what side they might be on. He had known admirable Cubans in Spain, first and foremost the abolitionist creole Rafael Labra, and was generally familiar with "advanced" Cuba's political history up to the end of the 1880s. Perhaps he was curious as to what could be learned from the experience of the Philippines' sister colony. What is likely, in any case, is that his years of isolation in Mindanao left him poorly informed on what was now happening in the Caribbean island under "Su Excelencia" Weyler.

In the event, Blanco promptly sent Rizal's letter on to Madrid with his personal stamp of approval. But for months there was no reaction from the imperial capital. Meanwhile, in Cuba itself, Weyler and *weylerismo* had replaced Martínez Campos.

NEW CONJUNCTURES

Rizal's deportation to Dapitan in July 1892 had led to the immediate collapse of the infant Liga Filippina. But soon afterwards, a very small group of activists in the Liga's orbit decided at a secret meeting in Manila to replace it by a clandestine revolutionary organization which they called the Kataastaasan, Kagalanggalang Katipunan ng mga Anak ng Bayan (perhaps Most Illustrious, Respectable League of the Sons-and-Daughters of the People). Its leader Andrés Bonifacio, two years Rizal's junior, was then twenty-nine years of age. The Katipunan does not seem to have achieved very much beyond survival until the end of 1895, when its membership was still less than 300 persons.[43] But new international conjunctures in that year encouraged an

---

43. In fact, the Liga had been reconstituted on its original bases in April, 1893. In Isabelo's words, Bonifacio, who headed the branch in the neighborhood of Trozo, "viendo que los trabajos de la Liga se esterilizaban con las continuas discusiones de sus ilustrados compañeros que parecían tener más egoísmo pueril que verdadero patriotismo, los mandó á paseo y elevó á Consejo Supremo del Katipúnan el popular que él presidía" [observing that the work of the league was losing its vigor thanks to the endless discussions of its *ilustrado* comrades, which seemed more characterized by puerile egoism than true patriotism, he set them aside and elevated the popular council over which he presided to become the Supreme Council of the Katipunan (a slip, he means the Liga)]. De los Reyes, *Sensacional memoria*, p. 87. The alarmed *ilustrados* declared Bonifacio in rebellion and tried to dissolve the Trozo branch, but Bonifacio refused to obey. This led the Liga to dissolve itself in October, but not before giving the Captain-General some internal Liga files. What is clear from this is that, so long as it was possible, Bonifacio tried to use the Liga he despised as cover for consolidating the clandestine work of the Katipunan.

energetic expansion of its cadres, said by some enthusiasts to have reached 10,000 by August.[44]

The key conjuncture for the Katipunan underground is best symbolized by the fact that Martí's landing in Cuba on April 11, 1895 occurred just six days before the signing of the Treaty of Shimonoseki between Tokyo and Peking after the former's crushing victory in the Sino-Japanese War of 1894–95 in Korea. In the case of Cuba, it was not just a matter of Martí's electrifying example, and the spectacular early military successes of Maceo and Gómez. Bonifacio and his comrades were keenly aware of the difficulties Spain would face if it had to confront two anticolonial insurrections on opposite sides of the world. They also knew that in such an eventuality Madrid would attach overwhelming military priority to money-making Cuba over the generally money-losing Philippines. On the other hand, Taiwan, whose southern tip lay only 250 miles from the northern shores of Luzon, was now the property of the Japanese state. If the Cubans could get support in the neighboring United States, might it not be possible that the Filipinos could do the same in the empire of the Rising Sun?

In fact, the geopolitical positions of the two "neighbors" were very different. The United States was by then the almost uncontested hegemon in the western hemisphere, while eastern Asia was an arena packed with competing, ambitious "white" imperialisms—British, French, German, Russian, and American. Almost immediately after the conclusion of the Treaty of Shimonoseki, intervention by Germany, France, and Russia forced the Japanese government to return the just-acquired Liaotung Peninsula to the Ch'ing regime. Furthermore, Japan was still burdened with the unequal treaties imposed on it over the previous three decades, giving its competitors substantial extraterritorial rights. An Anglo-Japanese agreement signed shortly before the outbreak of the Sino-Japanese War did look forward to the elimination of such treaties, but not before 1899. Yet where London led the way, the other imperial capitals would inevitably follow. The late 1890s were thus not—yet—a time for reckless Japanese adventures.

While official relations between Tokyo and Manila were generally correct, the Spanish authorities became more and more worried about the future.[45] Japanese ships swarmed into Philippine waters, and the trade balance was

---

44. See, for a succinct account, Teodoro A. Agoncillo, *A Short History of the Philippines* (New York: Mentor, 1969), pp. 77–81. The 10,000 figure may well be an exaggeration, but probably not too much so, given the astounding early successes of an insurrectionary movement primarily armed with machetes.

45. In the section on Japan that follows, I have relied heavily on Josefa M. Saniel's pioneering *Japan and the Philippines, 1868–1898* (third edition) (Manila: De La Salle University Press, 1998), which is based on thorough research in the Japanese, Spanish, and English-language sources.

ever more sharply in Japan's favor.[46] Japanese started to emigrate into the Philippines, and Tokyo pressed hard for relaxation of the colony's immigration laws. Japanese elites were increasingly well informed about the Philippines, while the Spanish diplomatic corps, without a single person capable of reading or speaking Japanese, was forced to rely on the British and Americans for what they understood about Japanese policies and intentions. By the beginning of the 1890s an increasingly vocal lobby—of opposition parliamentarians, newspapers, militarists, business interests, and ideologues—was pushing for Japanese expansion in the Pacific and Southeast Asia (partly to forestall German and American advances). The weakness and decrepitude of Spanish colonialism in the Philippines were becoming widely known.[47] And obscurely connected adventurers, civilian and military, were travelling in and out of the colony.

In Spain itself, Tokyo's military triumph over China brought the *espantajo Japonés* to the centre of public attention.[48] In February 1895, Moret, Sagasta's former minister for overseas territories, wrote that the rise of Japan to the status of a first-class power "implies a radical transformation in the relations of Europe with the Orient, and especially with the possessions of Spain in those seas. To refuse to recognize this fact, waiting for events which will not delay in coming, would be equivalent to a man sleeping on the rails of a railroad track, confident that the vibrations on those tracks by the oncoming train will warn him of the danger."[49] The radical republican newspaper *La Justicia* commented sarcastically not much later: "A beautiful future of simultaneous war in Cuba, the Philippines . . . it is sufficient that the government of the Restoration [i.e. of Cánovas] may write on the ruins of the Spanish nation the historic epitaph Finis Hispanae."[50]

Under these circumstances, it is not surprising that Filipino nationalists

46. Between 1890 and 1898 Manila's trade decifit with Japan increased sixtyfold. *Ibid.*, Appendix IX, p. 101.

47. The prominent Meiji writer and publicist Fukumoto Makoto made two extended trips to the Philippines, in 1889 and 1891. In a series of articles written after the second trip, he described the feebleness of the Spanish colonial military, manned by a few Spanish officers uneasily commanding native troops. In particular, he pointed out that when in 1890 Weyler sent a second expedition to the Carolines to repress renewed rebellion there, for a while not a soldier was left in Manila. *Ibid.*, p. 68.

48. This "Japanese spectre" appears in the section entitled "El espantajo Japonés y la revolución de 1896," in L. González Liquete's compilation *Repertorio histórico, biográfico y bibliográfico* (Manila: Impr. Del Día Filipino, 1930), cited in Saniel, *Japan and the Philippines*, p. 186.

49. Saniel, *Japan and Philippines*, citing Moret's "El Japón y Las Islas Filipinas," originally published in *La España Moderna*, LXXIV (February 1895).

50. *Ibid.* Note that by "war in . . . the Philippines" is meant one between Japan and Spain, not a Filipino insurrection.

began trying to establish useful contact with the Japanese. The first to do so was José Ramos, from a family rich enough to have had him educated in London. In the summer of 1895, tipped off that he was about to be arrested for spreading nationalist propaganda, he escaped the Philippines, posing as an Englishman, on a British ship headed for Yokohama. There he married a Japanese woman, took her name (Ishikawa), and eventually became a naturalized subject of the Emperor Meiji. Much of his time was spent in fruitless attempts to purchase surplus rifles left over from the war in Korea, and to send them to the Philippines.[51] Other rich Filipinos followed on the pretext of tourism or furthering their education.

Then on May 4, 1896, the Japanese naval training ship *Kongo*, with thirty-three cadets and twenty students of a Japanese naval school aboard, sailed into Manila's harbor, where it was promptly sequestered by the Spanish authorities on the pretext of possible infringement of the rules of quarantine.[52] Though the existing Japanese, Spanish, and Filipino accounts vary in their details, all agree that Katipunan leaders Bonifacio, Dr Pio Valenzuela, the young firebrand Emilio Jacinto, and Daniel Tirona made personal contact with the captain of the *Kongo*, and presented him with a written petition asking for Japanese aid and guidance in their "desire to rise up against the government." They were accompanied by "José" Tagawa Moritaro, a long-time resident in the colony, married to a Filipina, who had alerted Bonifacio to the *Kongo*'s arrival, and acted as interpreter. Nothing significant came of this encounter, except that the colonial police got wind of it, and redoubled their watchfulness.[53] Captain Serada did not mention the meeting when he reported to his superiors.

LEAVING DAPITAN

Such was the immediate background for a meeting of the Katipunan's top leadership later in May, where it was decided that an armed uprising was feasible, that a mission would be sent to Japan to ask for substantial support, and that an emissary would leave for Dapitan to get Rizal's endorsement.

51. *Ibid.*, pp. 180–82.

52. The following account of the *Kongo* affair is drawn from Saniel's careful and judicious reconstruction. *Ibid.*, pp. 192–4.

53. Tagawa, a carpenter from Nagasaki, was one of the first Japanese to settle in the Philippines, arriving there in the early 1870s. Eventually he became a moderately successful businessman. It appears that in July 1895 Bonifacio asked him to create a trading company exporting hemp, sugar, tobacco, and other products, the income of which would be used to buy Murata rifles in Japan. The Katipunan offered to pay all expenses if Tagawa were willing to go to Japan to arrange the purchase. But nothing seems to have come of this scheme. *Ibid.*, pp. 249–50.

(Without the novelist's knowledge, he had been made the Katipunan's honorary president; and its speeches are said to have ended customarily with a rousing "Long live the Philippines! Long live Liberty! Long live Dr Rizal!") At the end of the month, the only *ilustrado* among them, Dr Pio Valenzuela, sailed to Mindanao on the pretext of bringing a blind servant of his to be treated. It is important to note that Rizal did not know Valenzuela, either in person or by name, and it must have crossed his mind that the doctor might be an agent-provocateur. There is no certainty about the terms in which the short conversation between the two men was framed. When his interrogators later asked him for details, Rizal's recorded reply was as follows:

El médico D. Pio le habló al declarante de que iba á llevarse á cabo un levantamiento y que les tenía con cuidado lo que pudiera ocurrirle al declarante en Dapitan. El dicente le manifestó que la ocasión no era oportuna para intentar aventuras, porque no existía unión entre los diversos elementos de Filipinas, ni tenían armas, ni barcos, ni ilustración, ni los demás elementos de resistencia, y que tomaran ejemplo de lo que ocurría en Cuba, donde á pesar de contar con grandes medios, con el apoyo de una gran Potencía y de estar avezados á la lucha, no podían alcanzar sus deseos, y que cualquiera que fuera el resultado de la lucha, á España le convendría hacer concesiones á Filipinas, por lo que opinaba el declarante debía de esperarse.

Doctor Don Pio told [him] that an uprising was going to take place, and that they were worried about what might then happen to [him] in Dapitan. [He] declared that the occasion was not opportune for attempting adventures, because no unity existed between the various elements of [society in] the Philippines, nor did they have arms, ships, education, or any of the other requirements for a resistance movement. They should heed the example of what was happening in Cuba, where the people, despite abundant resources and the backing of a great Power, and being experienced in battle, were unable to achieve their desires. Whatever the outcome of the struggle there, it would be to Spain's advantage to make concessions to the Philippines. For this reason [he] believed that they ought to wait.[54]

This is the stilted language of a military stenographer, but to the trial court Rizal provided a brief "Additions to My Defence," which were written in his characteristically elegant manner. There he wrote:

Avisado por Don Pio Valenzuela de que se intentaba un levantamiento, aconsejé lo contrario tratando de convencerle con razones. D. Pio Valenzuela se separé de mí convencido al parecer, tanto que en vez de tomar parte después en la rebelión, se presentó á indulto á las Autoridades.

---

54. De la Costa, ed., *The Trial*, p. 9.

Advised by Don Pio Valenzuela that an uprising was being prepared, I counseled against it, trying to convince him by rational arguments. Don Pio Valenzuela took his leave persuaded, it appears, since instead of later taking part in the rebellion he presented himself to the authorities, asking for pardon.

A later sentence adds some complicating ambiguity:

D. Pio Valenzuela venía á avisarme para que me pusiese en seguro, pues según él, era posible que me complicaran.

Don Pio Valenzuela came to warn me to be on my guard, since, according to him, it was possible that they [presumably the Spanish, not the Katipunan] would implicate me.[55]

This testimony is pretty plausible. In Rizal's negative advice to the doctor one can hear echoes of Blumentritt's reasoned comparative warnings against revolutionary adventures. It is not clear how much he knew of what was really happening in Cuba, but the difficulties of the island's struggle are rhetorically deployed to reinforce that advice. It is plain, however, that Valenzuela cautiously presented himself as seeking not an endorsement for the insurrection, but merely counsel as to its opportuneness. Whether or not he was really convinced by the novelist's arguments, he appeared to accept them if for no other reason than that he could not be sure Rizal would not say something to other visitors, his family, or even the authorities in Dapitan.[56] What exactly Valenzuela told the comrades on his return to Manila is by no means clear: did he accurately report that Rizal's advice was to wait, since conditions for a successful uprising were not yet present, or did he simply say that Rizal flatly refused to endorse Bonifacio's project? The latter is perhaps more likely, since it is said that Bonifacio was at first incredulous, and then livid, calling Rizal a coward. But such was Rizal's prestige that the two men agreed to conceal his "rejection" from their Katipunan comrades.[57]

Then, out of the blue, on July 1, Blanco received a letter from minister of war Azcárraga saying that, since Weyler had raised no objection to Rizal coming to Cuba to work as a doctor, he should be permitted to depart for the Caribbean. The Captain-General's official letter to Rizal arrived in Dapitan

---

55. *Ibid.*, pp. 67 and 68.

56. Valenzuela was one of the *katipuneros* whose confessions were used against Rizal at his trial. When the Revolution broke out, he went into hiding, and was among the first to give himself up when Blanco offered amnesty to those rebels who surrendered. He told his interrogators all he knew and more, implicating many former comrades. His memoirs, published many years later, are notorious for their unreliability and selfservingness.

57. Guerrero, *The First Filipino*, pp. 381–3.

on the 30th. The following day Rizal left for Manila on the same boat that had brought Blanco's missive. The abrupt speed of this decision cannot be explained simply by his eagerness to escape the boredom and isolation of the Jesuit settlement—or by any urgency in Blanco's message. At his trial Rizal explained that his firm decision to go to Cuba came out of purely private reasons which led to difficulties with a missionary priest.[58] This must refer to the priest's refusal to marry Rizal and Josephine Bracken unless the former recanted all his heretical opinions. But the real reason was surely fear of being implicated in an impending Katipunan uprising which he was sure would be a bloody failure. At this point, however, his luck ran out.[59]

On June 7, just seven weeks earlier, a huge bomb was thrown during the annual Corpus Christi ceremonial procession in Barcelona. Six people were killed instantly, and a number of the forty-two wounded subsequently died in hospital. The following day martial law was declared in the city, then under the control of none other than General Despujol. It would remain in force for a year. The bomb was particularly frightening since it seemed aimed at no prominent political or religious personality, and its victims were ordinary citizens.[60] The police, egged on, hysterically or rusefully, by the Church and various rightwing groups and their press, ran riot, arresting about three hundred people—anarchists of all types, anticlericals, radical republicans, progressive intellectuals and journalists, and so on. Most of them were imprisoned in the gloomy fortress of Montjuich, which would soon become notorious all over Europe for the tortures practiced in its dungeons.[61] The principal (eventual) suspect turned out to be a twenty-six-year-old Frenchman. Thomas Ascheri,

58. De la Costa, ed., *The Trial*, p. 68.

59. So, alas, did that of Marcelo Del Pilar, who died of poverty and ill-health in Barcelona on June 4. He was just forty-six years old. Despite his differences with Rizal, Filipinos have always included him among the chief heroes of the Revolutionary generation.

60. Police sources claimed that the *attentat* was aimed at the clerical and military dignitaries at the head of the procession, but was bungled, killing instead people at the rear. Ramón Sempau, in his *Los victimarios*, p. 282, gives reasons for strongly doubting this theory. As we shall see, Sempau himself later tried his hand at an assassination, which targeted the right man, the chief Montjuich police torturer, but failed to kill him.

61. The origin of this curious name is contested. The more likely explanation is that it is a corruption of the Latin *Mons Jovis* (Jove's Mount or Hill). The steep, high escarpment overlooking the city was an appropriate site for sacrifices to the Romans' *capo di tutti capi*. But some Catalans believe that it refers to an old Jewish cemetery on the site. Eighty-seven prisoners were eventually tried—the first on December 15 (as we shall shortly see, Rizal's own court martial opened on the 26th). Most of the rest were summarily deported to Spanish Africa. The generally cautious, careful Esenwein, as well as other scholars, believe that the real mastermind was a Frenchman, Jean Girault, who escaped to Argentina. See Esenwein, *Anarchist Ideology*, p. 192; and Núñez, *El terrorismo*, pp. 96–7, 161–4.

born in Marseilles, ex-seminarist, ex-sailor, deserter from the French army, and informer for the French police, was also a man who claimed really to be an anarchist spy whose job it was to give the police false information and forewarn the comrades of imminent razzias.[62] After undergoing excruciating tortures, and trial before a military court, he and four almost certainly innocent Spaniards were executed on May 5 the following year.

Cuba was effectively under martial law, now Barcelona—and the Philippines would shortly follow. Domestic repression, the most severe in Europe, as well as the widening domestic awareness of the grimness of Weyler's methods in Havana, now polarized Spanish politics. Cánovas was admired or hated for both, and among his many enemies fury over Montjuich bled quickly into firmer sympathy for Cuba.

LAST JOURNEYS

Rizal sailed for Manila on July 31, 1896 expecting to catch the official monthly mailboat to Spain. But his ship ran into difficulties, and by the time it reached the Philippine capital on August 6, the mailboat was gone. Pending the departure of the next, scheduled for September 3, he was kept comfortably aboard off the Cavite shipyard, barred, at his own request, from contact with anyone but his immediate family. If the Katipunan rose while he was still in Manila, he wanted to be certain that he could not be implicated. There is no way to be sure what he knew of the events transpiring in Manila, let alone Cuba, Madrid, and Barcelona. But it is unlikely that he understood what was clear to Bonifacio—that with 200,000 Spanish troops tied down in Cuba, Madrid did not have the capacity to send an overwhelming military force to the Philippines. Blumentritt's hour for a successful liberation struggle now appeared on the rebel horizon.

From late 1895 Captain-General Blanco had been receiving reports from his secret agents that an underground, revolutionary Katipunan was becoming seriously active. Given the small number of troops at hand, and anxious not to panic the Spanish community in Manila, he gave orders that suspect persons be shadowed and suspect premises quietly searched. In the spring of 1896 members of the Katipunan had started disappearing, unobtrusively deported to remote islands. The Katipunan leadership's growing awareness of all this was one reason for Valenzuela's mission to Dapitan. In mid-July Blanco's agents came across a secret list of the full membership of one branch, and

---

62. Ascheri's nationality was a real asset to the authorities. It reminded the Spanish public of Ravachol, Vaillant, and Émile Henry, and pushed the source of the outrage across the Pyrenees. Furthermore, as an indigent foreigner, he could count on very little political help in Spain.

arrested or hunted them all. Some of the arrestees started to talk. The Captain-General's plan to break up the Katipunan on the quiet had, however, failed to take women into account. Some of the wives and mothers of the arrestees turned to their parish priests in the hope of getting their men released. On August 19, *El Español* published a sensational story by a parish priest who said he had discovered in the confessional—so much for the inviolability of confession in the Catholic colony!—that a revolutionary uprising was about to take place. The Spanish community went into an angry panic. Blanco was now forced to order massive open raids and searches, while to his fury the Orders began claiming that only their patriotic vigilance had prevented a massacre, while the feckless Captain-General had done nothing.[63] Bonifacio, on the run, had now to advance his timetable, and he issued orders for a general meeting of the *katipuneros* on the 24th, in Balintawak, a village just north of Manila, to decide what to do next. But the pressure was such that the meeting had to be moved up to the 23rd, and over to the village of Pugadlawin. The gathering agreed to begin the insurrection on the 29th, with those present tearing up their *cédulas* (tax payment receipts required to be carried by all natives as a form of identification) and shouting "Long live the Philippines! Long live the Katipunan!" Neighboring provinces were called on to rise and converge on the colonial capital at the same time.[64]

On the given day Bonifacio led an assault on the arsenal in the Manilan suburb of Marikina. Two days later the province of Cavite passed into the hands of the poorly armed rebels, and the other provinces surrounding Manila were soon—for a while—in rebel hands.

Blanco found himself in a difficult position. The panicked Spaniards in the colony (about 15,000 all told, including women and children, in a population of about 7,000,000), and even more the powerful Orders, demanded immediate and violent repression.[65] To a large extent, and perhaps against his

---

63. See the lucid account in Onofre Corpuz, *The Roots of the Filipino Nation* (Quezon City: Aklahi Foundation, 1989), vol. 2, pp. 217–19.

64. See the vivid, detailed account given in Teodoro Agoncillo's opinionated but ground-breaking *The Revolt of the Masses* (Quezon City: University of the Philippines Press, 1956), chapter 9. This shouting has gone down in nationalist history as the Grito of Balintawak, though it occurred in Pugadlawin. The terminology is clearly a reference to the *Grito de Yara*, the popular Cuban phrase for Céspedes's proclamation of insurrection on October 10, 1868. But it is probable that the locution was invented much later than August 1896. In any event, at this moment the Philippines was still "28 years behind" Cuba. But two years later they would become close contemporaries, as we shall observe.

65. Demographic data on the Spanish Philippines are notoriously uncertain and contradictory, as the regime never got round to doing a good modern census, and its guesstimates rarely coincided with statistics compiled by the Church. The fullest and most detailed study of the various countings can be found in a   *cont'd over/*

own better judgment (the colonial military was very small, and he had to cable Madrid for reinforcements), he yielded.[66] Hundreds of Filipinos were arrested and some were executed, while "rebel" property was confiscated. Death by firing squad was ordained for all those found by military courts to have helped Bonifacio's men. But to the rage of the colonial elite, Blanco followed Martínez Campos's earlier Cuban policy by immediately offering full amnesty to any rebel who surrendered promptly, and he repeated this offer in a second decree the following month. At the end of October, Archbishop Nozaleda cabled the Dominican HQ in Madrid (for further dissemination within Spain's political class): "Situation worsens. Rebellion spreading. Blanco's apathy inexplicable. To avert danger, appointment new leader urgently necessary." Less than six weeks later Blanco was recalled.[67]

And Rizal? The striking thing is that on August 30, the day *after* Bonifacio opened the insurrection with his attack on the Marikina arsenal, the novelist was handed two personal letters of introduction from the Captain-General, one addressed to the Minister of War, the other to the Minister of Overseas Territories. The language is remarkable. In the first, Blanco wrote:

> [Rizal's] behavior during the four years he stayed in Dapitan was exemplary, and, to my mind, he is all the more worthy of forgiveness and benevolence in that he appears in no way implicated in the chimerical attempts which we all deplore these days, neither in any of the conspiracies nor in any of the secret societies which have been plotting.[68]

---

65 cont'd   56-page appendix to the first volume of Onofre Corpuz's *The Roots of the Filipino Nation*, pp. 515–70. The roughly seven-million figure he comes to for the country on the eve of the Revolution includes the Muslim south and the pagan populations of Luzon's High Cordillera, over both of which Spanish control was exiguous. As for the Spanish, he suggests (p. 257) for 1876 a figure of 15,327 (including Peninsulars, creoles, and Spanish mestizos), of whom 1,962 were in the clergy (approximately 15 percent). Most of these people lived in or near Manila. Without citing any sources, Sichrovsky (*Ferdinand Blumentritt*, p. 25) gives the following not implausible figures for the various Orders at the end of the nineteenth century: Augustinians 346, Recollects 327, Dominicans 233, Franciscans 107, Jesuits 42, Capuchins 16, and Benedictines 6. Total: 1,077.

66. When the Revolution broke out, Blanco had only about 3,000 troops to hand, officered by Spaniards, with a mercenary native footsoldiery. Four shiploads of Spanish conscripts would arrive in the course of October, giving him a troop strength of just under 8,000. Corpuz, *The Roots*, vol. 2, p. 233. Comparing Cuba and the Philippines, we can conclude that the former, with about a quarter of the latter's population, was faced with almost twenty-five times the number of imperial military adversaries.

67. Guerrero, *The First Filipino*, p. 409.

68. *Ibid.*, p. 391. I have tampered mildly with Guerrero's translation to correct the grammar.

The wording indicates that Blanco intended to show the Cánovas cabinet and the military high command in Madrid that Rizal had nothing to do with the uprising, and did so by praising his conduct in Dapitan and referring to various conspiratorial groups about whose activities he had been reporting home for some months.

The mailboat left on the scheduled day. When it anchored in Singapore, expatriate supporters visited Rizal on board and urged him to jump ship; they were ready to sue for a British-colonial writ of habeas corpus on his behalf. But he had given Blanco his word of honor that he would go to Spain, and so refused their help. Off Aden he crossed, on September 25th, a large Spanish troopship crammed with conscripts—something new for the Philippines but made necessary by the war in Cuba. By the time his ship reached Malta, three days later, he was ordered confined to his cabin, though he smuggled out one distressed letter to Blumentritt. On October 3, he reached martial law Barcelona. After three days' confinement in his cabin, he was taken under guard to the Montjuich fortress and put in a cell. The next day he was taken to see Captain-General Despujol, who spoke to him civilly and sadly, but told him he would have to return to Manila that day aboard yet another troopship full of reinforcements. On arrival in Manila he was imprisoned in Fort Santiago.

What had happened? So long as the Philippines was at peace, Cánovas did not have to worry about the contrast between Weyler's harsh policies in Havana, and Blanco's moderation in Manila. But with the outbreak of the Katipunan's armed uprising, the contrast was no longer tolerable. All the less so, when he received cables from Blanco asking for substantial military reinforcements, which threatened the human and financial resources that Weyler urgently needed. Furthermore, the Captain-General was pleading for Peninsular troops, not local native mercenaries, and these could only be supplied by conscription, which was already very unpopular and required constant public justification. Finally, perceived weakness towards the Philippines would undermine the rationale for the extreme harshness of *el Sanguinario* in Cuba. In effect, it was becoming politically impossible to pursue different policies in Spain's last two big colonies.

There were other problems too. Legally speaking, it would have been out of the question, even in martial law Barcelona, to put Rizal on trial—not only because his "offences" had not been committed in Spain but also because witnesses were not available there. Politically speaking, a capital trial in Spain would have been a disaster. Rizal was a well-known figure there. Crucifying obscure anarchists was one thing, but doing the same to a man who was a personal friend of Moret, Morayta, and Pi y Margall was quite another. Outside Barcelona itself, Spain was not under martial law, and a case of this kind would have generated huge unwanted publicity, certainly amplified by the international media already beginning an onslaught on what Tarrida del Mármol would soon term the new Inquisition in Spain. Even martial law Barcelona was not necessarily reliable. The cabinet was aware of Despujol's earlier relationship with Rizal, and could not be sure that he could be entrusted with a kangaroo court martial of the young Filipino. Yet the regime was determined to strike hard at the symbolic leader of the Philippine movement for independence, and to effect this he had to be returned to his place of origin. The instruments were fortunately at hand.

Shortly after the outbreak of Bonifacio's insurrection, Blanco had appointed as head of a powerful commission of inquiry into its origins, plans, and resources a certain Colonel Francisco Olivé, unaware that this man, half a decade earlier, had been sent by Weyler to Calamba with orders to use all force necessary to evict the Dominicans' recalcitrant tenants, including Rizal's family and kinfolk. The colonel, Madrid behind him, insisted that Rizal be immediately interrogated and put on trial, and Blanco, paralyzed by the new Madrid policy, the hatred of the Spaniards in Manila, and his own imminent recall, felt helpless. On December 2, the severely Catholic General Camilo Polavieja arrived in the colonial capital with a flock of trusted subordinates, and ten days later took over power and charge of policy from Blanco.

WEYLERISMO IN MANILA

The new Captain-General had never previously served in the Philippines, but was a capable veteran of the Ten Years' War in Cuba against Céspedes. During the Guerra Chiquita he had served as Captain-General in Havana but had resigned before his term was up, out of frustration with the massive, deeply entrenched corruption of the colonial civil bureaucracy.[69] Nor did he lack political foresight. While in Cuba he had openly stated that "instead of trying to prevent at all costs and for always the independence of Cuba, which it would be useless to attempt, we should prepare ourselves for it, remain on the island only so long as it is reasonable to do so, and take the necessary measures to avoid being thrown out by force, to the prejudice of our interests and our honor, before the time when we must leave in all friendliness."[70] He came to Manila from the position of head of the Queen Regent's military household, and seems to have been picked for his probity, loyalty, and military toughness. He was believed ready to carry out Cánovas's orders *sin contemplaciones*.

---

69. Thomas, *Cuba*, p. 299.
70. Guerrero, *The First Filipino*, p. 411.

It cannot be clearly determined whether, in his cell, Rizal was aware of the implications of these events. But it is striking that on December 10, two days before Blanco fell from power, he wrote a petition to the Captain-General, sent through the investigating judge who was preparing the dossier for his trial. The core of this petition, as recorded by his interrogator, ran as follows:

> Suplica á Vuestra Señoría se sirva manifestarle, si en el estado en que se encuentra le sería permitido manifestar de una manera ó de otra que condena semejantes medios criminales y que nunca ha permitido que se usase de su nombre. Este paso sólo tiene por objeto el desengañar á algunos desgraciados y acaso salvarlos, y el que suscribe no desea en ninguna manera que influya en la causa que se le sigue.

> He entreats Your Honor to be willing to let him make a statement of one kind or another, if a statement were to be permitted to someone in his situation, condemning such criminal methods and [stating] that he had never given permission for the use of his name. This step [is taken] solely to undeceive some unfortunate men and perhaps to save them. The undersigned in no way desires that this influence his case.[71]

Blanco approved this petition the next day, his last in office. On the same day, the investigating officer made the formal decision "to omit the confrontation of the accused and the witnesses, considering such confrontation unnecessary for the proof of the crime, since he regards this to be sufficiently proven."[72]

We cannot be sure when Rizal learned that Blanco was gone, and it may be that when he wrote his "manifesto," on December 15, he was still in ignorance. Or he may have been told that Polavieja had endorsed Blanco's letter of permission. The *Manifiesto á Algunos Filipinos* was the last political text that he wrote, and for this reason, as well as its content, it is worth quoting in full:

> Paisanos: Á mi vuelta de España he sabido que mi nombre se había usado entre algunos que estaban en armas como grito de guerra. La noticia me sorprendió dolorosamente; pero, creyendo ya todo terminado, me callé ante un hecho que consideraba irremediable. Ahora percibo rumores de que continúan los disturbios; y por si algunos siguen aún valiéndose de mi nombre de mala ó de buena fé, para remediar este abuso y desengañar á los incautos, me apresuro á dirigiros estas líneas, para se sepa la verdad. Desde un principio, cuando tuve noticia de lo que se proyectaba, me opuse á ello, lo combatí y demostré su absoluta imposibilidad. Ésta es la verdad, y viven los testigos de mis palabras. Estaba convencido de que la idea era altamente absurda, y, lo que era peor, funesta. Hice

---

71. De la Costa, ed., *The Trial*, p. 32.
72. *Ibid.*, p. 30.

más. Cuando más tarde, á pesar de mis consejos, estalló el movimiento, ofrecí espontáneamente, no sólo mis servicios, sino mi vida, y hasta mi nombre, para que usasen de ellos de la manera como creyeren oportuno á fin de sofocar la rebelión; pues convencido de los males que iba á acarrear [iban à arreciar?], me consideraba feliz si con cualquier sacrificio podía impedir tantas inútiles desgracias. Esto consta igualmente.

Paisanos: He dado pruebas como el que más de querer libertades para nuestro país, y sigo queriéndolas. Pero yo ponía como premisa la educación del pueblo para que por medio de la instrucción y del trabajo tuviese personalidad propia y se hiciese digno de las mismas. He recomendado en mis escritos el estudio, las virtudes cívicas, sin las cuales no existe redención. He escrito también (y se han repetido mis palabras) que las reformas, para ser fructíferas, tenían que venir de *arriba*, que las que venían de *abajo* eran sacudidas irregulares é inseguras. Nutrido en estas ideas, no puedo menos de condenar y condeno esa sublevación absurda, salvaje, tramada á espaldas mías, que nos deshonra á los filipinos y desacredita á los que pueden abogar por nosotros; abomino de sus procedimientos criminales y rechazo toda clase de participaciones, deplorando con todo el dolor de mi corazón á los incautos que se han dejado engañar. Vuélvanse, pues, á sus casas, y que Dios perdone á los que han obrado de mala fé.[73]

Countrymen: On my return from Spain I learned that my name had been used as a war cry among certain people who were up in arms. The news was for me a painful surprise, but believing that all was over, I kept my silence in the face of what I considered an irremediable fact. Now I observe rumors that the disturbances continue; since some people still continue to make use of my name—in bad or good faith—in order to remedy this abuse and to undeceive the unwary I am hastening to direct these lines to you, so that the truth may be known. From the beginning, when I got word of what was being planned, I opposed it, I fought against it, and I demonstrated its absolute impossibility. This is the truth, and there are living witnesses to my words. I was convinced that the idea was highly absurd, and, still worse, calamitous. And I did more. Later, when despite my advice the movement erupted, I spontaneously offered not only my services, but my life, and even my name, to be used in whatever manner they deemed opportune, in order to suffocate the rebellion. For, convinced of the evils thereby entailed, I considered myself fortunate if some sacrifice on my part could prevent such useless misfortunes. I am still of this opinion.

Countrymen: I have given proofs, as much as anyone, of my desire for liberties for our country, and I continue to desire them. But I held as the necessary premise the education of the people, so that by means of instruction and work, they would hold on to their own personality and make themselves worthy of those liberties. In my writings I have recommended study, and the civic virtues without which no redemption can exist. Furthermore I have written (and my

---

73. *Ibid.*, pp. 172–3. Words in italics were underlined in the original text.

words have been repeated) that for reforms to bear fruit, they must come from *above*, since those that come from *below* will be irregular and uncertain shocks. Nurtured on these ideas, I can do no less than condemn, and I do condemn, this absurd, savage insurrection, plotted behind my back, which dishonors the Filipinos and discredits those who could be our advocates. I abominate its criminal procedures, and reject every type of participation, deploring, with all the pain in my heart, those unwary people who have allowed themselves to be deceived. So, return to you homes, and may God pardon those who have acted in bad faith.

If Rizal believed that this manifesto would be broadcast to the people of the Philippines, he was fooling himself. The military Judge-Advocate General, Nicolás de la Peña, writing to Polavieja, dryly observed: "His manifesto can be reduced to the following words. Faced with failure, countrymen, lay down your arms; later on, I will lead you to the Promised Land. Without being at all beneficial for the peace, it could in the future inspire the spirit of rebellion." He therefore proposed its suppression, and the Captain-General agreed.[74]

On December 19, Polavieja ordered that Rizal be promptly put on trial for sedition and treason before a military court. The trial itself opened on the 26th, and after summary proceedings lasting one day, the military judges recommended that the accused be executed. Polavieja approved the recommendation on the 28th. When handed the death warrant for his signature, the prisoner looked it over, and noticed that he was described in it as Chinese. He crossed out the word and replaced it, not by *filipino*, but by *indio*.[75] In his last hours, when his sister Trinidad came to see him, he gave her a small lamp, whispering that there was something in it for her. When she got home, she found hidden inside it a small piece of paper on which a 70-line poem of farewell to his country was inscribed in tiny letters. Known as "Mi último adiós," this beautiful, melancholy poem was soon translated into Tagalog, ironically enough by Bonifacio. (Over the next century translations appeared in some sixty-five foreign, and forty-nine Philippine, languages.)[76] At dawn on December 30, Rizal was led from his cell to the open space called Bagumbayan—now Luneta Park—where the three secular priests had been garroted a quarter of a century earlier. There he was shot to death by a Spanish-officered, native-manned squad before the eyes of thousands of spectators. Just thirty-six years old, he faced his

---

74. *Ibid.*, p. 173. In these sentences there is a curious echo of Lete's lampoon of 1892.

75. Information kindly provided by Ambeth Ocampo who has seen the original document.

76. See National Historical Institute, *Dr José Rizal's Mi Último Adiós in Foreign and Local Translations* (Manila: National Historical Institute, 1989–90), 2 vols.

At dawn on December 30, Rizal was taken to Bagumbayan (now Luneta Park) and shot by firing-squad.

death with dignity and equanimity. His body was not returned to his family, but buried secretly, for fear that a visible tomb would become a mecca for nationalist pilgrims.

But the mean calculation was in fact irrelevant. Rizal's public execution created exactly the opposite effect to what Cánovas had hoped to achieve by it. Far from extinguishing the insurrection, let alone Filipino aspirations for independence, Rizal's exemplary death created instantly a national martyr, deepened and widened the revolutionary movement, indirectly led to Cánovas's own assassination the following year, and paved the way for the end of the Spanish empire.

THREE REFLECTIONS

By way of reflection on this chapter, in order to bring it to a conclusion, one could make three observations.

First, what was Rizal waiting for when he returned home in 1892 along with almost the entire edition of *El Filibusterismo*? The most striking thing about the four years he spent in Dapitan is that this enormously gifted writer wrote practically nothing beyond a few censor-shadowed letters. Yet there can be no doubt that he could have written manuscripts and concealed them locally or smuggled them out with the sisters who came to visit him. The projected third "beautiful" and "artistic" novel came to nothing, and the fragments of *Makamisa* mark only a reversion to *Noli me tangere* rather than a step beyond *El Filibusterismo*. Possibly, another great novel was beyond him. Meantime, the Sandakan and Liga Filipina projects had been quickly aborted by the colonial regime. Offered by Regidor the chance of being rescued by ship, he turned it down, as he also did Blanco's offer to send him back to Spain. He was sure that nothing useful was possible there. He had no enthusiasm about going to Cuba until after Valenzuela's visit. And when he hurriedly decided to take up Blanco's offer, it was less to do something than to flee from something.

One could say that in the summer of 1896 he was experiencing what happens to a good number of original writers: that once their works leave the printery for the public sphere they no longer own them or control them. Rizal mistakenly regarded himself as a political teacher of his people, but his power did not come from his sermons and critical articles, which were not too different from the productions of other gifted *ilustrados*. It came from his novels—no one else attempted them. What he had done in *Noli me tangere* was to create in the imagination a whole (and contemporary) Philippine "society," with its intermeshed high colonial officials, village gamblers, dissident intellectuals, gravediggers, friars, police informers, social climbers, child acolytes, actresses, small-town caciques, bandits, reformers, carpenters, teenage girls, and revolutionaries. And its true hero, Elias the revolutionary, in the end sacrifices his life for the reformer Ibarra. What Rizal had done in *El Filibusterismo* was to imagine the political collapse of this society and the near-elimination of its ruling powers. Perhaps no Filipino had even dreamed of such a possibility till then, let alone entered the dream into the public domain. It was as if the genius's genie was out of the bottle, and the contrasting figures of Elias and Simoun had begun to assume a life of their own. Rizal did not know Bonifacio personally, and Bonifacio perhaps listened to Rizal speak on one single night. But when the Katipunan made Rizal its honorary president, and ended its discussions with the cheer "Long live Dr Rizal," it was surely because Elias and Simoun, and many other of the novels' figures of action now belonged to them.[77] Novelist and novels had parted company. José Rizal was one thing, Dr Rizal was another. Perhaps it

77. As we shall see in the next chapter, Bonifacio survived Rizal less than five months. There are extremely few documents which can be unassailably attributed to him, and his life in the shadows of clandestinity offers room for countless conjectures. But at least some copies of *El Filibusterismo* quietly circulated in Manila even before Rizal came home. It is a moral certainty that at some point between 1892 and 1896 the Katipunan leader found a way to read it.

was the discovery of this distance that so enraged Bonifacio on receiving Valenzuela's report. It was surely the deep reason for Rizal's angry anxiety, in the last months of his life, about his *nombre*. So to speak, *Simoun, ce n'est pas moi.*

Looking ahead a little, one notes a peculiar irony. Rizal had repeatedly told the Pilaristas that nothing could be achieved in Spain, and that assimilation was a fantasy. But in the colony, he found he too could achieve next to nothing. He told Valenzuela that the Cuban war would force Madrid to make concessions to the Philippines, said no more about the dangers of the Spanish language, and disassociated himself from the Katipunan uprising: effectively, a Pilarist position. At the same time, the Cuban war destroyed the future of Del Pilar's campaign, already reeling from the financial collapse of *La Solidaridad*. In the last months of his life, Del Pilar had planned to move back to Hong Kong, a site where assimilation was irrelevant. It is not at all beyond the realm of possibility that if he had lived, this seasoned practical politician would eventually have supported the Katipunan. What else was there left?

A second reflection arises in relation to Cuba. Not only was Martí's 1895 insurrection an exhilarating example for nationalist Filipinos, it was also a deadly blow to the Restoration political system and to the empire as a whole. The huge number of troops Cánovas had to send to the island, the accompanying vast losses of human life, financial resources, and international respectability made it extremely difficult for Madrid to act effectively in the Philippines, as we shall discover in the following chapter. The rapid growth in the Katipunan from the end of 1895 indicates how awareness of Madrid's weakness was spreading through the print media—to which Bonifacio and his friends, but not Rizal in Dapitan, had ready access. That Rizal should have termed the Katipunan's uprising as "absurd" and an "absolute impossibility" shows clearly how little he understood the real conjunctures of 1895–96. It is extremely unlikely that the Katipunan would have rebelled in August 1896 if the bloody struggle between Weyler and Gómez was not at its height. If they nonetheless did rebel, they would have been quickly crushed by the kind of military power made available to Weyler. Once the Katipunan did revolt, however, it was virtually inevitable that *weylerismo* minus Weyler would arrive in Manila. Rizal was judicially murdered just for this *raison d'état*—as a minatory example, not as a revolutionary. Blanco's letters on Rizal's behalf were designed to demonstrate to the highest authorities the novelist's complete innocence of involvement in the insurrection. But between the lines was the fear that in the end Madrid could not care less. One could argue that Polavieja acted stupidly, or obeyed stupid orders. Would it not have been slyer to save Rizal's life but insist that he tour the Tagalog area proclaiming his prison manifesto? Would this not have ruined Rizal's reputation? The answer is probably yes, but it would have come much too late; the popular insurrection had been in full swing for three months and had its own momentum. Many people in any case would have believed that the manifesto was coerced. Beyond that, the questions do not take Cuba into account. Madrid's decision to kill Rizal was also intended to have an audience in the Caribbean island and in the world beyond it. Polavieja was not sent to replace Blanco because he was a better general, but because the Spanish state, struggling to maintain a dying transcontinental empire, saw in him a second Weylerian man of steel.

Last, in spite of its crucial importance for Rizal's fate, the Cuban war for independence was only one part of a rising world turbulence which would reach its climax in 1914. East Asia, dominated for half a century by the British, was becoming highly unstable as new competition emerged from Japan, the United States, and Germany. In southern Africa, the Boer War was about to begin. Nationalist struggles in central and eastern Europe were undermining the dominant multiethnic land empires controlled by Istanbul, Vienna, St Petersburg, and even Berlin. Socialism in the broadest sense was also on the national and international move, as we shall soon see. Martial law Barcelona, where Rizal spent his last night in Europe, was one key site on which this spreading movement pivoted.

5

Montjuich

TARRIDA'S CRUSADE

Among the more than 300 people imprisoned at Montjuich in the aftermath of the Corpus Christi bombing of June 7, 1896, most were still there when Rizal joined them for that one night in early October. The key exception was the remarkable Cuban creole Fernando Tarrida del Mármol, Rizal's exact age-mate, whom we last encountered accompanying Errico Malatesta on his abortive political tour of Spain at the time of the Jerez *émeute* of 1892. Arrested late—July 21—on the steps of Barcelona's Polytechnic Academy, where he served as Engineer-Director and distinguished professor of mathematics, Tarrida was released on August 27. He was lucky that a young lieutenant warden, recognizing his former teacher, had the courage to sneak down into Barcelona on pretext of illness and wire the news of Tarrida's incarceration to the national press and to any influential figure he could think of. The Cuban was no less fortunate that his cousin, the Marquis of Mont-Roig, a conservative senator, then used his influence and contacts to spring the prisoner. (Tarrida was utterly unembarrassed by this kind of help from the Right, but one can be sure that it impelled him to be maximally active on behalf of his less well-connected prison-mates.) On his release, he very quietly made his way across the Pyrenees to Paris, taking with him letters and other documents from his fellow prisoners that he had managed to smuggle or have smuggled out.

Tarrida's "Un mois dans les prisons d'Espagne" appeared in *La Revue Blanche*, France's leading intellectual fortnightly, exactly at the time Rizal was being taken back from Barcelona to Manila under heavy guard. It was only the first of fourteen articles Tarrida wrote for this journal over the next

Execution of anarchists in Barcelona.

fifteen months.[1] They covered in detail not only the gruesome atrocities being practiced in Montjuich, but also the Cuban War of Independence, the nationalist movements in the Philippines and Puerto Rico, abuse of prisoners

---

1. See *La Revue Blanche*, 11: 81 (October 15, 1896), pp. 337–41. This review was originally the brainchild of two pairs of brothers, one Belgian, the other French (the cadet was only sixteen) who met in—where else?—Spa in the summer of 1889. The four secured the financial backing of the Natanson brothers, wealthy, cultivated, Polish-Jewish art dealers, who had moved to Paris in 1880. The boys published the first number in December 1889 in Liège. In 1891, however, the review moved to Paris, with the middle Natanson brother, Thadée, assuming direct charge, and in October the fortnightly started appearing in a much more lavish and elegant format. In January 1895, Félix Fénéon, recently acquitted of terrorism and sedition in the notorious Trial of the Thirty, took over the main editorial work. As we shall see, he was a committed cosmopolitan anarchist and anti-imperialist and made the journal more visibly leftwing than it had been before. *La Revue Blanche*'s last issue (no. 312) came out on April 15, 1903. It had always run a deficit, and now Thadée had lost a fortune by unwise investments in eastern Europe, while his beautiful Polish wife, Misia Godebska, had left him for a millionaire newspaper magnate. Elder brother Alexandre, a first-class financier and stockbroker, felt he could not afford to bear the entire financial burden alone. See Halperin, *Félix Fénéon*, pp. 300–14.

from the Caribbean in Ceuta, America's noisy imperialist scheming, and, perhaps surprisingly, a pre-Wright Brothers equation-filled professional text on "aerial navigation." The second in the series, published on December 15, two weeks before Rizal's execution, was in fact devoted to "Le problème philippin" (the novelist himself was briefly described as a political deportee). One could venture to say that in this period Tarrida was the review's most frequent contributor. The extraordinary space given to him was certainly at the start the result of his personal testimony on Montjuich. This was the onset of what would become an Atlantic-wide movement of protest against the Cánovas regime, dubbed by the writer, with his usual media flair, "the Inquisitors of Spain." Tarrida was a real find for *La Revue Blanche*, since he was that rare bird who was not only an open-minded, French-speaking anarchist intellectual from Catalonia, but also, as a Cuban patriot, perfectly positioned to link Montjuich systematically to the independence struggles in Cuba, Puerto Rico, and the Philippines.

How did this conjuncture come about? Tarrida's own past career was of decisive importance.[2] He was born, as we have noted, in Havana in 1861, and lived there till the spectacular fall of Queen Isabel in 1868. It is not clear why his father, eventually a wealthy Catalan manufacturer of boots and shoes, should have gone to live in Cuba at all. But the date of the family's return suggests that it may have been one of the many likely targets of the regime in its final repressive years.[3] The young Fernando was then packed off to the *lycée* in Pau—where many decades later Bourdieu was to suffer. At this school a classmate, the future French prime minister Jean-Louis Barthou, converted Tarrida to republicanism. On his return to Spain, Fernando moved further to the Left, frequenting working-class meetings and clubs. By 1886 (a year before *Noli me tangere* appeared) he had become a confirmed anarchist, a magnetic lecturer, and a regular contributor of articles to the leading anarchist publications *Acracia* and *El Productor*. In July 1889 he was chosen by the Barcelona workers to represent them at the new International Socialist Congress in Paris.[4] In a public lecture in November of that year, he coined the inimitable slogan "anarquismo sin

---

2. For this, and the following paragraph I am relying on the splendidly detailed chapter VIII ("Anarquismo sin adjetivos") in Esenwein's *Anarchist Ideology*.

3. Fernández hints at a different possibility. Tarrida's mother, very probably a creole, had a first cousin called Donato Mármol, who came from Oriente province, and was one of the first to rally to Céspedes's side. During the Ten Years' War he rose to the rank of general. If Tarrida's family left for Europe immediately after the insurrection started, this would mean that his father feared the consequences of this dangerous kin connection. *La sangre de Santa Águeda*, p. 25.

4. This occurred in the midst of the Great Exposition of that year, at which the Eiffel Tower—which Joris-Karl Huysmans called a "spread-legged whore," but Georges Seurat rather liked—was unveiled. Halperin, *Félix Fénéon*, p. 204.

adjetivos" as part of a sustained campaign to heal sectarian squabbles on the Left. "Of all the revolutionary theories that claim to guarantee complete social emancipation, the one that most closely conforms to Nature, Science, and Justice, and that rejects all dogmas, political, social, economic, and religious, is called Anarchism Without Adjectives." The idea was to end the bitter quarrels between Marxist and Bakuninist partisans: as he put it, true anarchism would never impose a preconceived economic plan on anyone, since this violated the basic principle of choice. But his campaign was no less directed against the whole idea of the solitary "propaganda by the deed."

Tarrida was promptly denounced by Jean Grave—often jokingly called the Pope of Anarchism—in *La Révolte*, as representing the wrongheaded Spanish anarchist tradition of "collectivism," that is, attachment to an organized working-class base. It says a good deal for this pope's sane rejection of infallibility that he immediately published Tarrida's toreador reply. The twenty-eight-year-old Tarrida, already a mathematics professor, wrote persuasively that small groups using propaganda of the deed without any collective organization behind them stood no chance against the centralized power of the bourgeoisie. Spanish anarchists believed, on the basis of long experience, that coordination was essential, since the organized resistance of the working classes was the only productive instrument for fighting state repression. It was completely wrong, therefore, to condemn the *centros obreros* out of hand as naturally authoritarian "hierarchies"; they had, on the contrary, proved indispensable to the growth of the revolutionary movement in Spain. Grave's demand that workingmen's associations be abolished was senseless. At the same time, however, Tarrida was ready to concede that in the case of the moribund FTRE (Federación de Trabajadores de la Región Española—ashes of the First International), bureaucratism had become deep-rooted, and the organization had lost any usefulness.

Tarrida's arguments were important in their own right (and fairly soon convinced Malatesta, Élie Reclus, and others), but in the present context the key thing is that they were published in *La Révolte*, to which, as we have seen, many of the leading novelists, poets, and painters of Paris were loyal subscribers. When Tarrida arrived in Paris after his release from Montjuich, he was therefore a familiar (printed) figure. That he was a Cuban in the time of Weyler's massively publicized repression on his native island further secured his entrée.

It should be further noted that Tarrida did not emerge in Paris as a lonely victim. Violent as the martial law regime in Barcelona was, Cánovas was wily enough not to extend it to the rest of Spain; but in September he forced through the Cortes the most punitive legislation of that time in western Europe against terrorism and subversion. Still, according to statistics compiled by Ricardo Mella (a careful comrade-in-arms of Tarrida) for Paris's

L'Humanité Nouvelle in 1897, the distribution of serious anarchist activists and sympathizers in Spain was as follows: Andalusia 12,400 anarchists (+ 23,100 sympathizers); Catalonia 6,100 (+ 15,000); Valencia 1,500 (+ 10,000); and New and Old Castile 1,500 (+ 2,000). Totals: 25,800 and 54,300.[5] The social isobars revealed by the Carlist Wars could not be mapped more clearly: cold reactionary and clerical weather in the North and Northwest, torrid rains and storms in the South and East, with the prime minister's Andalusia, not Barcelona, as their eye. Besides, Cánovas's enemies—in his own party, and among the liberals, federalists, republicans, and Marxists—found the occasion ripe, for principled or opportunistic reasons, to take up the Montjuich scandal, exposed in searing terms in "civilization's capital." It helped that among those imprisoned in Barcelona were at least one ex-minister, and three parliamentary deputies.

Furthermore, Paris was becoming an increasingly important site for political action by subjects of the Spanish empire. The radical republican leader Zorrilla had been settled there for a long time, plotting against the Restoration. His personal secretary, Francisco Ferrer Guardia, a seasoned leftist whom we shall encounter again, taught Spanish at the famous Parisian Lycée Condorcet, where Mallarmé was employed until his early death in 1898. After Martí's initiation of the independence war in Cuba in the spring of 1895, Spain was too hot for nationalists and radicals from the Caribbean, and they gathered, under the energetic leadership of the legendary Puerto Rican revolutionary Dr Ramón Betances, in the French capital, propagandizing and conspiring against Cánovas and Weyler. Finally, after the Corpus Christi razzias, many metropolitan radicals fled across the Pyrenees. Only the Filipinos were poorly represented in Paris. Rizal and Del Pilar were dead, and Mariano Ponce had left for Hong Kong. The painter Juan Luna remained as the sole well-known senior nationalist personality.

PARIS RADICALIZED

To grasp why the Paris of 1897 was open to Tarrida's hugely successful campaign, it is necessary to go back in time to consider the earlier careers of two men of different generations who played central roles in creating a new intellectual and political climate.

Georges Clémenceau was born in 1841, and grew up under the repressive and imperialist regime of Louis-Napoléon.[6] By 1861, just as Rizal was being

---

5. Quoted and discussed in Esenwein, *Anarchist Ideology*, p. 202.

6. The following account of Clémenceau's political career (to 1900) is based primarily on Gregor Dallas, *At the Heart of a Tiger: Clémenceau and his World, 1841–1929* (New York: Carroll & Graf, 1993), esp. at pp. 30–38, 97–120, 185–7, 212–340.

Ramón Emeterio Betances (left); his residence in Rue Chateaudun, Paris (right).

born, he was moving in the circles of the radical republican Left, where he encountered Henri Rochefort—the *ci-devant* Marquis de Rochefort-Laçay—who would later become his brother-in-law and a famously erratic radical journalist and editor. In 1862, Clémenceau was jailed by the Emperor for his critical articles, and on his release worked in a hospital next to the Sainte-Pélagie prison for "politicals," where he got to know and become fascinated by Blanqui. He even smuggled in a printing press from Belgium for the eternal conspirator. After Sedan, he became mayor of Montmartre, the *arrondissement* where the Commune would break out the next spring. Clémenceau was strongly opposed to the post-Louis-Napoléon government's groveling to Bismarck, and worked hard against the German siege of Paris. He created an arms factory in the mayoral office which made no less than 23,000 Orsini bombs for use against the invader. At this hour he became very close to Louise Michel. This remarkable woman, eleven years older than he, was the illegitimate daughter of a provincial aristocrat and a chambermaid, and had started sending her poetry to Victor Hugo when she was only fourteen. In the 1860s she was in Paris, moving steadily leftward in her politics, and in 1870–71 became famous for her devoted work in Montmartre for the wounded and the starving. Clémenceau stayed on the job till the last minute, saying to himself—imagines Dallas—as he left the capital, "They are going to shoot all my constituents. But for all that, I can't let my name bear the blame."

Clémenceau was among the first Third Republic parliamentarians to press for a general amnesty of the *communards*, tried to get Blanqui out of prison, and helped Louise Michel after she returned from New Caledonian imprisonment in 1880. When the Red Virgin was sentenced in 1883 to another prison term, this time for anarchism, Clémenceau led the press campaign that forced the Third Republic to release her. A strong supporter of the workers' rights to organize and to unionize, he was also a committed opponent of colonialism and imperialism—including brutal French adventures in Indochina, Africa, and Oceania. No prominent French politician–publicist was more sympathetic to the Cuban cause. His newspaper, *La Justice*, which folded only in October 1897, was the most powerful and respected opposition organ of the post-Commune period. Clémenceau moved to Ernest Vaughan's new *L'Aurore* just in time for the explosion of the Dreyfus affair.

Félix Fénéon, two decades younger than Clémenceau, was born in Turin in 1861, ten days after Rizal was born in Calamba. A brilliant provincial schoolboy, he moved to Paris when he was twenty, took a job at the War Department, and started an astonishing career as art critic, literary editor, and (by the mid-1880s) active anarchist.[7] At the age of twenty-three, he founded the avant-garde *Revue Indépendente* (in its first incarnation it lasted a year), of which Huysmans's stories were the mainstay, but which also featured the writings of Proudhon, Blanqui, Bakunin, and Kropotkin. It was extremely hostile to French imperialism in Indochina, as well as *revanchiste* French nationalism. Fénéon wrote sarcastically of the war minister that he was "sending new troops to the Far East, with the intention of decimating and pillaging the Chinese—who have all our best wishes."[8]

In the second half of the 1880s, the time of Rizal's *Noli me tangere* and Isabelo de los Reyes' *El folk-lore filipino*, Fénéon became a central figure—in some ways the central figure, though he preferred to work behind the scenes—of the Parisian *avant-garde*. He managed simultaneously to edit (with the help of Laforgue among others) the original *La Vogue* (1885–89)—which went out of its way to combat French nationalist provincialism by publishing Keats, Dostoievsky, and Whitman, as well as Laforgue's most

---

7. Fénéon's father was a French traveling salesman and his mother a young Swiss. Halperin, *Félix Fénéon*, p. 21.

8. *Ibid.*, p. 56.

A police photograph of the widely admired French anarchist,
school teacher and aid worker Louise Michel.

oneiric poetry—and a revived *Revue Indépendante* (1885–89). It was Fénéon
who meticulously edited and organized the poetic chaos Rimbaud left behind
into the bombshell *Illuminations* of 1886.[9] In the same year, the Salon des
Indépendents held its second exhibition, the first in which Seurat (two years
older than Fénéon) and Signac (two years younger) were spectacularly
featured. Fénéon not only coined the term "post-impressionists" for the
young rebels, but became their determined and brilliant champion.[10] It is
characteristic of his political outlook that he sent his path-breaking "high-
brow" review of the exhibition to the Belgian avant-garde, socialist journal
L'Art Moderne, and published another, entirely in Parisian argot, for the
radical tabloid *Le Père Peinard*. If all this were not enough, he took over the
job of theatre critic for *L'Art Moderne* from his close friend Huysmans,
championing new playwrights writing under the powerful influence of Ibsen.

In the early 1890s—the time of *El Filibusterismo*—Fénéon veered back to

---

9. *Ibid.*, pp. 62–7.
10. T.J. Clark, in his *Farewell to an Idea* (New Haven: Yale University Press,
1999), p. 62, calls him the "best art critic after Baudelaire," which is high praise.

Paul Signac's avant-garde painting of Félix Fénéon.

radical politics without abandoning his other avocations. In August 1891 he met the bizarre figure who called himself Zo d'Axa (aka Alphonse Gallaud de La Pérouse), who had founded the violently anarchist/avant-garde journal *L'Endehors* three months earlier.[11] It lasted less than two years. Six months after its launching, Zo was indicted for "outrages on morals" because of his journal's scathing articles on the French army, judiciary, and parliament; he fled to England, returned to Paris worried about his wife's fidelity, was arrested and held incommunicado for two weeks, got released pending trial, and disappeared for good.[12] Many of his comrades, however, went to prison for many years. Fénéon was not arrested, but his police dossier was started that year (1893). He took over the journal for the rest of its life, bringing in the great radical Belgian poet Emile Verhaeren, as well as Octave Mirbeau and Paul Adam, two young French anarchist-sympathizing writers in Mallarmé's circle.[13]

---

11. Halperin, *Félix Fénéon*, pp. 245–6.
12. *Ibid.*, p. 252.
13. Maitron, *Le mouvement*, p. 137.

"In the Cell" by Maximilien Luce depicts Fénéon in prison in 1894.

It was at meetings of the Zo group that he met, and was fascinated by, Émile Henry, whom in a letter to Signac he described as "the most anarchist of all" because his acts were addressed to the electors ultimately responsible for the Third Republic. (Fénéon was also writing to Signac that "the anarchist acts have done more by far for propaganda than twenty years of brochures by Reclus or Kropotkin.")[14] On April 4, 1894, after Henry's arrest (with swift execution certain), Fénéon planted a bomb on the window-sill of the fashionable Foyot restaurant opposite the Senate, which killed no one, but caused some grave injuries.[15] As we have seen earlier, he was soon arrested. It is typical of his sang-froid that while awaiting trial on capital

---

14. Eugenia Herbert, *The Artist and Social Reform: France and Belgium, 1885–1898* (New Haven: Yale University Press, 1961), p. 113. She draws the second quotation from John Rewald, "Extraits du journal inédit de Paul Signac," in *Gazette des Beaux-Arts*, 6:36 (1949), p. 113.

15. See the vivid reconstruction in Halperin, *Félix Fénéon*, pp. 3–4. It was not until many years later that he confessed what he had done to the anarchist Alexander Cohen, a cultivated Dutch Jew who had first translated Douwes Dekker's *Max Havelaar* into French.

A contemporary depiction of Émile Henry's arrest (left); Élisée Reclus, the famous theorist of anarchism (right).

charges, he set to translating *Northanger Abbey*, a copy of which he surprisingly found in the prison library.[16] In the dock as one of the seditious Thirty, he was acquitted, after running brilliant and hilarious rings around the judges and having many intellectual celebrities, as well as Clémenceau, testify on his behalf.[17] Mallarmé described Fénéon to the judges as *cet homme doux*, and when asked by journalists what his general opinion was of the art critic and his co-defendants—a strange mix of intellectuals, criminals, and anarchists—calmly replied that "he did not wish to say anything about these saints."[18] But Valéry in 1895 was closer to the mark, when he characterized him as "one of the most intelligent men I have ever met. He is just, pitiless, and

16. David Sweetman, *Explosive Acts: Toulouse-Lautrec, Oscar Wilde, Félix Fénéon and the Art and Anarchy of the Fin-de-Siècle* (London: Simon and Schuster, 1999), p. 375. The translation later appeared in *La Revue Blanche*.

17. Halperin's detailed account of the trial in chapter 14 of *Félix Fénéon* is masterly, and wildly funny. Although the police found detonators in Fénéon's War Department office, they could not produce any direct evidence linking the accused to the Foyot bombing.

18. Joll, *The Anarchists*, pp. 149–51.

gentle."[19] On his release, Fénéon found it hard to get open work to his liking, so he went to *La Revue Blanche* as behind-the-scenes part-time editor. It was not long before he became the journal's driving force.[20]

Clémenceau and Fénéon, from different generations, with strong but contrasting personalities, and only partly overlapping political outlooks, were in the later 1890s poised to become interacting allies. One immediate reason, aside from hatred of the Third Republic's imperialist brutalities in Asia and Africa, was anger at the so-called *lois scélérates* enacted after the *attentats* of Ravachol, Vaillant, and Henry. These laws banned all revolutionary propaganda, and made those assisting, or even in sympathy with, "revolutionaries" liable to severe punishment. (Camille Pissarro, who had a large police dossier, fled early to the safety of Belgium.)[21] But there was also a wider political transformation afoot, which can be symbolized by the birth of the Parti Ouvrier Belge in 1885, and the publication of Zola's novel *Germinal* the following year.

THE PARTI OUVRIER BELGE AND *GERMINAL*

For much of the nineteenth century Belgium was second only to Britain in its level of industrialization. Politically, however, it was generally backward, with a highly restricted suffrage, and domestic power largely in the hands of devotedly free-trade liberal magnates. Its late-century head of state, Léopold II, compensated himself for this situation by the notorious diplomatic and military interventions that made him absolute personal ruler of the Congo in 1885. That same year, however, the remarkable Émile Vandervelde created the Parti Ouvrier Belge and mobilized the working class to such effect that within a decade the suffrage was radically expanded, and the party's parliamentary presence surpassed that of the once all-powerful liberals.

---

19. Halperin, *Félix Fénéon*, p. 6.

20. After *La Revue Blanche* closed down, Fénéon began to withdraw from political life, though in 1906 he started to contribute satirical and often moving minimalist contributions to *Le Matin* under the title "Nouvelles en trois lignes." *Ibid.*, chapter 17. He became a key figure in one of the most successful art-dealing houses in Europe, and retired in 1924. For the last twenty years of his life he lived in such complete solitude that many people assumed he was dead. Having for decades shown little interest in Marxism, he joined the French Communist Party after the end of the Great War, when he was almost sixty. He died in 1944, and but for the German occupation of Paris, would have left his magnificent art collection to the Soviet Union. Sweetman, *Explosive Acts*, pp. 493–5.

21. Pissarro (and his son Lucien) were serious radicals. Camille was a Jew and born in the Danish Antilles, so he had bad experiences of the brutal suppression of a slave revolt in the Caribbean, and of anti-semitism in French schools. Degas and Renoir regularly referred to him as "the Jew Pissarro." *Ibid.*, p. 220.

Vandervelde regarded himself as an open-minded Marxist who was respectful of the Belgian workers' Proudhonian traditions, and he kept up amicable relations with many peaceful anarchists. Perhaps even more significant, he was a keen art lover with close friends among his country's radical avant-garde. Accordingly, he opened a very successful Maison du Peuple in Brussels, and hired Emile Verhaeren to run its Section d'Art. Verhaeren in turn brought into the party's orbit the country's avant-garde painters, grouped together as Les Vingt, of whom the best-known member was the *anarchisant* visionary James Ensor. On the literary front Verhaeren was just as successful, winning the adherence of, among others, Maeterlinck, whom Vandervelde later remembered fondly as "an aggressive revolutionary."[22] The arts journal *L'Art Moderne*, and the literary periodical *La Revue Rouge* not only fostered local talents but were also firmly internationalist. It was under the aegis of Verhaeren and Vandervelde that Huysmans and Fénéon were invited to serve as reviewers, as we have noted earlier, while French Impressionists and Postimpressionists came eagerly to offer their latest work for exhibition in Brussels. (This was the Brussels where Rizal came in January 1890 to compose *El Filibusterismo*—one month after *La Revue Blanche* was born in Liège.) French and Belgian writers published in each other's magazines, and William Morris's ideas and work received a very warm welcome. The impact of the Parti Ouvrier Belge's leaders and policies in France was substantial. Where the sternly philistine Jules Guesde had avoided almost all contact with the Parisian intelligentsia, by the mid-1890s he was starting to be supplanted by Jean Jaurès, who worked hard to emulate the Belgian model.[23]

Though Zola was generally scorned by the literary radicals of Paris, his *Germinal*, based on intensive research on a bitter and tragic strike in the Anzin coalfields of the Northeast, proved a political sensation, with an impact that followed every translation into another European language. (As quite often happened in the nineteenth century, a "social" novel could have much deeper and longer political effects than fact-based journalism.) While Zola depicted the "revolutionaries" among the coal-workers in a hostile manner, nonetheless *Germinal* offered readers a terrifying picture of the miners' poverty, industrially caused disease, absence of safety measures, and

---

22. We may think of Maeterlinck primarily as the author of the misty-medievalist *Pelléas et Mélisande*, but he was one of the first members of the Cercle des Étudiants et Anciens Étudiants Socialistes in Brussels in 1889. As late as 1913, he was still writing for the Parti Ouvrier's *Album du premier mai*, at the time of the great general strike of that year. Herbert, *The Artist*, p. 99.

23. The above paragraph is largely based on *ibid.*, pp. 9, 27–34, 67–71.

exploitation by the mine-owners.[24] Clémenceau himself visited striking miners and was appalled by what he observed. It is notable that coalfields were also connected—perhaps also via Zola—with one of Henry's more deadly *attentats* in 1894. Disguised as a woman, he left a bomb at the offices of the Société des Mines Carmaux to punish the owners of the Carmaux coalfields who had responded to a workers' strike in which machinery was smashed by bringing in armed police. Despite promises by socialist parliamentarians to mediate, months passed with no results, while the workers starved. Henry's bomb was discovered and taken to a police station, where it exploded, killing five policemen, and a boy.[25]

THE DREYFUS AFFAIR

Nothing shows better the change in the political atmosphere in the less than three years that followed the enactment of the *lois scélérates* than the *Revue Blanche*'s publication in the early spring of 1897 of a huge "Enquête sur la Commune," with contributions by the well-known anarchists Élisée Reclus, Louise Michel, and Jean Grave, as well as one by Clémenceau's radical-aristocratic brother-in-law Henri Rochefort. Tarrida was also prominently on view, and there were also texts by Mallarmé, Laforgue, Jarry, Daniel Halévy, Nietzsche, the deceased Eduard Douwes Dekker, Paul Adam, and Huysmans's homosexual friend Jean Lorrain. Many years later Léon Blum, who was born in 1872, would write: "the whole literary generation of which I was part was . . . impregnated with anarchist thought."[26]

Captain Alfred Dreyfus's initial kangaroo court martial on charges of spying for Germany, and his subsequent deportation to Devil's Island, which took place in the autumn of 1894—only three months after the guillotining of Carnot's young assassin and the trial of the Thirty—had attracted very little engaged attention, though the following year Fénéon had attacked the verdict in the pages of *La Revue Blanche*. But by 1896, evidence that the Jewish Dreyfus had been framed by antisemitic, aristocratic, high-ranking army officers began to leak out, leading in time to an intense press campaign that forced the state to arrest the real culprit, Major Marie-Charles Esterhazy, in October 1897, and try him the next January. His brazen acquittal the day after the trial began led to Zola's famous "J'accuse" open letter, published in Clémenceau's *L'Aurore*. The embattled regime saw no way out but to put Zola on trial in February 1898. Fined and sentenced to prison,

---

24. *Ibid.*, p. 162. Herbert goes so far as to say that *Germinal* was the first major novel directed at the working class. Zola was changing.

25. Halperin, *Félix Fénéon*, pp. 272–3.

26. Quoted in Herbert's *The Artist*, p. 12.

the "bourgeois novelist," as he was termed by critical leftwing intellectuals, suddenly found himself a hero to the Left.[27] Out of all this came a massive political confrontation between Right and Left, in which many avant-garde intellectuals became politically active for the first time in their lives, and the more fiery among them, such as Octave Mirbeau, almost got themselves murdered by antisemitic mobs.[28]

Meanwhile, the Cuban exiles in Paris became increasingly active after the onset of Martí's uprising and lobbied (with growing success) such leading journalists as Clémenceau to show anti-imperialist support for the cause of their country.[29]

As noted earlier, Tarrida did not stay long in Paris. Spanish diplomatic pressure got him expelled to Belgium.[30] From there he crossed the Straits of Dover. This is why many of his later articles for *La Revue Blanche* came from London, politically still the most important capital in the world, as well as a popular safe haven for anarchists on the run from their own repressive governments. There the overlapping Montjuich and Dreyfus scandals aroused widespread indignation, and the young Cuban anarchist was welcomed enthusiastically for a lengthy publicity tour arranged by Keir Hardie, Ramsay MacDonald, and others.[31] In a country with a long history of animosity to Spain, accounts of the doings of the "New Inquisition" found ready ears. Tarrida made adept use of his multiple contacts across oceans and state boundaries to spur the creation of a broad press coalition of liberals, freemasons, socialists, anarchists, anti-imperialists, and anticlericals against the Spanish prime minister. Consider the following (very partial) list of newspapers and periodicals that joined the campaign:[32]

---

27. Many writers who had looked down on Zola as "bourgeois" and philistine rushed to testify on his behalf. The sentence was overturned in April by the Cour de Cassation. A second trial was then instituted, but Zola, his political objectives achieved, decamped to England where he remained till an amnesty was declared.

28. Herbert, *The Artist*, p. 203. Mirbeau was then working for *L'Aurore*.

29. According to the right-wing Eduardo Comín Colomer, Tarrida met the anarchist Francisco Ferrer Guardia (of whom more later), then teaching Spanish at the Lycée Condorcet, and a group of strong Cuban supporters including Clémenceau, Aristide Briand, Charles Malato, and Henri Rochefort, as well as Caribbean radicals led by Betances. See his *Historia del anarquismo español* (Barcelona: Editorial AHR, 1956), Tomo I, pp. 180–81.

30. Fernández, *La sangre de Santa Águeda*, p. 27.

31. Tarrida found he liked England, and eventually settled down there, becoming, alas perhaps, a Fabian. He died, too young, during the Great War.

32. Comín's *Historia del anarquismo español*, vol. l, pp. 173–5; and Esenwein, *Anarchist Ideology*, p. 194. Fernández, *Santa Águeda*, p. 31, quotes the work of Paul Avrich, *An American Anarchist: The Life of Voltairine de Cleyre* (Princeton: Princeton University Press, 1978), pp. 112–13, as claiming that 50,000 copies of the English translation of *Les Inquisiteurs* were distributed in Philadelphia alone.

France: Clémenceau's *La Justice*, Rochefort's *L'Intransigeant*, *Le Jour*, *L'Écho de Paris*, Jean Grave's *Les Temps Nouveaux*, *Le Libertaire*, *La Petite République*, and *Le Père Peinard*.

Britain: *The Times*, *The Daily Chronicle*, *Freedom*.

Spain: *El País, La Justicia, La Autonomía, El Imparcial* and Pi y Margall's *El Nuevo Régimen*.

Germany: *Frankfurter Zeitung*, *Vorwärtz*, and *Der Sozialist*.

Italy: *La Tribuna* in Rome and *L'Avvenire* in Messina.

Portugal: *A Libertade*, *O Caminho* and *O Trabalhador*.

Rumania: *Miscarea Sociala*.

Argentina: *El Oprimido*, *La Revolución* and the Italian-language *L'Avvenire*.

USA: Boston's *Liberty*, New York's Cuban *El Despertar*, and Tampa's Cuban *El Esclavo*.

Cánovas found himself without much effective external support, even in Catholic Europe. Austro-Hungary was preoccupied with its own militant nationalisms and with the Balkans, France with the Dreyfus affair, and Italy with the effects of the disastrous March 1896 defeat at Adawa at the hands of the Abyssinian ruler Menelik. But Cánovas' nerve did not fail him. As we have seen, a few relatively prominent Montjuich prisoners were allowed to go into exile, but most of those not tried before military courts were deported, along with some Cuban "troublemakers" sent in from Havana, to harsh camps in Spanish Africa. On May 5, 1897 Ascheri and the four Spaniards, sentenced to death for the Corpus Christi "outrage", were executed, but not before letters describing the tortures they had undergone, and proclaiming their innocence, had been smuggled out by a few of those released. Three months later, Cánovas' own turn came to meet a bloody political death at the Basqueland spa of Santa Águeda.

PATRIOT OF THE ANTILLES: DOCTOR BETANCES

Ramón Emeterio Betances was born in Cabo Rojo, Puerto Rico, on April 8, 1827—a year and a half before Tolstoi. How he came by his part-African descent is not clear, not least because he seems to have been born on the wrong side of the blanket. In any case, his father was rich enough and modern enough to send this precociously intelligent son to study medicine at the Collège de Toulouse, where he became fluent in French. Thereafter, he continued his medical education at the Sorbonne, graduating in 1853. On returning to Puerto Rico, he made a name for himself in the cholera epidemic of 1855. Child of Diderot and Byron, he was swept up by the Revolution of 1848—which also abolished slavery in the French

Caribbean—and may even have fought on the barricades of the capital.[33]
For the remaining fifty years of his life he devoted himself to doctoring
(like Rizal he specialized in ophthalmology) and to radical republican and
anticolonial politics. An abolitionist from the start, he was also captured
by the Bolivarian vision of a vast transcontinental movement of liberation
aimed both against the decrepit and brutal colonialism of Spain, and the
hungry imperialism of what he called the American Minotaur.[34] Though a
patriot for Puerto Rico, he was convinced that the Caribbean islands,
geographically scattered, multiply colonized, and militarily insignificant,
could only survive and progress if bound together in a "Bolivarian"
Federation of the Antilles, which would include Haiti, the Danish colony
of St Thomas, and other non-Anglo-Saxon controlled territories.[35] One
condition for the realization of this dream, he believed, was what he
termed the total de-hispanization of Cuba, Puerto Rico, and Santo
Domingo; hence his complete hostility to "assimilationist" ideology
among the colonials, and complete lack of belief in either Spanish or
American good intentions.[36]

Back in the Caribbean in the 1860s, he actively supported the armed
struggle for the restoration of Dominican independence in 1863–65 (see
Chapter 3), and circulated radical propaganda in Puerto Rico itself, until he
was forced to flee. Prior to his return to Paris in 1872, he was constantly on
the move—St Thomas, Haiti, the Dominican Republic, Venezuela, and even
New York—pursued by Spain's spies, threatened by venal post-independ-
ence dictatorships, and evicted by non-Spanish colonial authorities bending

---

33. "Participa activamente en la Revolución Francesa de 1848 . . . revolución que se le presenta cual una revelación misteriosa" (He participated actively
in the French Revolution of 1848 . . . a revolution which came to him like a
mysterious revelation). Félix Ojeda Reyes, "Ramón Emeterio Betances, Patriarca de la Antillanía," in Félix Ojeda Reyes and Paul Estrade, eds., *Pasión por
la libertad* (San Juan, P.R.: Editorial de la Universidad de Puerto Rico, 2000), p.
32.

34. In a letter written to fellow Puerto Rican Francisco Basora, from Port-au-
Prince, April 8, 1870, cited in Paul Estrade, "El heraldo de la 'independencia
absoluta'," in Ojeda and Estrade, eds., *Pasión por la libertad*, p. 5.

35. Betances lived in Haiti from February 1870 to the early autumn of 1871,
helping to fight a cholera epidemic and composing his remarkable essay on Alexandre
Pétion, the Haitian patriot who sheltered Bolívar when he had had to flee Venezuela,
and provided crucial military support for his later comeback. Betances's book was
published in New York in 1871. A contemporary edition can be found in a collection
of his major writings, edited by Carlos A. Rama and titled *Las Antillas para los
Antillanos* (San Juan: Instituto de Cultura Puertorriqueña, 1975). Lauding Pétion led
him to some overly severe criticism of Toussaint.

36. "Es igual yugo por yugo" (One yoke is the same as another). Estrade,"El
heraldo," p. 5.

to pressure from Madrid.[37] He spent his time treating patients among the poor, writing powerful polemical articles, and trying to buy, and safely cache till the time for insurrection was ripe, what arms he could manage. He also largely inspired the first armed uprising in Puerto Rico itself, which occurred in the mountain township of Lares on September 9, 1868—just four weeks before Céspedes's proclamation of Cuban independence—and which lasted barely twenty-four hours.[38] Nothing really worked, not least because of his single-minded commitment to armed insurrection, and his methods of clandestine organizing about which the scent of Masonry, *blanquismo*, and 1848 continued to hang.[39] But in the process he became a legend.

Betances returned to Paris at the end of 1871, eight months after the fall of the Commune, and remained there for most of the rest of his life.[40] His medical research eventually earned him membership in the Légion d'Honneur, but he never ceased writing polemical articles—we have seen already one fine example in the case of the *princesas* of Manila—and cultivating political allies in Paris and other parts of Western Europe. Between 1879 and 1887, he even held a high post in the Dominican legation in the French capital, with responsibility also for London and Bern.[41] Inevitably, as time passed, he became the doyen of the "Latin community" in Paris (and to a lesser degree in other neighboring countries.) This was not an easy role to play for a man of Betances's views and temperament. In the mid-1890s, there were about three hundred Cubans and Puerto Ricans in the City of Light, aside from hundreds of other Latin Americans. Almost all were very rich, hacienda rentiers, bankers, doctors, industrialists and playboys, whose politics were either completely conservative or, at best, liberal assimilationist. Ojeda notes sarcastically: "No hay un solo negro en su seno. Los artesanos brillan por su ausencia" (There was not a single negro in [the "Latin" community's] midst. Artisans sparkled by their absence).[42] Nothing could be

---

37. It was in New York that Betances helped found the Comité Revolucionario de Puerto Rico on July 16, 1867. The CRPR's manifesto denounced slavery, Peninsular commercial monopolies, hunger, absence of schools, and total lack of progress in the colony. A month later he coolly swore before a court of law that he intended to become an American citizen—calculating that this would keep him out of Spanish clutches—and left for Danish St Thomas the next day! Ojeda, *El desterrado*, pp. 98–9.

38. Betances himself was off hunting up guns in the Dutch colony of Curaçao, so missed the historic event.

39. See Ojeda, *El desterrado*, pp. 349–51, for an interesting look at the affinities between Betances and Blanqui.

40. *Ibid.*, p. 221.

41. Estrade, "El heraldo," p. 10.

42. Ojeda, *El desterrado*, p. 338.

more different from the largely poor, working-class Cuban communities in Tampa, Cayo Hueso, and New York where Martí found his supporters. But Betances held the community more or less together by force of personality, medical services, and weekly social gatherings (*tertulias*) at his spacious office at 6 bis Rue Chateaudun, curiously enough only a door or two away from the residence (at 4 bis) of Rizal's rich friend Valentín Ventura, the financier of *El Filibusterismo*'s publication.[43]

In his own way, the elderly Betances was a practical man and welcomed whatever allies might be available. It turned out, perhaps to the surprise of a man very far from being an anarchist himself, that the most energetic of these allies were anarchists or anarchist-inclined. Martí had frequently and acerbically attacked anarchism for what he regarded as its contempt for politics in the normal sense of the word, and its negation of the concept of *patria*. On the other hand, there were plenty of anarchists who saw in the nationalist leaders' hunger for state power and the fetishism of elections a sign that independence would do little to ameliorate the real lives of presently existing working people.[44] In Paris, Betances's political friends were former *communards* and anarchist intellectuals. Élisée Reclus (born in 1830) and Louise Michel (born in 1830) were of his generation, as was Henri Bauer, illegitimate son of Dumas, *communard*, and alumnus of New Caledonia's penal settlement. Rochefort was there, and the French anarchist Charles Malato, whom Betances persuaded to go to Barcelona to try and start an uprising of workers to weaken Weyler's campaign in Cuba.[45] (Malato got nowhere, of course.) None of these people had been to Cuba or the Philippines, and they had no emotional investment in their nationalisms. But they had had many bitter experiences at the hands of the French state, both domestically, and imperially (New Caledonia, Devil's Island). Cánovas and Weyler could be seen as Thiers and Galliéni (respectively the French president who crushed the Commune and the general who conquered most of what became French Africa) Iberianly transplanted. Less than the beauties of Cuba Libre and Filipinas Libre, what drew them into Betances's orbit was loathing

43. See Ventura's letters to Rizal of February 5 and May 19, 1890, the first reporting that he has signed a two-year lease, and the second saying he is about to move in. Rizal stayed with him there in October 1891, prior to leaving for Marseilles and Hong Kong. *Cartas entre Rizal y sus colegas*, pp. 493–4 and 531.

44. This important point is well brought out in Francesco Tamburini, "Michele Angiolillo e l'assassinio di Cánovas del Castillo," *Spagna contemporanea* [Alessandria, Piedmont] IV:9 (1996), pp. 101–30, at p. 117. So it might be theoretically. But Cuban nationalism brought many local anarchists to Martí's side, and Spanish nationalism subterraneanly reinforced Spanish anarchism's distrust of Cuban (bourgeois) nationalism's separatist utopianism.

45. Ojeda, *El desterrado*, pp. 339 and 348; Estrade, "El heraldo," p. 9.

of the barbarities committed in Montjuich, Cuba, and the Philippines.

Outside France, Betances's closest links were to Italian anarchists with Garibaldian traditions, enraged by prime minister Francesco Crispi's Canovism, and the repulsive fiasco in Ethiopia. The spirit of 1848, the "springtime of nations," also had its role to play. A man of 1848 himself, Betances supported the efforts of a number of these comrades to go to Cuba and fight Garibaldi-style for the revolution, but he was usually thwarted by the policy of the New York headquarters of Martí's revolutionary organization, run by Tomás Estrada Palma, which was to prevent any "foreigners" meddling in the island's struggle.[46] Curiously enough, one of Betances's most energetic sub-groups was in Belgium, run by the young Cuban engineer Pedro Herrera Sotolongo, who was a classmate and friend of Rizal's protégés Alejandrino and Evangelista.[47] Needless to say, the task of yoking a rich Cuban community which not only had no negroes or artisans, but lacked a single anarchist, with his non-Cuban anarchist friends was rather Sisyphean, but the Puerto Rican somehow, minimally, managed it.

Betances's moment finally came with the onset of Martí's war of independence in 1895. The two men seem never to have met, and little survives of their correspondence. But despite the fact that Betances was more than twice Martí's age, and endured a life experience utterly different from that of the younger man, they respected each other.[48] Martí's revolutionary headquarters in New York had always included Puerto Ricans at the highest levels, and Puerto Ricans had played their own role during the Ten Years' War. Accordingly, on April 2, 1896, Betances was appointed officially as the top diplomatic agent of the Cuban Revolution in Paris, not merely in recognition of his age and his reputation, but also because of his unrivalled knowledge of, and political alliances in, Western Europe.

It remains only to add, parenthetically, that Betances maintained a lively

---

46. See Francesco Tamburini, "Betances, los mambises italianos, y Michele Angiolillo," in Ojeda and Estrade, eds, *Pasión por la libertad*, pp. 75–82; and Ojeda, *El desterrado*, pp. 362–71.

47. This committee was composed of two Cubans, two Belgians, and a young Englishman called Ferdinand Brook, whose brother had gone to fight in Cuba against the Spaniards. Paul Estrade, *Solidaridad con Cuba Libre, 1895–1898. La impresionante labor del Dr Betances en París* (San Juan: Editorial de la Universidad de Puerto Rico, 2001), p. 143. Herrera kept in close touch with Alejandrino when the latter moved to Hong Kong. He passed on to Betances information he received about the progress of the Philippine revolution. In 1897, Betances's journal, *La República Cubana*, published two letters from Alejandrino, postmarked Hong Kong, one in July and one in September. Rizal's protégé also used his link with Herrera to urge the Cubans in New York to help with arms. It is not clear whether Alejandrino was acting on his own, or on instructions from his titular boss Mariano Ponce.

48. On their relationship, see Ojeda and Estrade, eds., *El desterrado*, pp. 329–33.

interest in the Philippine revolution, partly because it was diverting Spanish troops away from Cuba, but also for its own sweet-nationalist sake. As early as September 29, 1896, a month after Bonifacio started his uprising, the good doctor wrote to Estrada in New York that the insurrection was much more serious than the Spanish public realized, and that 15,000 troops were already on the way to suppress it.[49] In the same month, Betances's journal *La República Cubana* published two articles on the Philippines—titled "¡Viva Filipinas Libre!" and "¿Qué quiere Filipinas?" (Long Live the Free Philippines! What does the Philippines Desire?)—expressing strong support for the uprising.[50] Learning from Herrera how desperately the Filipinos needed arms, he passed the news on to Estrada in New York, urging him to do what he could to help.[51] He also mailed to Florida Rizal's last poem, which appeared in the *Revista de Cayo Hueso* on October 7, 1897, under the title "Mi último pensamiento."[52]

ANGIOLILLO: FROM FOGGIA TO SANTA AGUEDA

Michele ("Miguel") Angiolillo was born on June 5, 1871, just after the bloody end of the Paris Commune, in the *mezzogiorno* township of Foggia, 112 kilometres northeast of Malatesta's Naples.[53] Angiolillo was thus forty-four years younger than Betances. While attending a technical institute he became politically conscious as a radical republican militant deeply hostile to the monarchy. Conscripted in 1892, he was observed attending a commemoration of the Parthenopean Republic of 1799, and was brutally punished for this by his military superiors.[54] He returned to civilian life a committed anarchist. During the elections of 1895, he published a manifesto against prime minister Crispi's version of the *lois scélérates*, for which he was arrested on charges of fomenting class hatred. Briefly at liberty pending his trial, he sent the Minister of Justice a blistering letter of complaint about the prosecutor. For this he was sentenced to eighteen months in prison and a

---

49. *Ibid.*, p. 372. According to Estrade, *Solidaridad*, p. 147, Betances told Estrada that he had a spy in the Spanish embassy who passed on a lot of confidential information.

50. Estrade, *Solidaridad*, p. 147.

51. Ojeda, *El desterrado*, p. 373.

52. *Ibid.*, p. 374.

53. In the following account of Angiolillo's brief life, I have relied heavily on Francesco Tamburini's "Michele Angiolillo." This article is based on a thorough study of Italy's hitherto largely unexamined state archives on the Foggian and his assassination of the Spanish prime minister.

54. The Parthenopean Republic was the last of the four Italian republics formed between 1796 and 1799 under the protection of Napoléon's armies. It was based in Naples.

Michele Angiolillo (left); the influential Fernando Tarrida del Marmol (right).

further three years of internal exile. At this point he went to see a friend and former classmate, Roberto d'Angiò, who was already a correspondent of Jean Grave's *Les Temps Nouveaux* (*La Révolte*'s new name after the Trial of the Thirty). D'Angiò took him to see Oreste Ferrara, then an obscure law student, but soon after to become famous as a recruit to the Cuban Revolution, a trusted aide to General Máximo Gómez, and eventually Cuba's foreign minister during the brutal presidency (1925–33) of General Gerardo Machado.[55] Advised by Ferrara to flee Italy, in early 1896 he arrived, using a false name, in Barcelona via Marseilles. The city had a considerable colony of Italian workers and artisans, as well as a deserved reputation for anarchist activism. Angiolillo had barely settled down to his trade as a freelance printer (and to acquiring Spanish) when the Corpus Christi bombing occurred, and the city was put under martial law. A number of his friends were incarcerated in Montjuich, including Cayetano Oller, with whom he had worked at Tarrida's and Sempau's journal *La Ciencia Social*. The grim rumors about the tortures inflicted on prisoners there persuaded

---

55. On Ferrara's career, see Tamburini, "Betances," pp. 76–7.

the young printer to flee Spain for France. He was arrested in Marseilles for having forged papers, spent a month in prison, and was then expelled to Belgium, where he found temporary work with a printing press owned by a senior member of Vandervelde's Parti Ouvrier Belge, before moving to London in March 1897: three months after Rizal's execution, and with Tarrida's crusade against the Cánovas regime at its height.

As mentioned earlier, London was the safest haven for Continental anarchists on the lam. The Spanish anarchist contingent was by now being augmented by people like "Federico Urales," as well as Oller, who after being terribly tortured, was released for lack of evidence, then expelled from his country. Angiolillo resumed his work as a printer, helped by his membership in a little-known institution, Typographia, which was a special section of the British printers' union reserved for foreigners. He certainly attended the huge demonstration of ten thousand people in Trafalgar Square on May 30, organized by a Spanish Atrocities Committee led by the English anarchist Joseph Perry. The crowd was addressed by a wide range of political notables, including Europe-famous Tarrida, who spoke not in the name of anarchism, but as the representative of *La Revue Blanche* and in the name of Betances's Cuban Revolutionary Delegation in Paris.[56] Malato made a passionate speech in which he asked who would avenge José Rizal and so many others murdered by the Cánovas regime. But the most emotional moments came when the maimed victims of Montjuich rose to tell their stories and bare their bodies. Not long afterward, Angiolillo personally met Oller and Francisco Gana, another horribly maimed victim, at the house of a friendly Spanish anarchist exile. The German anarchist Rudolf Rocker, who was present, described the scene as follows:

> That night when Gana showed us his crippled limbs, and the scars over his entire body left by the tortures, we understood that it is one thing to read about such matters, but quite another to hear about them from the very lips of the victims . . . We all sat there as if turned to stone, and it was some minutes before we could utter a few words of indignation. Only Angiolillo said not a word. A little later, he suddenly rose to his feet, uttered a laconic goodbye, and abandoned the house . . . This was the last time I saw him.[57]

---

56. Estrade, *Solidaridad*, p. 146; Tamburini points out that in *Les Inquisiteurs* Tarrida described himself rather disingenuously as "a Cuban, but not a filibustero, a federalist but not an anarchist, a freethinker but not a freemason." "Michele Angiolillo," p. 114, referring to p. 36 of Tarrida's famous book.

57. Fernández, *La sangre de Santa Águeda*, p. 40, quoting from the Spanish version of Rudolf Rocker's memoirs, *En la borrasca (Años de destierro)* (Puebla, Mexico: Edit. Cajica, 1967), pp. 118–20. He also quotes a letter *cont'd over/*

Not too long after this event, Angiolillo somehow made his way to Paris, with vengeance on his mind and a London-acquired pistol in his pocket. By this time he had read Tarrida's hastily assembled *Les Inquisiteurs d'Espagne* which more than any other text of its time linked in detail Manila, Montjuich, and Havana.[58] He is said to have attended lectures by Rochefort and Betances on the transcontinental crimes of the Spanish government. It was at this point that he went to see the Puerto Rican at one of the regular *tertulias* on the Rue Chateaudun. Initially suspicious of a police plant, Betances was reassured by Tarrida and Malato, both of whom had talked with Angiolillo in London. What actually transpired when Betances and Angiolillo finally met *tête-à-tête* remains shrouded in uncertainty. Betances later said that Angiolillo told him that he planned to go to Spain to assassinate the Queen Regent and the infant Alfonso XIII. The good doctor replied that this would be a mistake: killing a woman and a child would be "terrible publicity"; besides, neither was responsible for the cruelty of the Spanish regime. The true villain was Cánovas.[59] On the face of it, this account is a little implausible. Angiolillo was not an ignoramus. He had lived in martial law Barcelona, had talked with tortured former comrades, and had attended the demonstration in Trafalgar Square. He knew perfectly well that Cánovas was the master of the Spanish empire. Perhaps the old Puerto Rican wished to leave posterity with the idea that he had saved the lives of a woman and her child, while taking credit for aiming Angiolillo at the Spanish prime minister.[60] Almost thirty years earlier, he had written to his great friend the Dominican patriot Gregorio Luperón about the need to arrest and try for treason the corrupt dictator Buenaventura Báez:

> No me parece imposible coger á Báez, y puesto que la República Dominicana necesita incontestablemente una reforma radical, yo digo con Diderot, que parecía

---

57 *cont'd* from Cleyre to her mother after seeing Gana personally, to the effect that his hands had been burned with red-hot irons, his fingernails torn out, his head put in a metal compressor, and his testicles ripped off. This account comes from Avrich's above-cited *An American Anarchist*, p. 114.

    58. It came out in early mid-June, according to Max Nettlau, citing Jean Grave's *Les Temps Nouveaux* of June 19, 1897.

The reference here is to p. 116 of the manuscript of the as yet unpublished second volume of his *Anarchisten und Syndikalisten*, a copy of which was kindly provided to me by Mieke Ijzermans of the Internationaal Instituut voor Sociale Geschiedenis in Amsterdam.

    59. See Fernández, *La sangre de Santa Águeda*, p. 45, for lengthy excerpts from Betances's account.

    60. It should be added that a key element in Tamburini's study is a forceful demolition of the often-repeated story that Betances (or Rochefort) gave Angiolillo a substantial amount of money (variously 1,000 and 500 francs).

preveer la muerte de Luis XVI: "el suplicio de un Rey cambia el espíritu de una nación para siempre."

I don't think it is impossible to get Báez, and since the Dominican Republic needs a radical reform, I say with Diderot, who seemed to have foreseen the death of Louis XVI: "The punishment of a king changes the spirit of a nation forever."[61]

In any event, Angiolillo then made his way to Madrid via Bordeaux, where he was briefly taken care of by Antoine Antignac, a young anarchist in the Proudhonian tradition.[62] In the Spanish capital he learned that Cánovas was at the spa of Santa Águeda with his new, much younger Peruvian wife. Checking in at the same hotel, he watched his target's movements for a day or two, and then, on August 8, shot him dead with the pistol he had brought from London. Angiolillo made no attempt to escape. His three-day trial, by a military court, *in camera*, was held the following week. In his defence speech, he spoke mainly of Montjuich, with vague allusions also to the wars in Cuba and the Philippines.[63] He also said that Cánovas "personified, in their most repugnant forms, religious ferocity, military cruelty, the implacability of the judiciary, the tyranny of power, and the greed of the possessing classes. I have rid Spain, Europe, and the entire world of him. That is why I am no assassin but rather an executioner."[64] The court then sentenced him to death, and he

61. Ojeda, *El desterrado*, p. 121, citing the second volume of Manuel Rodríguez Objio's *Gregorio Luperón e Historia de la Restauración* (Santiago, Dominican Republic: Editorial El Diario, 1939), pp. 167–8.

62. Tamburini quotes from Antignac's memoirs these mournful sentences: "Le livre qu'il lisait et relisait était intitulé *Montjuich*", par Tarrida del Mármol, sa valise ne contenait que celui-là . . . Quelques heures avant son départ nous dîmes à Angiolillo 'Au revoir, camarade.' 'Non, pas au revoir, Adieu!' À ce moment son œil flamba sous les lunettes. Nous fûmes stupéfaits." [The book that he read and reread was Tarrida del Mármol's *Montjuich*, his suitcase contained nothing else . . . Some hours before his departure, we said to him "Till we meet again, comrade." "No, we shall not meet again. Farewell." At this moment his eye blazed behind his spectacles. We were stupefied]. "Michele Angiolillo," p. 118.

63. It is a curious fact that in London, both *The Times* and the *Daily Telegraph* published on August 10 a Reuters report that the man it called Michele Angino Golli "has admitted that he shot Señor Canovas in order to avenge the Barcelona Anarchists, and Dr. Rizal, the insurgent leader who was executed in the Philippines." The following day the *Telegraph* gave its readers another Reuter's report according to which "Golli is said to have expressed regret that he did not kill General Polavieja, for having caused the filibustering leader, Rizal, to be shot." No mention of Weyler or Cuba at all. My thanks to Benjamin Hawkes-Lewis for this information.

64. Tamburini, "Michele Angiolillo," pp. 123 and 129. The quotation is my translation of the Italian original that Tamburini takes from the article "La difesa de Angiolillo," published (after undergoing Crispi regime censorship) in Ancona's *L'Agitazione* on September 2, 1897.

was garroted on August 20. At the last moment of his life, he is said have cried out: "¡Germinal!"[65] Pío Baroja imagined him thus:

> Era un tipo delgado, muy largo, muy seco, y muy fino en sus adelantes, que hablaba con acento extranjero. Cuando supe lo que había hecho, me quedé asombrado. ¿Quién podía esperar aquello de un hombre tan suave y tan tímido?

> He was a slender fellow, very tall, very dry, very courteous in his gestures, who spoke with a foreign accent. When I learned what he had done, I was stunned. Who would have believed it of so gentle and timid a man?[66]

Cánovas's death did not only sound the knell for Restoration "cacique democracy" in Spain. It also brought with it the fall of Weyler in Havana, as the general immediately understood.[67] An interim government under war minister Azcárraga lasted only until October 4, when it was replaced by that of the eternal Sagasta, who made Segismundo Moret once again his minister for Overseas Territories. Both had been strong public opponents of Cánovas's policies in Cuba and Barcelona (though Sagasta, in power when Martí's uprising began, had at least talked in just as hardline a manner). On October 31, Weyler handed over command in Cuba to none other than Ramón Blanco—the man who had tried to save Rizal and who had been forced out of Manila by the clerical lobby's working on the Cánovas cabinet and the Queen Regent.[68] Blanco came with a mandate for leniency, compromise, and

---

65. "Germinal" was a war cry popular in the anarchist movement, probably as a result of the huge success of Zola's novel. Tamburini, "Michele Angiolillo," p. 124. But the symbolism goes back to the calendar of the French Revolution, in which the first month of spring went by that name. So to speak, "if Winter comes, can Spring be far behind?"

66. Pío Baroja, *Aurora roja* (p. 160), cited in Núñez, *El terrorismo*, p. 131.

67. The general—whom Betances liked to call a mini-Attila (*pequeño Atila*)—may even have been partly relieved. Fernández reports that he had been lucky not to have been blown to pieces in April the previous year. With the help of two Asturian anarchists, a young Cuban nationalist called Armando André hid a bomb in the roof of the ground-floor toilet of the Captain-General's palace. The device was supposed to explode when Weyler sat down on the pot, bringing the whole second floor down on his head. The plotters were unaware, however, that Weyler suffered so severely from haemorrhoids that he almost never used the facility, preferring an earthenware field-potty when he had to relieve himself. The bomb went off, but no one was hurt, and Weyler decided to inform Madrid that the explosion had been caused by stoppages which prevented the latrine's gases from escaping normally.

68. The enthusiastic popular reception of Weyler's return to Spain on November 19 panicked the new Liberal government, which feared he would lead a *coup d'état*. But the general, who was no fool, stood by the constitution and did nothing to encourage his supporters, who then began to look to the strongly Catholic Polavieja as a possibility. See Martín, *Valeriano Weyler*, chapter xiii.

reform, but it was now too late. The diehard colons greeted him with the organized mob violence that Guy Mollet would experience six decades later in Algiers; the revolutionaries had no taste for a second Zanjón; and American imperialism was on the move. Eight months later the United States was master of Cuba. It is probably true that only Weyler had the capacity and determination to give McKinley, Roosevelt and Hearst a serious run for their money.

INTO THE MAELSTROM

In the seven months between the execution of Rizal and the assassination of his political executioner what had been happening in the Philippines?

Camilo Polavieja stayed in the Philippines only four months, but this short reign was to have long-lasting consequences. Twelve days after Rizal's death, twelve prominent Filipinos, "led by" the millionaire Francisco Roxas, went before a firing squad at the place where the novelist had died. *Weylerismo* had arrived in Manila.[69]

But Polavieja's main task was to crush the rebellion militarily, and in this he was successful except in the hilly province of Cavite. There his troops were held up by a complex system of trenches and fortifications, planned and built on the orders of Rizal's former *protégé* Edilberto Evangelista, back from Ghent with a civil engineering degree in his pocket.[70] The political consequence of Polavieja's offensive was to force Bonifacio out of the Manila area where his authority was undisputed and into Cavite, a province unfamiliar to him and famous for the clannishness of its people.[71] There he ran foul of an ambitious *caviteño* clique led by Emilio Aguinaldo, the 27-year-old mayor of the small township of Kawit. Aguinaldo belonged neither to the highly educated ilustrado elite exemplified by Rizal, nor to the often autodidact Manilan artisanate, like Bonifacio. His Spanish was mediocre, but he was a member of the commercial-farming, medium landowning provincial gentry, and his family was widely connected in the Cavite region. He had joined the

---

69. There is no reason to believe that the charges were true. Some of these men had been involved with Rizal's abortive Liga Filipina in 1892, corresponded with Del Pilar and the circle of *La Solidaridad*, and were cautious nationalists with plenty to lose. Ocampo reports that Bonifacio asked Roxas for funds to help the Katipunan, but the millionaire refused. The angry revolutionary then told his trusted aide Emilio Jacinto to forge the signatures of people like Roxas on the Katipunan's membership lists, and leave them where the Spanish police could find them. He seems to have thought that they would be arrested and tortured, and thus be converted to the rebel cause. Ocampo, *Rizal without the Overcoat*, p. 246; see also Teodoro Agoncillo's *A Short History*, p. 86, based on his pioneering two-volume study of the Philippine Revolution.

70. Evangelista was killed in action on February 17, 1897.

71. The language of the province is a distinct dialect of Tagalog. The local notables, then and now, are well-known for their complex intermarriages.

The founder of the Katipunan revolutionary society, Andrés Bonifacio.

Katipunan in March 1895 in a junior capacity, but once the fighting started, he demonstrated that he was a capable soldier.

In March an election was held in the town of Tejeros to decide who would be the Revolution's president and who the members of his government. Bonifacio could rightly claim that he had formed the Katipunan—which Aguinaldo had joined—and had initiated the insurrection. But Aguinaldo's supporters felt that Bonifacio's uprising in Manila had proved a fiasco and was a thing of the past; the task ahead was to run an effective war. Cavite had shown what needed to be done. In the end, Aguinaldo won the election and picked a cabinet almost entirely composed of fellow *caviteños*. In addition, the former Supremo was openly sneered at for his irregular education and low-class origins. Bonifacio did not take this denigration lying down and started to rally what supporters he could. The Aguinaldo group then arrested him, tried him in April, and sentenced him to death for treason to the Revolution he had initiated. He and a brother of his were executed on May 10.

Whether Polavieja was aware of these developments, and, if he knew, whether he cared, is unclear. In April he resigned his post (as he had earlier done in Cuba) in disgust at Madrid's unwillingness or inability to send the military reinforcements that he believed necessary to finish off the rebellion. By the end of 1896, his forces had risen to 16,000, and he received 13,300 more in January 1897, for a total of 29,300. After that, nothing.[72] If the insurrection spread to further parts of the archipelago, he would not have the manpower to fulfill his mission. Cánovas seems to have understood that the time for *weylerismo* in the Philippines had passed. Knowing the conditions that had caused the capable Polavieja to resign, no senior general would take the job of Captain-General without a change of policy. In April, Fernando Primo de Rivera arrived to take Polavieja's place. He had been a mildly popular Captain-General during the calm early 1880s when Rizal was setting off for Europe. With his knowledge of the colony, his military experience, and his political flexibility, he could be expected to pursue both a policy of attraction towards local elites, and of continuing the war, even if now with *contemplaciones*. A sort of revived *blanquismo*, one might say. In fact, the new Captain-General did manage to retake Cavite, but Aguinaldo and his generals eluded capture, and, making a wide detour around Manila, ensconced themselves in a rocky fastness well north of the capital, from which no succeeding military efforts managed to dislodge them.[73]

On May 17, a week after Bonifacio's execution, Primo made what he thought was a major conciliatory gesture, pardoning 636 people who had been incarcerated either by Blanco or Polavieja. He further invited a delegation from this group to his palace, expecting expressions of gratitude and renewed loyalty. He was in for a disagreeable surprise. Prominent in the delegation was none other than Isabelo de los Reyes, who had been arrested in the immediate aftermath of Bonifacio's uprising. The busy folklorist and journalist had been taken completely aback by the insurrection. Prison was a terrible shock. Mariano Ponce wrote to Blumentritt a few months later:

> el pobre Isabelo, tan pacífico y de carácter tan calmoso, por la serie de desgracias por que ha pasado, siendo la principal la muerte de su mujer, y los agudos sufrimientos morales y materiales que venía padeciendo, ha tenido accesos de irritabilitad nerviosa hasta el punto de maldecir en voz alta y en público lo que él creía injusto y bárbaro, y á las órdenes religiosas como origen de tamañas iniquidades

> poor Isabelo, so peaceable and of so calm a character, as a result of a series of calamities, the gravest of which was the death of his wife, and the acute moral and

---

72. Corpuz, *The Roots*, vol. 2, p. 239.
73. Today Biak-na-Bató (Split Rock) is an infrequently visited official heritage site. Some wading up a small winding river will take one to the bat-filled limestone caves where Aguinaldo and his men are thought to have hidden out.

material sufferings he had just undergone, was affected by attacks of nervous irritability to the point of damning out loud and in public what he believes to be unjust and barbarous, as well as the religious Orders as the root of such enormous iniquities.[74]

Indeed his ailing wife had died while he was behind bars, and he was not permitted by Polavieja to attend her funeral or to do anything for his many children.

In any event, Isabelo brought with him to the meeting a blistering memorandum, which he had already sent to friends in Spain, outlining what he believed were the *ilustrados'* conditions for a peaceful settlement. Above all, he demanded the immediate expulsion of the Orders, whose abuses of power he listed in great detail. He then insisted that Primo explain how the government planned to respond to the colony's aspirations, or at the very least those of the assimilationist "party" (in the nineteenth-century sense) to which he belonged. The Captain-General reacted "as if he had been bitten by a snake."[75] Furious at Isabelo's insolence—"the audacity of his temperament and his love of notoriety"—he ordered the folklorist re-arrested three days later and clapped into irons in Manila's Bilibid prison.[76] Soon afterward, Isabelo was secretly deported to martial law Barcelona. The ship's captain was told to keep the young villain isolated from any contact with Filipinos "over whom he exercises considerable influence."[77] On arrival in Barcelona a month later—Cánovas was still alive and well—Isabelo was put in the municipal jail, where, after some money had changed hands, he was contacted by another prisoner, the veteran Catalan anarchist-republican journalist Ignacio Bó y Singla. This admirable figure, who was serving a six-year sentence because he had called for Cuban independence and protested against the sending of Spanish troops to Weyler's Havana, told the bewildered young Filipino that "the advanced Republican party" supported the independence of the Philippines.[78] But this was only the beginning.

---

74. Letter from Ponce in Hong Kong to Blumentritt, dated September 22, 1897 in Ponce's *Cartas sobre la Revolución, 1897–1900* (Manila: Bureau of Printing, 1932), pp. 42–5. Ponce noted that he heard about the delegation's encounter with Primo from one of the people who was a member.

75. Ponce, *Cartas*, p. 24. Letter to Blumentritt, written in Hong Kong on August 18, 1897. The phrasing is: *el General saltó como picado por una culebra.*

76. Scott, *The Unión Obrera Democrática*, p. 14, quoting from Primo's correspondence with his superiors in Madrid.

77. *Ibid.* It is interested that, in his August 18 letter to Blumentritt cited above, Ponce said he had not seen Isabelo's name on any passenger list, meaning that he had someone in Manila to monitor outgoing shipping. He expressed his fear that the folklorist had been "disappeared," as we say nowadays.

78. *Ibid.*, p. 14. Isabelo recalled in 1900 that "estaba rigurosamente incomunicado en las cárceles nacionales de Barcelona, en un calabocillo á donde, para llegar, había que pasar por tres puertas cerradas con llave *cont'd over*/

After a week, Isabelo was transferred to Montjuich, whose commandant calmly (and falsely) assured him that only those facing the death penalty were incarcerated in its cells. He was not—by a long chalk—the first Filipino since Rizal to be sequestered there. The anarchist "Federico Urales"—who had been arrested after the Corpus Christi bombing because he had courageously adopted Pallás's orphaned daughter, had opened a highly popular secular school for children, and had published an attack on trials by military courts in Barcelona—gave, in his memoirs, this touching account. He said that

> el partido colonial logró del gubierno que fuese destituído el general Blanco por demasiado transigente y que en su lugar se nombrase al general cristiano Polavieja, asesino del poeta y doctor filipino Rizal. Tan pronto Polavieja llegó á Filipinas, empezó á fusilar y á embarcar gente para España y un barco cargado de insurrectos llegó á Barcelona, siendo encerrados en la cárcel donde nosotros lo estábamos. Ello occurría en invierno, y aquellos pobres filipinos fueron deportados llevando el mismo traje del país, que consistía en unos pantalones que parecían calzoncillos y en una camisa de telaraña. Y era vergonzoso y triste á la vez ver á los pobres filipinos en el patio de la cárcel de Barcelona, paseándose, formando círculo y dando patadas en el suelo para calentarse los pies y tiritando de frío . . . Lo noble, lo hermoso fué ver á toda la población penal de la cárcel tirando al patio zapatos, alpargatas, pantalones, chalecos, chaquetas, gorras, calcetines para que se abrigaran los pobres deportados filipinos, en cuyo país no se conoce el frío.

> The colonial lobby succeeded in getting the government to dump General Blanco for being too lenient, and to replace him with the Christian general Polavieja, the murderer of Rizal, the Filipino poet and doctor. On his arrival in the Philippines Polavieja immediately began executions and deportations to Spain. One ship laden with insurrectionaries having arrived at Barcelona, the prisoners were incarcerated in the same prison as ourselves. This happened in winter, and those poor Filipino deportees were [still] clothed in their native attire, which consisted simply of drawer-like pants and a cobweb-thin shirt. It was both shaming and melancholy to see the poor Filipinos in the courtyard of the Barcelona prison, pacing about in a circle,

---

78 *cont'd*   que, cuando, por arte de birlibirloque, un distinguido periodista federal, que estaba también preso por revolucionario, D. Ignacio Bó y Singla, logró introducirse en mi prisión" [I was kept rigorously incommunicado in the national prisons of Barcelona, in a cell entry to which required passing through three locked doors; but obtaining the key by abracadabra means, the distinguished federalist journalist, D. Ignacio Bó y Singla, also a prisoner because taken for a revolutionary, managed to introduce himself into my place of incarceration]. *Filipinas ante Europa*, March 25, 1900. Federico Urales, *Mi vida* (Barcelona: La Revista Blanca, 1930), Tomo I, p. 218, wrote that though Bó was physically insignificant (*casi ridículo*), he had enormous courage. He began his political life as a federalist with Pi y Margall, but moved on to anarchism and committed atheism. He also later published a lacerating book on Montjuich.

to warm their feet and shivering with cold. It was a noble, beautiful sight to see the prison inmates throwing down into the courtyard shoes, rope-sandals, trousers, vests, jackets, caps, and socks to warm the poor Filipino deportees, in whose country the cold is unknown.[79]

In September Isabelo received a new cellmate, Ramón Sempau, who on the 4th of that month had tried to assassinate Lieutenant Narciso Portas, the torturer-in-chief of Montjuich, aka the "Spanish Trepov," whose name Tarrida, via the European press, had made synonymous with the New Inquisition. (The lieutenant had been appointed head of a special political intelligence unit by Weyler during his tenure as Captain-General of Catalonia, prior to reassignment to Havana.) Sempau was basically a bohemian literary figure, a journalist and poet with anarchist leanings.[80] If Urales's memoirs are to be trusted, the plan to kill Portas was hatched originally in Paris, and after Sempau's arrest the French anarchist Charles Malato came to Barcelona to carry out what proved to be an abortive attempt to arrange his escape.[81] In any case, Isabelo was enchanted by the failed assassin. In old age, he wrote that the Catalan was

very well educated; he knew by heart the scientific names of plants in the Philippines, and later translated Rizal's *Noli me tangere* into French. In his fight with some hundred police agents, he showed an absolute lack of fear. His very name caused terror in Europe. Yet in reality he was like an honest and good-natured child—yes, even a true Christ by nature . . . I repeat, on my word of honor, that the so-called anarchists, Nihilists, or, as they say nowadays, Bolsheviks, are the true saviors and disinterested defenders of justice and universal brotherhood. When the prejudices of these days of moribund imperialism have disappeared, they will rightfully occupy our altars.[82]

79. Urales, *Mi Vida*, Tomo II, pp. 196–7, and 200. Urales's real Catalan name was Joan Montseny, but he took on the Ural Mountains (Siberia!) for his first *nom de guerre* and *nom de plume*. He was originally to be deported to Rio de Oro; but at the last minute he was sent into exile in London, where he immediately helped to organize the Committee on Spanish Atrocities. He returned to Spain in 1898 and founded *La Revista Blanca* in homage to *La Revue Blanche* (but it was more oriented to *obreros conscientes* than to leading intellectuals). He recalled, rather touchingly, that when he started *La Revista Blanca* he wrote very popular articles on diseases and the social conditions that caused them, under the pseudonym Dr Boudin. He did so because the "intellectuals of the working class did not believe in the talent of Federico Urales, whom they knew to be Juan (sic) Montseny," but they thoroughly trusted "Dr Boudin." *Ibid.*, p.206

80. See Núñez, *El terrorismo*, pp. 55 (Narciso Portas), and 60–61 and 158 (Sempau). Nettlau rather cattily described him as "ein zwischen Anarchismus und Catalanismus flukturierender Einzelgänger" [a go-it-aloner fluctuating between anarchism and Catalanism] (Nettlau ms, p. 116). Sempau later became part of the Catalan Revival of the turn of the century, collaborating on the Catalan-language review *Occitània*.

81. *Ibid.*, p. 158, quoting from the third volume of Urales's *Mi vida*, pp. 80–81.

82. Isabelo, quoted in Scott, *Unión Obrera Democrática*, p. 15.

Perhaps with Sempau's help, Isabelo further got a friendly guard to pass him books and newspapers, which, as he later recalled, "really opened my eyes." He learned that anarchism "espoused the abolition of boundaries; that is, love without any boundaries, whether geographic or of class distinction . . . with all of us associating together without any need of fraudulent taxes or ordinances which trap the unfortunate but leave the real criminals untouched."[83]

With Cánovas dead, and Sagasta's opposition coalition in power, while Tarrida's campaign was going full blast,[84] the situation of the Montjuich prisoners started to change. The demands of the army and the police that Sempau be tried by a military court, which would certainly have sentenced him to death, were rejected by the new government. Such was the odium in which Portas was held that no civilian judge wished or dared to declare the would-be assassin guilty. On January 8, 1898, Isabelo was freed. Thanks to letters of reference from Pi y Margall, Alejandro Lerroux (the head of the populist Radical Republican Party in Barcelona), and Federico Urales, he quickly got a minor sinecure in the propaganda section of Moret's Ministry for Overseas Territories. Isabelo's articles on the Philippines, especially his tirades against the Orders, were published in Lerroux's party organ, with Grand Mason Professor Miguel Morayta polishing their language. Best of all, armed with a revolver, Isabelo plunged happily into the radical demonstrations of the times, without shooting anyone, but not without getting an occasional bloody nose.[85]

GO EAST, YOUNG MAN

Mariano Ponce, two years younger than Rizal, and one year older than Isabelo de los Reyes, came from the province of Bulacan, adjoining Manila on its northeast side (Aguinaldo's guerrilla hideout Biak-na-Bató is located in this province). While still a student at Santo Tomás, he had become a

---

83. *Ibid.*, p. 14.

84. The committedly anarchist Theâtre Libertaire opened its doors in 1898 with a drama entitled "Montjuich," which remained popular for several years thereafter. Herbert, *The Artist*, p. 39. Herbert comments that in the 1890s Paris was very short of competent French playwrights, and Ibsen—often interpreted anarchistically—towered over everything.

85. Scott describes the delicious welter that attended a lively demonstration against "Montjuich" in February 1898—in which Isabelo joined. Organized by a group close to Lerroux (including a woman journalist for his newspaper *El Progreso* who would become the Filipino's second wife), it was composed of: the Association of Freethinkers, the Barcelona Centre for Psychological Studies, *El Diluvio*, the Kardesian (Cartesian?) Spiritists' Union, Liberal Students of the Faculty of Law, the Marxist Center, the Progressive Feminist Society, Republican Youth, *Revista Masónica*, the Society of Stevedores, the Society of Lumber-loading Labourers, the Union of Workers' Societies, and *La Voz del Pueblo. Unión obrera Democrática*, p. 16.

*Meeting of Mariano Ponce (right) Dr Sun Yat-Sen
(left) in Ponce's Yokohama home.*

nationalist activist under the tutelage of Del Pilar, and continued with his
activism after arriving in Madrid to study medicine at Rizal's and Unamuno's
Central University. Ponce and his mentor were the driving forces in founding
La Solidaridad in Barcelona in February 1889, and in moving it to the Spanish
capital nine months later. Though he wrote articles under various pseudonyms, he discovered that his real talents were working as managing editor,
treasurer, and archivist. More and more Del Pilar turned managing the journal
over to him. It says a great deal for his calm, honest, and modest character that
even when relations between Rizal and Del Pilar were at their most fraught,
Ponce remained the close and trusted friend of both.

   After Rizal's arrest and deportation to Dapitan, *La Solidaridad* began a
slow decline, and its last issue appeared in October 1895. One difficulty was
that it depended financially on contributions from well-off sympathizers in
Manila, and these were increasingly difficult to extract. But the main
problem was that after six years of intensive labor, Del Pilar's policy of
strategic assimilationism still had little impact on the Spanish government,
and there was a growing feeling in the Filipino colony that it was a dead-end.

Accordingly, in the spring of 1896, Ponce and Del Pilar decided to move to Hong Kong, where they could be safe from persecution but close to their homeland. But Del Pilar's health was by then broken, and, as noted earlier, he died a miserable death in martial law Barcelona on July 4. Ponce, who had faithfully nursed him, stayed on to settle their remaining affairs. When Bonifacio's uprising erupted at the end of the following month, the police raided the house where he was living and the premises of the Hispano-Philippine Association, removing many documents. Ponce himself was imprisoned, but only for one night, as the police found nothing seriously compromising. When things quietened down, he slipped across the French border to Marseilles and set sail for the Far East on October 11.

In the spring of 1897, at the age of thirty-four, he began there the work that occupied him for the next four years: raising money for what was by then Aguinaldo's revolutionary government, attempting to buy guns and ammunition to be smuggled into the Philippines, and engaging in a ceaseless propaganda campaign on behalf of his country's independence. (In June 1898, Ponce was sent by Aguinaldo to represent the Philippines in Japan.) In accomplishing the first two tasks Ponce had little success. His *Cartas sobre la Revolución* contain a number of letters to wealthy Filipinos residing outside the country, begging them to show their patriotism by substantial financial contributions, and other letters, to close friends, complaining how odiously selfish and unpatriotic these people mostly turned out to be. The search for arms was even less successful. But the correspondence shows in fascinating detail how Ponce conducted his propaganda campaign, and tried to adapt to the hectic events of 1897–1900. Before undertaking an analysis of the texts, a brief recapitulation of these events is necessary.

WHO IS THE ENEMY?

While Isabelo was still languishing in Montjuich, the military impasse in the Philippines continued. Primo Rivera was unable to destroy Aguinaldo, and the man from Cavite was unable to make any serious break-out from his Biak-na-Bató redoubt. It was time for political initiatives. Aguinaldo's civilian associates advised him that his position would be greatly strengthened if a democratic constitution were enacted to create a legal revolutionary government competing with the colonial regime. The task was assigned to Félix Ferrer and Isabelo Artacho. Teodoro Agoncillo dryly described the process this way:

> Ferrer and Artacho lifted the contents of the Constitution of Jimaguayú, Cuba, drawn up in 1895, and passed it off as their brain work . . . [A] contemporary scholar, Clemente José Zulueta, once calmly told a friend who expressed fear that

the only copy of the Biak-na-Bató Constitution might be lost: "Don't worry, we have a copy of the Constitution of Jimaguayú."[86]

The only local addition was a then-divisive clause making Tagalog the national language. The caudillo, whose Spanish was weak, and who knew little about the world beyond the Philippines, proudly proclaimed the enactment of this "Filipino" constitution on November 1. The next day he was sworn in as president.

But even before this grand gesture was being made, negotiations had begun with Primo de Rivera, who seems to have hoped, after Cánovas's death, Weyler's fall, and the return of Sagasta to power, to secure at best a sort of oriental version of the Pact of Zanjón. By the end of the year, it had been agreed that the rebels would lay down their arms and receive full amnesty; and that Aguinaldo and his officers would leave for Hong Kong with 400,000 pesetas in their pockets, and another 400,000 due when the surrender of arms was complete. A further 900,000 pesetas was to be allocated for the benefit of innocent Filipino victims of the fighting over the past fifteen months. Primo de Rivera, aware of intense Filipino suspicion of Spanish treachery, sent two of his generals to Biak-na-Bató as hostages, while his 27-year-old nephew, Colonel Miguel Primo de Rivera (the future dictator of Spain in the 1920s, much less intelligent than his uncle), would accompany Aguinaldo across the China Sea. Unsurprisingly, neither side lived fully up to the agreement—many rebels buried their weapons rather than surrender them, and the second *tranche* for the caudillo never materialized.[87]

Meanwhile Washington was on the move, above all in the person of Theodore Roosevelt. As early as November 1897 he had written that, in the event of war with Spain over Cuba, it would be advisable to send the American Asiatic Squadron, based in Japan, to Manila Bay; simultaneously, he arranged for the like-minded Commodore George Dewey to take over the squadron's command. At the end of February 1898, Roosevelt ordered Dewey to move his base of operations to Hong Kong. When war was finally declared on April 25, after the curious explosion of the warship USS *Maine* in Havana's harbor—it had been sent there to intimidate the Spanish—Dewey set off for the Philippines within an hour of getting the official cable. On May 1, he destroyed the obsolete Spanish fleet within sight of Manila's shoreline. (At this point there was still no attack on Cuba itself!) At Dewey's invitation Aguinaldo and his men followed from Hong Kong on the 19th. But Washington's real aims soon became clear. Aguinaldo was barred from entering Manila, while Dewey's people started to fraternize with the defeated Spaniards, and relations with the Filipinos steadily deteriorated. Aguinaldo

---

86. Agoncillo, *A Short History*, p. 102.
87. *Ibid.*, p. 103.

The assassination of President William McKinley brought Theodore Roosevelt to power. His maxim on US foreign policy, "Speak softly and carry a big stick," was widely lampooned in contemporary cartoons.

was forced to read the declaration of Philippine independence on June 12, not in the capital but from the balcony of his substantial home in Kawit. Shortly thereafter, he appointed Apolinario Mabini as his chief political adviser.

Mabini was an extraordinary figure.[88] Born three years after Rizal, he was the child of poor peasants in the province of Batangas, and throughout his brief life he never had a real penny to his name. He was a brilliant law student at Santo Tomás, as well as a member of Rizal's abortive Liga Filipina. Fluent in Spanish, he had neither the means nor, probably, the inclination to study overseas. The only time he would leave his country was when he was deported by the Americans to a political prison in Guam. In 1896 disaster struck when he became paralyzed from the waist down, perhaps from rheumatic fever, perhaps from polio, but the condition saved him from Polavieja's fury. In the first half of 1898, while Aguinaldo was ensconced in

---

88. The wonderful and indispensable source is still Cesar Adib Majul's *Mabini and the Philippine Revolution* (Quezon City: University of the Philippines Press, 1996)—originally published in 1960.

Hong Kong, Mabini became celebrated for the passionate revolutionary manifestos he wrote in defence of the Revolution. When the caudillo summoned him to Cavite, hundreds of people took turns to bear his litter from the spa of Los Baños to the revolutionary leader's headquarters. Mabini designed and wrote virtually all the Aguinaldo government's decrees, and effectively managed their execution for the crucial year when he remained in power as Aguinaldo's prime minister. A man of iron will, Mabini was also a dedicated patriot, and one of the very few top leaders of the immediate post-Rizal era who recognized that the popular movement was essential to the Revolution's survival, and predicted early on that it would be betrayed by most of the *ilustrados* and the wealthy.

But Mabini's rise to power came just at the point when large numbers of American troops landed in Cuba. Six weeks later the hostilities there between Spain and the United States came to an end, and Washington became effective master of the island. The turn of the Philippines was bound to come next. At the end of the year the Treaty of Paris was signed between the US and Spain by which Madrid "sold" the colony to Washington for $20 million. (Germany bought up most of the Carolines and Marianas for a much lower price.) In the meantime, a Philippine national assembly had assembled in Aguinaldo's temporary capital of Malolos (in Bulacan), created a new constitution, inaugurated the Republic of the Philippines, and elevated Mabini to the prime ministership. Every effort was made to mobilize political support in the islands outside Luzon, to reasonably good effect except in the Muslim far south.

The Filipino-American War broke out in February 1899. The Filipino soldiers fought bravely but, poorly armed, were no match for their new enemies in conventional warfare. Worse was to follow. Mabini was driven from power in May by a cabal of wily *ilustrados* who were eager to collaborate with the Americans. Antonio Luna, chief of staff and the only Filipino general with a clear strategic vision of how to conduct guerrilla warfare against the new colonizers, was assassinated in June by Aguinaldo and his clique, who were afraid that the Ilocano would eventually take power. The war officially ended in March 1901, when Aguinaldo was captured in the high Luzon Cordillera—and promptly swore allegiance to Washington. But other generals fought on for another year, and armed popular resistance was not finally stamped out till the end of the decade. The details of all this have been amply studied and need not detain us here. For present purposes only two things ought to be underlined.

First, on the eve of the second anniversary of Rizal's execution, Aguinaldo issued a proclamation that the entire population should thereafter mourn, on each subsequent anniversary of his death, the country's National Hero. The earliest monument, two small Masonic pillars inscribed with the titles of

Rizal's novels, still survives in the small hurricane-haunted town of Dáet on the Bicol peninsula of southeastern Luzon. Second, the Americans, having ferociously denounced Weyler's "concentration of populations" in Cuba, ended up by adopting this same policy—in spades—in the Philippines. A large number of Filipinos died of malnutrition and disease in these concentration zones, as well as in a merciless counterinsurgency warfare during which torture of prisoners was commonplace.[89]

A GENTLEMAN GLOBALIZED

With this background in mind, it is possible to return productively to Ponce's correspondence in his role as one of the most important overseas emissaries of the Philippine regime. Before doing so, one has to emphasize that his *Cartas*, published long after his death, contains only letters that Ponce himself wrote. Both the original letters from which they were culled, and all the letters of his correspondents, have long disappeared. There is no way to determine for certain whether they have been bowdlerized, and how many letters were omitted. (The editor, Teodoro Kalaw, a conventional mainstream post-revolutionary nationalist and politician, was probably not eager to have the revolutionary movement's dirty laundry hung out for public consumption. The collection as printed is notable for the absence of personal letters to Ponce's kin, of letters in any way critical of Aguinaldo, and of correspondence about the intrigues and financial manipulations—well known from other sources—of unprincipled "leaders," primarily in Hong Kong, but also elsewhere.)

There are 243 letters in all, beginning in May 1897 and ending in March 1900. Two tables (see over) will give the reader a general statistical picture of the character of Ponce's correspondents. It should be noted that some of these correspondents used one or more pseudonyms (as did Ponce himself) to elude the monitoring of Spanish, British, and American spies. Not all of the real people behind these pseudonyms have been firmly identified.

Almost 50 percent of the letters were addressed to just five people: Galicano Apacible (who took over from Ponce in Hong Kong after the latter left for Japan) 43; Blumentritt 39; Vergel de Dios (Ponce's main contact with the Cubans in Paris) 15; "Ifortel" (who may have been Rafael de Pan

---

89. See Leon Wolff, *Little Brown Brother* (New York: Doubleday, 1961), and more recently Celerina G. Balucan's "War Atrocities," *Kasaysayan*, 1:4 (December 2001), pp. 34–54. But in his *Battle for Batangas: A Philippine Province at War* (New Haven: Yale University Press, 1991), based in fine-grained study of parish records in the worst-hit province of Batangas, Glenn May has shown conclusively that Wolff's "half a million" dead was an exaggeration, and a sizeable part of the deaths occurred before the American counterinsurgency began, caused by crop failure, cattle disease, and climate irregularities.

Table 1 Nationality of correspondents (where known):

Filipinos	28	Dutch	1
Japanese	17	Portuguese	1
Spanish	5	British	1
Cuban	4	American	1
Unknown	3	Canadian	1
Austro-Hungarian	2	Chinese	1

Table 2 Addresses of correspondents by country or state:

Japan	18	(at least half in Tokyo)	Austro-Hungary	2 (Dresden and Leitmeritz)	
Spain	9	(evenly divided between Barcelona and Madrid)	Macao	12	
Philippines	6	(various)	Singapore	1	
Unknown	6		The Netherlands	1	
Hongkong	5		Mexico	1	
France	5	(all in Paris)	Canada	1 (Montreal)	
United States	5	(New Orleans, New York, and 'Pennsylvania')	Germany	1 (Berlin)	
			China	1 (Shanghai)	

and whose address is unclear) 12; and Francisco Agoncillo (Aguinaldo's frustrated representative in the US) 11.

The languages used are also revealing. Generally speaking, Ponce used Spanish when writing to Spaniards, Cubans, Puerto Ricans, and Filipinos, with three interesting additions. All the lengthy correspondence with Blumentritt was in Spanish, as well as that with his own Japanese translator "Foujita" and Miura Arajiro, the Japanese diplomat to whom he wrote while the latter was on a reconnoitering mission to Manila, and later in Mexico. On the other hand, Ponce used an English painfully acquired in Hong Kong to address all but two of his Japanese correspondents, as well as a Briton, a Dutchman, an American, a Canadian, a German, and an Austro-Hungarian. Most strikingly the only letters wholly in Tagalog are the two he sent to Aguinaldo (though a few sentences in otherwise Spanish letters are also visible). He was plainly aware of the caudillo's shaky command of the imperial language.

Comparison between the two tables makes other things very clear. First is the extent of the Filipino and Cuban diaspora—Ponce was communicating with Filipinos in New Orleans, Paris, Hong Kong, Barcelona, Shanghai, Madrid, Yokohama, and Macao, and with Cubans in New York and Paris, but not in Havana or to any real extent in Spain. There is something else of special interest. When writing in Spanish, Ponce normally used the ultra-polite terms of address of nineteenth-century Spain. But to the two Antilleans to whom he felt closest, Betances and José Izquierdo in Paris—and only to them—he addressed his letters with the phrases *mi distinguidísimo correligionario*, and *mi querido correligionario*—where the playful coreligionist clearly meant "fellow (non-Filipino) nationalist."

If one steps back from the *Cartas* and considers their circumambience, the limits of their "globalization" are revealed by the absences. Ponce had no contacts in the capitals of the New World, including Havana and Washington. In Europe, the biggest absence is London, followed by Vienna, Rome, Brussels, Lisbon, and Belgrade. In Asia, his important contacts with Chinese were in Japan, not China itself, while India and neighboring Southeast Asia are almost invisible, though Ponce mentions a certain Matias González working for the cause in Java. Politically, it is plain that he had very little communication with the Left. Clémenceau, Dreyfus, Tarrida, Vandervelde, Keir Hardie, as well as Malatesta, and the anarchists of Catalonia and Andalusia are never mentioned, and seem to be off his screen. The people he wrote to were overwhelmingly liberal scholars and newspaper people in the West, and fellow nationalists in the Cuban and Chinese diasporas. It is only in the case of the Japanese that the picture becomes more blurred.

BLUMENTRITT

On December 16, 1896 Blumentritt wrote a quite uncharacteristically obtuse and emotional letter to Pardo de Tavera in Paris:

> Celebro también que le haya gustado mi artículo que ha publicado en la Política de España, p[or?] q[ue?] [para?] condenar los que ahora se han rebelado en Filipinas. No puedo hallar bastante numeros de voces en el diccionario castellano que pudieran expresar bien la indignación que me inspira aquella nefanda revolución. Sus instigadores merecen no solamente el castigo que pone la ley sino también el odio y desprecio de parte de los filipinos, pues la felonía de aquellos ha llevando al país á la sangre, desgracia y ruina. Todo la Europa simpatiza con la causa española y admira los esfuerzos heróicos con que España defiende en el Occidente y el Oriente la gloriosa bandera de su nación. Espero que en el momento cuando V. habrá recibido esta carta, será suprimida por completo aquella loca rebelión.

> I am delighted that you enjoyed the article I published in the *Política de España* condemning those who are now in rebellion in the Philippines. I cannot find enough words in the Spanish dictionary properly to express the indignation that this calamitous rebellion arouses in me. Its instigators deserve not only the punishment laid down by the law, but also the hatred and the contempt of the Filipinos, for these men's treachery has led the country to bloodshed, misfortune, and ruin. All Europe sympathizes with the Spanish cause and admires the heroic efforts by which Spain is defending, in the West and in the East, the glorious flag of its nation. I trust that by the time you receive this letter, this insane rebellion will have been annihilated.[90]

90. Taken from a retype of the original letter, found in the Ateneo de Manila's Pardo de Tavera Collection.

Doubtless, Blumentritt was agitated by the thought of what might happen to his bosom friend Rizal in Fort Santiago. It is also possible that he was sending other letters of this kind to friends and colleagues in Spain in the hope of getting their help in saving Rizal's life. But some time in January 1897 he got the last letter Rizal wrote, saying he would be dead by the time it arrived. More than anything else the execution changed the Austrian scholar's mind, and from then on he was an intelligent and tireless supporter of the Revolution.

Although Ponce and Blumentritt had never met face to face, the two men had corresponded for years, since the latter wrote frequently for *La Solidaridad* and always sent to the editors copies of his latest scholarly texts on the Philippines. Now the relationship became extremely close. For Blumentritt, Ponce in Hong Kong was a generally well-informed and reliable source of detailed information on the ups and downs of the Revolution at a time when the Philippines itself was under martial law, and the European press was generally ignorant and indifferent. In return, Blumentritt appears to have given Ponce good advice on the world political situation, warning particularly against any naïveté about American intentions and ambitions.[91] Blumentritt not only used Ponce's reports to write regularly for the press, but, aware of Ponce's unfamiliarity with the international academic world, used his scholarly contacts—in Pennsylvania, Berlin, Dresden, the Netherlands—to put Ponce directly in touch with sympathetic and active professors.[92]

THE ANTILLEANS

Ponce's *Cartas* contain eleven letters to diasporic Antilleans, dated between May 1897 and November 1898, most sent prior to the American conquest in August 1898. They were written, therefore, in the period when Cuba was seen as a shining example for Filipino nationalists, Spain as the enemy, and the United States as a potentially benevolent ally. Most of them were addressed to the Cuban José Izquierdo, who was evidently a good personal friend—Ponce

91. In a letter of September 28, 1898, Ponce wrote to Blumentritt saying he shared the scholar's view, and had repeatedly warned his countrymen that "while doubtless under the Americans the country would grow rich in agriculture, industry and commerce, yet *esa riqueza no será nuestra, sino que estará en manos americanas* [the riches will not be ours, but will be in American hands]." *Cartas*, pp. 195–205.

92. Specifically Dr Eduardo Soler in Berlin, Dr Daniel Brenton in Pennsylvania, Dr A.H. Meyer in Dresden, and the intellectual publisher A. Tjeenk Willink in the Netherlands. In an effusive letter of September 9, 1897 Ponce thanked Tjeenk Willink for publishing in his *Op de Uitkijk* a laudatory memorial article on Rizal by the famous Javanologist R.A. Kern. *Cartas*, p. 34. Later Blumentritt pushed Ponce to write for this periodical himself.

mentions their time together as members of the Ateneo club in Madrid. Izquierdo was a young lawyer and assimilationist liberal on the outer edge of Betances's nationalist circle in Paris.[93] Sent on May 11, 1897, the first letter shows a pattern repeated regularly thereafter: Ponce updates his friend on the progress of the Philippine Revolution, and asks for publications of the Cubans, especially Martí's Manifesto and the writings of General Máximo Gómez on the principles of (guerrilla) war. He then proceeds to ask Izquierdo to put him in touch with the Cuban Delegation in New York to get advice on whether an armed expedition to the Philippines could be organized over there. It is telling of the way in which Ponce thought about the United States at that time that he wrote: "No hemos dado aún paso para conseguir la protección de los Estados Unidos" (We have yet to take any steps to seek the protection of the United States). He went on to observe:

> No se olvide de que son Vdes nuestros hermanos mayores y que somos nuevos y sin experiencia aún en estas empresas colosales, ya por lo tanto muy necesitados de ayuda, consejos, instrucciones, que sólo podemos esperar de Vdes. Cuba y Filipinas han recorrido juntas el doloroso camino de su historia de vergonzosa esclavitud, juntas deben también pulverizar sus cadenas.

> We do not forget that you are our elder brothers and that we are new and still without experience in these colossal enterprises, and, just for that reason, we are in need of the aid, advice, and instructions which we can hope for only from you. Cuba and the Philippines have together trodden the tragic path of shameful enslavement, and together we should also smash our chains.[94]

Izquierdo must have been discouraging about prospects in America, since in the second letter, of September 8, Ponce asks whether in that case Mexico might be willing to permit "expeditions" from one of its Pacific ports.[95] There is as yet no evidence that the Ponce–Izquierdo contacts were the cause, but it is interesting that some time in June 1898, shortly before the American onslaught on Cuba, a letter was sent to Mabini—only just in power, so the senders were *au courant*— by the Cuban Bureau of General Information, at Room 45, 81 New Street, New York, offering to sell the Philippines the "latest" (*de nueva invención*) in arms, along with manuals showing how to use them. The details have their melancholy interest: a light mortar with its carriage, for $125; a carton containing ten dynamite bombs with gunpowder, for $40, at from 10–20% in discounts. "The carton in addition contains 12 capsules and 12 fuses for the bombs. The cover

---

93. Izquierdo is mentioned only a couple of times in the hundreds of pages of *El destierro*.

94. Ponce, *Cartas*, pp. 5–9.

95. *Ibid.*, pp. 28–32.

has a clasp and hinges, and is provided with handles and a leather strap so it can be carried on the shoulder and thus transported easily."[96] Ponce's later letters were mainly asking help from the Cuban Delegation in New York (Gonzalo de Quezada) and Izquierdo in Paris for Agoncillo, whom Aguinaldo had sent to America to lobby the press and legislators, and on to Paris to try to be heard at the talks leading to the Treaty of Paris. Neither mission had fruitful results. Strangely enough, the most touching correspondence arose from something of no political importance at all. On September 13, 1898 Ponce wrote a letter from Yokohama to Apacible in Hong Kong, addressed to "Kanoy." (Today *kanoy* is contemptuous Tagalog for "American," derived from *amerikano*, but here it is only an affectionate Filipinization of Galicano.) He told Apacible that he had received a letter from Betances—who died a few days later—making two enquiries. The first was about a young Puerto Rican lawyer, Manuel Rovira y Muñoz, working as a registrar of land holdings in the province of Laguna, whose long silence had deeply worried his parents in Puerto Rico.[97] Betances's second request was more complex and shows beautifully how "globalization" worked at the end of the nineteenth century. He told Ponce that he was very concerned after hearing from a Cuban prisoner about the misery of five Cubans, including himself, and seven Filipinos incarcerated in Valladolid. Betances said he himself could help the Cubans, but he could find no representation of the Filipinos either in London or Paris, so asked Ponce to do what he could. Betances's letter included a transcript of the "Cuban" prisoner's letter, a wonderful document in its own right. It is written in Spanish but with a peculiar orthography. Valladolid appears as *Balladolid*, Capablanca as *Kapablanca*, *aquí* as *akí*, and *cómo* as *komo*. There is no "v" sound in Tagalog, and no letter "k" in the standard Spanish alphabet. The spelling is impossible for Spanish-speaking Cubans, even with a low level of literacy, but it is close to the one already aggressively pushed by Rizal at the time of *El Filibusterismo* (as noted earlier).[98] The person who actually wrote the letter to Betances must have been a Filipino, probably following the dictation of an illiterate Cuban. This is nice anecdotal confirmation of Schumacher's claim that in 1900 literacy

96. The letter does not mention Mabini by name, and is addressed tactfully to Muy Sr nuestro. But the Americans who later captured it were almost certainly right in thinking it was meant for the man of the hour. The letter is on microfilm at the National Library in Manila.

97. Ponce, *Cartas*, pp. 174–6. That same day Ponce wrote a strong letter to Mabini asking his help, adding that Betances was an old comrade to whom our "sacred cause owes much." *Ibid.*, pp. 177–9. Later it transpired that the youngster had been detained by the Philippine government, but was in good health and spirits.

98. What we will probably never know is whether poor Tagalogs picked up Rizal's "innovation," or whether Rizal was borrowing from the practices of poor Tagalogs.

in the Philippines was as high as in Spain, and *a priori* much higher than in Cuba.

THE JAPANESE

Japan was initially a total shock to Ponce, even if the shock passed in time, so that in the end he happily married a Japanese woman. On July 8, 1898 he wrote to Blumentritt:

> Tiene razón. Destruye toda noción que hemos adquirido en Europa, pues todo esto revela un mundo desconocido, completamente extraño y exótico á todo lo que se podía imaginar antes de verlo.

> You are right. [Being here] destroys every conception that we have acquired from Europe, since everything discloses a world unknown, completely strange and exotic [compared to] everything that one might imagine before seeing [it] with one's own eyes.[99]

Knowing no Japanese—Ponce wrote to almost all his Japanese correspondents in English—and with no experience of the intricate conflicts and intrigues within the late-Meiji elite, he was an easy prey, at first, for speculators. It took him time to understand that the opposition—whatever it happened to consist of at any one moment—enjoyed blaming whatever coalition was in power for "weakness" towards the "white" Powers and unwillingness to help the exploited "Asian brothers," until the moment when the political wheel rotated, and opposition became government. Ponce cultivated high government officials (often discreetly sympathetic), opposition politicians (less discreetly so), the press, university professors, and shady adventurers, military and civilian, without getting very far, though he did persuade various periodicals to publish key documents of the Aguinaldo regime. (The reasons for Japanese caution have been laid out in Chapter 4.)

Then, on April 5, 1899, at the height of the Filipino-American War, Ponce wrote to Apacible in Hong Kong that he had found the sustained outlet he needed. The periodical he called *Keikora Nippo* (Kaika Shimbun) was publishing a long series of his articles under the rubric "Cuestiones Filipinas". The miracle was not only the contract itself, but that the journal had on its staff a man he called "Foujita Sonetaka" who was reasonably fluent in Spanish.[100]

---

99. Ponce, *Cartas*, pp. 124–6.

100. *Ibid.*, pp. 316–17. Fujita must have been an unusually cosmopolitan figure for the Japan of his time. Professor Umemori Naoyuki of Waseda University informs me that Fujita was listed as a Spanish translator for the Foreign Ministry during 1899–1900 in the contemporary government directory (*Shokuinroku*). In 1901 he became a language instructor in the Spanish language   cont'd over/

On the 25th, Ponce wrote again to Apacible about his pleasure at being invited
to give an address to what he called the Oriental Young Men's Society,
composed of "*indios* [Indians], *koreanos, chinos y japoneses*," after which
he was made an honorary member.[101] Shortly thereafter, Ponce had the
sensible idea of turning his series of articles into a book, revising, cutting
duplications and so on. "Foujita" was entrusted with the job of translating
and publishing the text, getting the Japanese copyright in return. It seems
probable that the articles, or news of the impending book, got "Foujita" into
hot water, since Ponce wrote to him on November 3 to say how badly he felt
that his friend had been harassed by the Japanese police "because of
our cause."[102] A week earlier he had written a chilly letter to Felipe
Buencamino, leader of the clique that had plotted Mabini's fall and now
Aguinaldo's right-hand man, to say curtly that, because of time constraints,
he would be unable to submit his manuscript to "la censura de nuestro
Gobierno".[103] The book did not appear until 1901, well after the

---

100 cont'd   department of the Tokyo University of Foreign Studies (Tokyo Gaiko-
kugu Gakko), according to the university's published history. He is mentioned as
teaching intensive courses for the Malay and Hindustani languages, at the same
institution, in Matsuno Akihisa, "Nihon no okeru Malay go no kaishi to tenkai" (The
beginning and development of Malay education in Japan), in Kondo Tatsuo, ed.,
Wagakunini okeru gaikokugo kenkyu/kyoiku no shiteki kosatsu (Osaka: Gaikokugo
Gakko, 1990). Also in 1908, he gave a lecture on "The Scripture of the Islamic
Religion" to the Toa Kyokai educational association founded by the influential
academic Inoue Tetsujiro. (Fujita was a member of this organization, and its rolls
indicate that he was a Tokyo-boy, of samurai background, but with no university
degree.) This lecture was then published in two parts in the association's journal as
"Huihuikyo no keiten ni tsuite," *Toa no Hikari* (Light in East Asia), 3:4 (pp. 50–56)
and 3:6 (pp. 78–85).

In this remarkable text, writes Umemori, Fujita mentioned that he had stayed
in Moscow, and given a talk there based on his experiences with Muslims within
the Tsar's domains, had then moved on to study Islam in China, and finally
broadened his interest to the whole Islamic world from the Philippines to North
Africa. He also underlined, giving concrete examples, the influence of Arabic on
Turkish, Spanish, Portuguese, and even Japanese. He argued that Europe's
religious biases made impartial study of Islam impossible there, but that the
Japanese were positioned to do so "without bias or favour," and should get
going.

After 1908 Fujita disappears from the known record as mysteriously as he entered
it. Umemori notes that it is obvious that archivists had no idea how to pronounce the
Chinese ideograph for his personal name, so that it variously appears as "Hideo,"
"Kiso" and "Suetaka."

101. *Ibid.*, pp. 333–6. In the meantime Ponce had met the 20-year-old "Iwo,"
second son of the Korean dynast, who was being touted by Korean progressives as the
best successor to the throne. Ponce was charmed by his youthful *élan* and liberal
ideals.

102. *Ibid.*, pp. 416–18.

103. *Ibid.*, p. 411. Letter dated October 26, 1899.

Suehiro Tettyo

Cartas come to an end.[104] (But it had consequences to be looked at later in this chapter.)

When Ponce asked the translators to include the original Spanish text of Rizal's last poem—here titled "Mi Último Pensamiento"—he probably believed that he was introducing the martyred novelist to the Japanese public for the first time. If so, he was deceived. In early 1888, when Rizal set off from Manila to London, he spent six weeks in Japan (February 28– April 13). Fascinated by the country, he immediately started to study not merely the Japanese language, but also Japanese painting and calligraphy.[105] On the liner that took him to San Francisco he met and befriended Suehiro Tettyo, who understood no foreign languages and felt miserably alone. The

---

104. On the inner title page it is described as *Cuestion Filipina: una exposition* (sic) *histórico-crítica de hechos relativos á la guerra de la independencia*, translated by H[eikuro] Miyamoto and Y.S. Foudzita. The publisher was Tokyo Senmon Gakko (an early name for Okuma's Waseda University).

105. See Caesar (sic) Z. Lanuza and Gregorio F. Zaide, *Rizal in Japan* (Tokyo: C.Z. Lanuza, 1961), for several photographs of Rizal's elegant calligraphy and impressive brush-paintings in the Japanese manner.

pair traveled together across the United States, and proceeded, via Liverpool, to London, where they parted ways.

Suehiro was a striking figure. Born twelve years before Rizal, in the legendary pirate town of Uwajima on the southwestern shores of Shikoku, he came from lower samurai stock. In 1875, at the age of twenty-six, he joined the staff of the liberal metropolitan newspaper *Tokyo Akatsuki Shimbun*, eventually becoming editor-in-chief. For his attacks on government repression of the movement for democracy and freedom of speech he was sent to prison. Plagued by ill-health, he was hospitalized, but from his sick-bed he wrote the political novel *Setchubai* (Plum in the Snow) which had a huge success among the young. It was the royalties from this novel that paid for his "political study" travel to the United States and Europe in 1888. He was enormously impressed by Rizal as a person, as an extraordinary linguist, and as a political idealist. The Filipino novelist featured centrally in the account of his travels—amusingly titled *Oshi no Ryoko* (Travels of a Deaf-Mute)—which was so popular that it ran through six editions between 1889 and 1894. Furthermore, in the same year as *El Filibusterismo*, Suehiro published two novels, *Nanyo no Daiharan* (Storm over the Southern Ocean) and *Arashi no Nagori* (Remains of the Storm).[106] Three years later he combined them into a single book entitled *Oonabara* (Big Ocean).[107]

The young hero of the novel, a Filipino named Takayama, living in Yamada-mura (Yamada village) near Manila, is engaged to Okiyo, the daughter of the boy's kindly patron Takigawa. But a well-placed prison official called Joji, also in love with her, believes that the engagement is Takigawa's doing. Joji therefore instructs Tsuyama, a notorious convict in his prison, to kill the old man, but to make it look like an ordinary, if bloody,

---

106. *Ibid.*, chapter VII. This text is full of errors, for the correction of which I thank Carol Hau and Shiraishi Takashi. The strange thing is that—so far as I can tell—Rizal only mentioned Suehiro once in his correspondence, in a letter to Ponce sent from London on July 27, 1888. The two offhand sentences read: "hice conocimiento con un japonés que venía á Europa, después de haber estado preso por Radical y ser director de un periódico independiente. Como el japonés no hablaba más que japonés, le serví de intérprete, hasta nuestra llegada á Londres" [I made the acquaintance of a Japanese who was going to Europe, after being imprisoned as a Radical and director of an independent periodical. Since the Japanese spoke only Japanese, I served as his interpreter up to our arrival in London]. *Epistolario Rizalino, 1887–1890*, p. 34.

107. For the following account of *Oonabara* I am very grateful to Umemori Naoyuki. He explains that up till about 1900 Meiji-era novelists regularly gave Japanese names to foreign characters and most foreign places, without this implying necessarily any "real" Japanese connection. Translators of favorite European authors, such as Zola, followed the same practice. The idea was to make the texts more accessible to the ordinary Japanese reader.

burglary. This is why one of the two elegant and mysterious swords in Takigawa's possession was stolen at the time of the murder. The hero responds by starting an insurrection in the colonial capital, but it fails and he is imprisoned. Fortunately, a huge earthquake breaks open the prison and allows him to escape. He and Okiyo, hunted by the colonial police, plan to flee overseas. They find a small rowingboat in a coastal swamp full of alligators. At this juncture the police catch up with them, but the helpful reptiles devour the pursuers to a man. Out on the stormy ocean the boat of Takayama and Okiyo capsizes, and they are parted. Takayama is picked up by a British vessel, and under the aegis of a kindly merchant is taken to London, believing that Okiyo has perished. But in fact she has been rescued by fellow Filipinos, and is put quietly on a ship to Hong Kong where she takes shelter in a convent.

In London, Takayama becomes well known as the author of a critical scholarly history of Manila. Meanwhile, Joji discovers Okiyo's whereabouts, and arranges for her former servant Kyuzo (who is his spy) to bring Okiyo a fake letter from Takayama saying that he is in prison in Madrid and in desperate straits. The pair then set off for the imperial capital, where they are met by Joji, who promptly confines Okiyo to an isolated suburban house. By chance, she comes across a newspaper article about the author of *A History of the Colonial Government in Manila*, and immediately realizes that Takayama is alive in London. She writes him a letter which is brought to her lover by Kyuzo, who reports that Okiyo is desperately ill in Bayonne. Noticing that Bayonne is close to the Spanish border, Takayama is at first hesitant, but eventually sets off in Kyuzo's company from Charing Cross Road. On the night train from Paris, Kyuzo slips the hero a sedative, so that he only wakes up when the train is a few miles from the border, and realizes that he has been tricked. Fortunately, the train has a terrible accident so he is able again to escape. A few days later, Okiyo reads about the disaster in a Madrid newspaper, which also reports that the police had been lying in wait for Takayama in San Sebastian. Takayama's body has not been found, but he must be dead, like all the other passengers in his carriage. With the help of a sympathetic servant, she flees from her confinement and ends up in Paris, where by chance she runs into a fully recovered Takayama. They leave for London at once.

In the Japanese section of the British Museum, they spot Takigawa's missing sword, and learning who had sold it to the curator, manage to have the killer arrested. They also find an expert who can read the mysterious (Chinese) characters in an ancient family document that Takayama has inherited. It transpires that the author was the celebrated "Christian daimyo," Takayama Ukon, exiled to Manila in 1614 by Ieyasu, founder of the

Tokugawa shogunate. The text also reveals that Ukon gave two magnificent swords to a faithful vassal called . . . Takigawa!

Soon after this happy discovery, the young Filipino patriot learns that a huge insurrection has broken out back home. He decides to return to the Philippines accompanied by his best (Filipino) friend, Matsuki, who enlists forty "real" Japanese *soshi* to fight for the cause.[108] Takayama succeeds in expelling the Spanish, and is elected Governor-General. On taking office he proposes to the Filipino people that their country become a protectorate of Japan. With full popular support, he writes to the Emperor Meiji, asking him to get the Diet to accept the plan. The novel ends with Madrid acknowledging the Philippines as a Japanese protectorate.

In the preface to this novel, Suehiro wrote that it was based on a story he had heard from an unnamed Philippine gentleman whom he had met in the West some years previously. But in two essays concerning his travels in the United States and Europe he gave the name of this "gentleman" as Rizal. Indeed, if there were no other indications, Antonio de Morga and *daimyo* Takayama Ukon were virtual contemporaries, and young Takayama's discovery of his personal ancestry and Rizal's hunt for his nation's origins perfectly coincide—in the British Museum!

It is worth remarking that the two novels wired together in *Oonabara* were written before the Sino-Japanese war that opened the era of Japanese imperialist expansion, and also before the insurrections of Martí and Bonifacio. Quite likely Rizal had told Suehiro of his immediate personal plans, and of his compatriots' eagerness to throw off the Spanish yoke. The sympathies of the former political prisoner were visibly engaged. If he wished to show his readers that Filipino patriots had blood connections to early Japanese victims of persecution, and that they thought about securing the disinterested help of Japanese volunteers and the protection of the Japanese state, he was trying to make his private sympathies broadly popular.[109] It was just what Blumentritt was doing in Austro-Hungary, one might say.

In any case, true to his lights, Suehiro returned from his travels to enter the political arena. He was elected to the Diet as a (genuine) liberal democrat, and even served briefly as its Speaker. Alas, he died of cancer just a few months before his Filipino friend's execution.[110]

---

108. Though the term *soshi* in the twentieth century acquired the negative connotation of "political bully," Suehiro used it in the older, more positive, sense of "defender of people's rights." See the discussion in Appendix VII of Saniel's *Japan and the Philippines*.

109. As we have seen, the Katipunan would, two years later, seek just such Japanese assistance.

110. Lanuza and Zaide, *Rizal in Japan*, chapter VII.

Takayama, the Filipino hero of Suehiro's political novel Oonabara, *asleep in his student digs. His story was partly based on Rizal's life and experiences.*

CHINESE CONNECTIONS

In his second letter to Aguinaldo, dated June 8, 1899, Ponce wrote:

> Malaki po ang tulong na ibinigay sa akin ng mga reformistang inchik, at si Dr Sun Yat-sen na siyang nangungulo sa kanila ang siya ko pong kasama at kagawad sa lahat.

> The Chinese reformists have given me a great deal of help, and Dr Sun Yat-sen, their leader, has been my companion and helper in everything.[111]

Two years younger than Ponce, Sun had been leading an adventurous, but as yet not very successful life. Leaving China in 1894, he had gone to Hawaii where he founded the Hsing Chung Hui (Revive China Society); he then moved its headquarters to Hong Kong early in 1895. That October, in alliance with various local secret societies, he launched a disastrous uprising in Canton. Hong Kong was now too hot for him, and he left for Europe. The following year he became internationally famous when agents of the Ch'ing

---

111. Ponce, *Cartas*, pp. 353–4.

regime attempted to kidnap him in London. Thereafter he spent most of his time in Japan, propagandizing and organizing among the large community of Chinese students, political exiles, and businessmen.

Ponce met Sun for the first time in early March 1899, when the Filipino-American War had just begun and the Filipinos were still holding their own. Sun was brought to Ponce's home in Yokohama by Hirata Hyobei, a Tokyo lawyer and political fixer who had earlier helped José Ramos become a naturalized Japanese citizen.[112] The two young nationalists (thirty-five and thirty-three years old), chatting in English, hit it off at once, and eventually became lifelong friends.[113] It is notable that Ponce, perhaps of partial Chinese descent, and in any case quite familiar with Chinese from his student days in Manila, found nothing in the least strange or exotic about his new comrade. Barely four months later, Sun made possible the only large shipment of arms that came close to being successful. He brokered a deal by which Wan Chi, a rich friend of his, joined hands with Nakamura Yaroku, a sympathetic Japanese nationalist, to buy a ship, which was then rented to the Filipino revolutionaries. Loaded at Nagasaki, the *Nunobiki Maru* had stowed on board six million cartridges, ten thousand Murata rifles, one fixed cannon, ten field-guns, seven field-glasses, a pressing machine for gunpowder, and another for making ammunition.[114] The passengers included Japanese military men knowledgeable in gunnery, engineering, and munitions manufacture.[115] Leaving Nagasaki, the ship detoured towards China to divert suspicion, but was caught in a typhoon and sank on July 19 off the Saddle islands, a hundred miles from Shanghai.[116]

112. In a March 6 letter to Apacible in Hong Kong, Ponce wrote that Sun and Hirata were currently visiting with him. It must have at this meeting that the famous photograph of the two men was taken—Ponce in European clothes, except for some very odd shoes, and with a fine moustache; Sun in Japanese clothes, and an even finer moustache. The photo is included with the letter in *Ibid.*, pp. 292–6.

113. Ponce published a biography of Sun in 1914, and was on his way to visit when he suddenly fell ill and died in Hong Kong on May 23, 1918. See the entry for Ponce in volume 2 of *Filipinos in History*, pp. 115–16.

114. Named after their inventor Murata Tsuneyoshi, a lower samurai from Satsuma, the Murata rifle was a creative mix of up-to-date French and German models. An improved version was a decisive element in Japan's victory over imperial China in 1895. It was superseded in 1897 by Arisaka Nariakira's Mauser-based rifle. This is why plenty of obsolete Murata rifles were available on the clandestine arms market. My thanks to Tsuchiya Kenichiro for his expertise on this subject.

115. Shiraishi Takashi kindly informs me that no less than Japan's Army Chief of Staff was behind this whole undertaking, and it was at his orders that the unlucky military officers were on board. Nothing in Ponce's correspondence suggests that he was aware of this.

116. See the succinct account in Silvino V. Epistola, *Hong Kong Junta* (Quezon City: University of the Philippines Press, 1996), pp. 123–4, which is based on letters Ponce sent to Apacible on July 25 and 26 (*Cartas*, pp. 364–81). The Americans had their spies in Japan, and also maintained effective naval patrols of Philippine waters.

Why did Sun Yat-sen go to all this trouble on the Philippines' behalf? Quite aside from the real friendship between the two men a revolution had been developing in the thinking of Chinese intellectuals, which has been splendidly described by Rebecca Karl. Such intellectuals had been accustomed to seeing China as far "behind" Western Europe, the United States, and Japan. But from about 1895 on, the telegraph was bringing to the local newspapers accounts and photographs of the Cuban insurrection (1895–98), the Philippine Revolution and war against American imperialism (1896–1902), and the Boers' armed struggle against the advancing British empire (1899–1902). On three continents, so to speak, small peoples previously ignored or despised by educated Chinese were showing themselves, thanks to their unity and courage, well "in advance of" China. Karl convincingly shows that as a result of following the close-by Filipino insurrection parts of the intelligentsia now started to view their struggle against the Manchus as anticolonial, and to visualize "revolution" for the first time.[117] Ponce, a humble man, was perhaps surprised that after the Japanese version of his book came out it was immediately published in Chinese and quickly went through several printings. But he should not have been.

PAWA: INTERNATIONALIZING THE WAR

In a letter to "Ifortel" of February 19, 1898, from Hong Kong, Ponce reported the arrival within Aguinaldo's entourage of three exceptional contributors to the armed revolution. Two were well-known *ilustrado* nationalists, Miguel Malvar and Del Pilar's nephew Gregorio Del Pilar. But the third was absolutely not. Ponce described him admiringly as "el coronel Pawa, un chino sin coleta, más valiente que el Cid y muy entusiasta" (Colonel Pawa, a Chinese without a pigtail, braver than The Cid, and very ardent).[118] José Ignacio Pawa was born in an impoverished Fujian village in 1872, with the name Liu Heng-fu.[119] At the age of eighteen he emigrated with his uncle to Manila, and became a skilled blacksmith, while taking up Chinese martial arts as a sideline. He was an early and enthusiastic recruit to the Revolution, and became a great favorite with Aguinaldo. While the general was still fighting in Cavite, the twenty-four-year-old immigrant recruited a number of his Chinese

117. See Rebecca Karl, *Staging the World* (Durham, N.C.: Duke University Press, 2002), especially chapter 4, "Recognizing Colonialism: The Philippines and Revolution."

118. Ponce, *Cartas*, pp. 190–91.

119. This name was kindly given to me by Carol Hau, reporting on recent research by scholars in China. The account of Pawa that follows is largely based on Teresita Ang See's article "The Ethnic Chinese in the Filipino-American War and After," *Kasaysayan*, 1:4 (December 2001), pp. 83–92.

*José Ignacio Pawa – "a dashing officer with a
colonel's uniform, but with a pigtail."*

blacksmith friends to set up an arms factory for the badly under-armed
Filipino troops. Teresita Ang See describes his activity like this:

> Under his skillful supervision, old cannon and broken Mausers captured from the
> enemy were repaired, large bamboo cannon taped with wires were manufactured,
> numerous *paltik* [crude firearms] were made, and thousands of cartridges were
> filled up with home-made gunpowder.

Pawa also trained Filipinos how to melt down metal objects, especially
church bells (!), to create weapons, and proved himself a very resourceful and
brave battlefield commander. See quotes the Filipino lawyer Teodoro
Gonzalez's unpublished memoirs as follows: "It was a strange sight in camp
to see him—a dashing officer with a colonel's uniform but having a pigtail.
His soldiers were Tagalogs, all veteran fighters, yet they were devoted to him,
and were proud to serve under his battle standard, notwithstanding the fact
that he was a Chinaman."[120] Finally, sent by Aguinaldo to Bicol to raise

120. If this description is accurate, Pawa must have cut off his pigtail on arrival
in Hongkong, where Aguinaldo needed him as an interpreter. (He probably spoke
only Hokkienese, perhaps a little Cantonese, and Tagalog, which made the caudillo
feel very comfortable with him.)

money for the Revolution among the local Chinese and Chinese mestizos, he managed to raise the staggering sum of 386,000 silver pesos.

Remarkable as Pawa was as a person, he was only one among many non-Filipinos who, for various reasons, joined or supported the Revolution. Immigrant Chinese, ghettoized, despised and often abused by the colonial regime, had plenty of reasons to want the Spaniards gone. And after the American conquest of Cuba, substantial numbers of young Spanish officers decided to "fight on" by joining Aguinaldo's forces. Antonio Luna, as Chief of Staff, happily took advantage of their professional training to put them to work as personal aides, instructors, and creators of fortifications. Quite a number served well as battlefield commanders when the Philippine-American War broke out. There were also a few Cubans in the Spanish military who joined the revolutionary cause, alongside Frenchmen, Italians (including a captain who later joined the Boer War on Kruger's side), a few Britons, quite a number of Japanese, and even deserters from the American forces, mainly blacks.[121]

MALATESTA TO MANILA

Meanwhile in Madrid, Isabelo de los Reyes had managed to put together the funds to start publishing a fortnightly that he named *Filipinas ante Europa*, with the impeccable editorial logo: "Contra Norte-América, no; contra el imperialismo, sí, hasta la muerte."[122] What Del Pilar had once maliciously called the folklorist's "deplorable fecundity" came in handy, as most of the contents had to come from his pen.[123] The loss of empire, and the humiliations inflicted by Washington, brought about a substantial change in public opinion in Spain. Anger at the Americans created a new sympathy for the Filipino cause. The change suited Isabelo's book, since he had plenty of Spanish friends, had just married a Spanish journalist, and had always attributed the evils of colonial rule mainly to the malign power of the Orders. Hence the aim of his fortnightly was to strengthen this convergence by blistering attacks on American imperialism and what he charmingly called *la codicia* (greed) underlying it. McKinley was a favorite target on account of his Tartuffian claims that the conquest was designed to bring liberty to the

---

121. This paragraph is a regrettable condensation of the splendidly detailed material in Dery, "When the World Loved the Filipinos" (see Chapter 3, n. 43).

122. *Filipinas ante Europa* ran for thirty-six issues between October 25, 1899 and June 10, 1901. After closing, probably because of trouble with the Madrid police, it reappeared as *El Defensor de Filipinas*, a monthly which ran from July 1 to October 1, 1901.

123. See Scott, *The Unión Obrera Democrática*, p. 13, citing the *Epistolario de Marcelo H. del Pilar* (Manila: República de Filipinas, Dept. de Educación, Oficina de Bibliotecas Públicas, 1955), vol. 1, p. 20.

Filipinos.[124] Isabelo regularly attacked the United States for its racism and lynch law, rightly saying that this was bound to affect how the Filipinos, as non-whites, would be treated.[125] Yet he also went out of his way to feature excited reports about the campaigns of the American anti-imperialists. Isabelo's other main target was what he regarded as the treachery of those wealthy *ilustrados* who, having supplanted Mabini in the Revolution's leadership, were the first to jump ship and grovel to the new colonial masters.[126] Mabini was constantly held up as a shining example of steadfast patriotic refusal to buckle to the *yankís*. The folklorist did not forget to underline that Cuban "independence" was turning out to be a complete sham. In the middle of this he still found space for an article on how much the Boers had learned from the Filipino guerrilla fighters, and now how much the Filipinos could learn from the sober discipline of the Boers.[127]

But by the summer of 1901, with Aguinaldo's capture and quick swearing of allegiance to Washington, the Revolution was over. Those prominent men who refused to swear—including the crippled Mabini—were packed off to the new tropical Siberia: Guam.[128] Isabelo saw no point in staying in Spain

124. Characteristic is the headline "Mac-Kinley, embustero ó criminal? [McKinley, Liar or Criminal?]," *Filipinas ante Europa*, March 10, 1900.

125. "Negro Porvenir de los filipinos bajo la dominación imperialista [Black Future for Filipinos under Imperialist Domination]," *ibid.*, November (exact date not given), 1899. "A los negros, les cazan como á fieras en las calles, si tienen la desgracia de enamorarse de una blanca" [As for the blacks, they are hunted down on the streets like wild beasts if they have the misfortune to fall in love with a white woman].

126. Alas, this group included Pardo de Tavera, who returned to the Philippines to become a member of the Republic's legislature. Later he justified going over to the Americans on the grounds that caudillism was already rampant, and the Philippines would suffer the fate of South America if it got its independence prematurely. Alas, too, the elderly Basa and Regidor also moved into the American column. Isabelo regularly called these people "Judases." A good example of the ferocity of his rhetoric is "Contra la traición [Against Treason]," *ibid.*, February 10, 1900.

127. "Organización del ejército boer [The Organization of the Boer Army]," *ibid.*, September 10, 1900.

128. Mabini was captured on December 10, 1899, and imprisoned in Manila. From jail he wrote his most powerful articles against American policy, some so fierce that the press refused to publish them. On June 21, 1900 a general amnesty was announced for political prisoners provided they took the oath of allegiance to the new colonial government. But Mabini still refused to do so. On October 3, he was briefly released, but continued his attacks on Filipino collaborators and the American regime's policies. On January 15, 1901, the man described by future Governor-General William Howard Taft as "the most prominent irreconcilable among the Filipinos" was put on a ship which left for Guam the following day, along with about sixty others, including nationalist militants—and their personal servants (Mabini had none). On July 4, 1902, President Roosevelt issued a further amnesty, which was sent to Guam; all but Mabini and one other man accepted its terms and sailed home. Finally, on February 9, 1903 Mabini was informed that he was no longer a prisoner of war, and could go freely anywhere he wished, but that   *cont'd over/*

The Boers: subject of an article by Isabelo, who stressed the mutual benefit that both Filipino guerrillas and Boers derived from studying each other's methods.

any longer. He had not seen his six children by his first wife in four years. Like Rizal in 1892, he would go back to face the colonialists, politely telling them that he was coming, and see what he could politically achieve, more or less within the law.[129]

Isabelo set sail for Manila in early October 1901.[130] In his bags he had

---

128 *cont'd*   he would not be allowed back to the Philippines without swearing the oath of allegiance. Feeling he now had no alternative, he agreed to do so on arrival in Manila. He died of cholera three months later, on May 13. His funeral was the largest mass gathering of Filipinos in the capital seen in many years. See the last chapter of Majul's *Mabini.*

129. In "A mi casa [Going Home]," in the final, October 1, 1901 issue of *El Defensor de Filipinas*, he gave a persuasive and modest account of his reasons.

130. The following section on what Isabelo did on his return to the Philippines is largely drawn from Scott's excellent book. Almost the last person Isabelo visited before going home was (the still controversial) Francisco Ferrer Guardia. Ferrer, born in 1859 to a well-off conservative Catalan family, left home at the age of fourteen to escape a "stifling religious atmosphere," and eventually made his way to Paris where he worked for a long time as the secretary of the veteran republican conspirator Zorrilla. After sixteen years in France, where he became a convinced   *cont'd over/*

packed a small idiosyncratic library: Aquinas and Voltaire, Proudhon and the Bible, Darwin and Marx, Kropotkin and Malatesta. There is every reason to believe that these were the first texts of Marx and the leading anarchist thinkers, perhaps even of Darwin, to enter the Philippines. Isabelo's reputation as a staunch adversary of American imperialism had preceded him. The *Manila Times*, mouthpiece of the swelling population of American business vultures, immediately denounced him as a dangerous agitator and bloody anarchist. Not by chance: the previous month President McKinley had been shot to death in Buffalo by the 28-year-old Polish-American anarchist blacksmith Leon Czolgosz. The new colonial regime immediately banned Isabelo's

---

130 cont'd anarchist, Ferrer returned to Barcelona in 1901 and started the influential anarchist publication *La Huelga General*, made possible, it is said, by a million-franc legacy from a Frenchwoman who had been his pupil. He also founded a model laicist and progressive Escuela Moderna, which interested Isabelo very much. Later Ferrer was tried, but acquitted, for supposedly masterminding two failed assassination attempts on Alfonso XIII (May 31, 1905 in Paris; May 31, 1906 in Madrid). In July 1909, in response to massive and unruly protests in Barcelona over the dispatch of Spanish troops to Morocco, the conservative government of Antonio Maura declared martial law in the city, closed all leftwing clubs and progressive, non-religious schools, and banned the anarchist and republican groups. Ferrer was again arrested, and this time convicted of sedition by a military court. He was executed on October 13. The Maura regime fell twelve days later. J. Romero Maura, "Terrorism in Barcelona," pp. 141–2, and 182–3; and Núñez, *El terrorismo*, p. 66. Núñez adds a disquieting note on Ferrer's end before a firing squad. On November 12, 1909, a month after the execution, Unamuno wrote to his friend González Trilla: "En efecto, querido amigo, ha sido España, la legítima España, la española, quien ha fusilado á Ferrer. Y ha hecho muy bien en fusilarle. Ferrer era un imbécil y un malvado, y no un inquietador. Sus escuelas, un horror. Pedagógicamente detestables. Su enseñanza, de un vacuidad y una mala fé notorias. Sus libros de lectura horrorizan por lo estúpido. Ferrer, una vez condenado por el Tribunal, no por instigador, sino por partícipe en los incendios, no debió ser indultado. Se trataba de la independencia espiritual de España, de que el gobierno no podía sucumbir á la presión de la 'golfería europa'—anarquistas, masones, judíos, científicos, y majaderos—que pretendía imponérsele y que 'antes del juicio' estaba ya pretendiendo trocarlo. Habían declarado 'a priori' inocente á Ferrer." [In effect, my dear friend, it has been Spain, legitimate Spain, Spanishness, which has shot Ferrer. And by shooting him has acted very well. Ferrer was an imbecile and a malefactor, not an awakener of consciences. His school, a horror. Detestable pedagogically. His teaching (was) of a frightening vacuity and bad faith. His texts make one's hair stand on end by their stupidity. Once sentenced by the Tribunal, not for being an instigator but for personal participation in arson, he did not deserve any indulgence. It was a question of Spain's spiritual independence, and of the government being obliged not to succumb to the pressure of the "European wave" (of indignation)—anarchists, freemasons, Jews, scientists and idiots—who had the presumption to impose their will and even before the sentence claimed the right to change it. They declared Ferrer innocent *a priori*.] Unamuno is said later to have regretted this Daily Telegraphese (Núñez, p. 150).

planned newspaper, *El Defensor de Filipinas*, and prohibited his proposed Partido Nacionalista.

But he was a man not easily put down. In old age he recalled that he "took advantage of the occasion to put into practice the good ideas I had learned from the anarchists of Barcelona, who were imprisoned with me in the infamous fortress of Montjuich." So he set himself, under the noses of the Protestant conquistadors, to radicalize and organize the working class in Manila. In this endeavor he had some perhaps unsuspected advantages. He had always been a partial outsider for the *ilustrado* nationalist intelligentsia, which was overwhelmingly Tagalog: not exactly aristocratic, since there had never been an indigenous feudal state in the Philippines, but with aspirations (above all the landowners among them) in that direction—especially in the face of a Spanish imperialism which both had strong feudal roots and continued to fancy itself in feudal fancy dress even when the reality was bare-faced corruption, shady caciquism, and Orderly landlordism. Isabelo was just the opposite: an honest businessman, publisher, printer, and journalist, who had employees rather than servants, and treated them in a democratic spirit. Better still, he was, as we have seen, an upcountry man from northern Luzon, the home of the Ilocanos, an ethnic group legendary for its thrift, hard work, plain speaking—and clannishness. (Ilocos is still the one area of the Philippines, aside from the mountain slopes south of Rizal's Calamba, where one sees every poor peasant home surrounded by a tiny, beautifully tended garden of flowers and flowering shrubs.) He was not the only Ilocano in the nationalist elite, but he was the only *provinciano* among them. The Luna brothers were also Ilocanos—Juan the painter, who in a jealous fit murdered his wife and mother-in-law, escaped heavy punishment in a Paris solicitous of *crimes passionelles*, especially by artists, and died miserably in Hong Kong; and Antonio, trained as a chemist, who became the most brilliant general in the war against the Americans, and was assassinated for his pains by Aguinaldo's clique. But both were Manila-bred, and assimilated themselves to elite Hispano-Tagalog culture.

The crucial thing was this: as Rizal had rather disdainfully put it to Blumentritt, the *Dienstleute* of late-nineteenth-century Manila were overwhelmingly industrious immigrants from hardscrabble Ilocos. The incipient working class were too, though one would never guess this from reading *Noli me tangere* and *El Filibusterismo*. Isabelo could talk to these people in their own language, which, in those days, virtually no educated Tagalog knew. (Did Rizal ever meet a Filipino urban worker and talk to him or her? No worker appears in his novels.) Isabelo was also perfectly familiar with their sturdy culture of the street and the *barrio*.

In classical fashion Isabelo first organized the printers. But his success with organized strikes encouraged other sectors to follow suit and the union became quite quickly a Barcelona-style free-wheeling central—a Unión Obrera Democrática that would have delighted the Tarrida of *anarquismo sin adjetivos*. The American rulers watched with disbelief and alarm a huge wave of strikes in Manila and its surroundings, many of them successful because they were unexpected by capitalists and administrators alike.[131] The Americans were also befuddled by some of Isabelo's methods. Street demonstrations he had learned in his revolver-waving days in Lerroux's Barcelona. But when he raised money for the strikers and his organization by holding a series of popular balls combined with lectures, and staging zarzuelas and other theatricals with themes hostile to the Americans and their elite Filipino collaborators, he was shrewdly tapping the Filipino passion for fiestas, dancing, theatre, and music.[132] The rulers eventually found various ways to bar Isabelo from the labor scene. In late June 1902 he was arrested and tried for "labor conspiracy," but he was sentenced to only four months in prison when it became clear even to the judge that many prosecution witnesses had been suborned. Before going to jail he threw a huge party at a newly formed workers' club in the working-class neighborhood of Tondo, and resigned his leadership. He was succeeded first by Dominador Gómez, a fellow returnee from Spain, active in the circle of *La Solidaridad*, and Isabelo's collaborator on *Filipinas ante Europa*, who soon lived up to his authoritarian name;[133] and eventually by his secretary, Hermenegildo Cruz, a slum boy still illiterate at the age of twelve, who became an admirable *obrero consciente* from his reading in Isabelo's little library. Aside from his organizing activities, Cruz would publish detailed notes on the Spanish translation of Élisée Reclus's anarchist *L'Homme et la terre*, as well as a Tagalog translation of parts of *La Ilustración obrera* by Pablo Iglesias, the old founder of Spain's Marxist Socialist Party. Isabelo, meanwhile, was getting alarmed by the possibility that the Americans would return to the Orders the estates which the Revolution had confiscated. So he turned to agitating against the Catholic lobby, and busying himself with the organization of the "schismatic" nationalist Aglipayan Church, formed by a fellow Ilocano, the revolutionary priest Gregorio Aglipay, in the time of the

131. See the chapter "The Strikes" (pp. 35–41) in Scott's *The Unión Obrera Democrática*.

132. Isabelo called these events, straight-faced, *veladas instructivo-recreativas*—perhaps "pedagogico-recreational soirées."

133. Gómez was also one of the very few Filipinos to go to Cuba. A former medical student in Madrid, he served, as Rizal was supposed to do, with the Medical Corps of the Spanish military forces there. Schumacher, *The Propaganda Movement*, p. 190, n. 12.

First Republic.[134] The UOD collapsed in 1903, but out of its ashes came many other labor organizations, and eventually a Socialist and a Communist party which merged in 1938, led the Hukbalahap guerrilla movement against the Japanese military invaders, and ultimately carried on a revolutionary war against the American-arranged Second Republic inaugurated on—when else?—July 4, 1946.

In 1912, perhaps as a way of distracting himself from the grief caused by the death of his second wife, Isabelo turned to the electoral arena, and ran successfully for membership of a Manila Municipal Council controlled by appointed Americans.[135] Serving in this capacity he was a consistent champion of the city's poor. In 1922 he returned to Ilocos to run as an independent for a seat in the Senate. Insisting, as he always did, in the manner of his old anarchist friends, that he was both an individualist and a collectivist, he was elected, to his own surprise, against the well-heeled machine of the dominant, cacique-ridden Nacionalista Party of Manuel Quezon. He appalled his fellow senators by coming to the assembly's session in a horse-drawn *calesa*, saying it was better to give money to a coachman than to throw it away on a car and its gasoline which would only benefit American business. At the same time, he insisted on living for the rest of his life in working-class Tondo, erecting an apartment building for poor tenants who were never evicted for being in arrears. After 1929, when he was partly paralyzed by a stroke, he confined himself to work for the Aglipayan Church. He died on October 10, 1938.

AFTERGLOW WEST: ISABELO DE LOS REYES

Isabelo had on occasion been treated disdainfully by Rizal, who disliked his Ilocano patriotism and thought he wrote too much, too fast, for any depth, but the folklorist was not the type to brood over slights and for the most part he greatly admired what Rizal had achieved. *Filipinas ante Europa* often ran articles about Rizal as the exemplary patriot, even if they rarely mentioned the novels. But appearances can always be deceiving. Already in 1899 the first

---

134. Aglipay was enraged by the Vatican's unconditional support for Spanish colonial rule, and the local (Peninsular) hierarchy's ferocious hostility to the revolutionary movement. His efforts were supported by Apolinario Mabini, who wanted to break Rome's hold over the more traditional sector of the indigenous population. If one goes to Sarrat in northern Ilocos, the site of the uprising of 1815, one will find as neighbors a Spanish-style Catholic church and its Aglipayan competition. In the first the crucified Counter-Reformation Christ is in blood-stained torment and clothed only in a tattered grayish loincloth. In the second, He is serenely bearing His suffering, has a svelte, mostly unbloodied body, and wears an elegant, embroidered, sky-blue satin pair of drawers. Perhaps this was Isabelo's cheerful doing.

135. This paragraph is drawn from Llanes's *The Life*, pp. 22–32.

translation of *Noli me tangere* into a non-Spanish language was published—in Paris (which must have delighted the martyr's shade).[136] It is very unlikely that Isabelo had no hand in this, since one of the two joint translators was his long-time Montjuich cellmate, Ramón Sempau, while the other was a Frenchman, Henri Lucas, who was also probably an anarchist. Under the slightly depressing title *Au Pays des Moines*, this translation was advertised in *La Revue Blanche* as volume no. 25 in the Bibliothèque Sociologique of Pierre-Victor Stock—who inherited a publishing company dating back to 1708, but between 1892 and 1921 issued a long line of anarchist titles under this rubric. The catalogue is riveting. No. 1 (1892) was Kropotkin's *La Conquête du pain*; it was followed by Jean Grave's *La Société mourante et l'anarchie* (1894), the French anarchist Charles Malato's *De la Commune á l'anarchie* (1895), Bakunin's *Oeuvres*, vol. 1 (1895), Grave's *La Société future* (1895), Kropotkin's *L'Anarchie: sa philosophie, son idéal* (1896), Georges Darien's *Biribi: armée d'Afrique* (1898), the Dutchman Ferdinand Domela Nieuwenhuis's *Le Socialisme en danger* (1897), Tarrida's *Les Inquisiteurs d'Espagne: Montjuich, Cuba, Philippines* (1897), Élisée Reclus's *L'Évolution, la révolution et l'idéal anarchique* (1897), and Louise Michel's *La Commune* (n.d.). Then Rizal's novel, wholly innocent of anarchism, appears sandwiched between the Italian historian Guglielmo Ferrero's *Le militerisme et la société moderne* (1899) and Charles Albert's *L'Amour libre* (1898).

Should we be surprised that the at least *anarchisant El Filibusterismo* did not follow? Probably not. As Jovita Castro points out, the Lucas–Sempau *Noli me tangere* was by no means a faithful translation. The narrator's seductively *narquois* asides to the reader were all eliminated, as well as references to Filipino folk tales and legends, and anything remotely erotic. The vitriolic attacks on the Orders were also, for reasons that are not clear, toned down.[137] The effect was to turn the novel into a flatly *sociologique* description of "a" colonial society. If *Noli me tangere* had to suffer this surely well-meaning bowdlerization, we can guess that its inflammatory sequel would have been hard to swallow now that anarchism (hand in hand with syndicalism) had, in France anyway, left the age of propaganda by the deed behind it.

---

136. The edition I have had access to was printed in 1899, but the front matter indicates that this was already the third printing, so that an original publication late in 1898 is just possible.

137. See Jovita Castro's introduction to her translation, *N'y touchez pas!* at pp. 31–5.

AFTERGLOW EAST: MARIANO PONCE

There are hundreds of statues of Rizal decorating the plazas of Philippine towns, crowned by an impressive monument erected in the American time—but not from an American initiative—on the spot where he was executed. In Spain and in Spanish America, it is common to find streets named after him. In the United States, however, there is little more than small statues in out-of-the-way places in San Francisco and Seattle and a larger one in Chicago. Perhaps this ignorance and indifference can be read as the world-hegemon's unconscious response to the novelist's own indifference to, and ignorance of, God's country.[138]

However, there is now a large, recently built, Rizal theme park in Amoy, financed mainly by wealthy Hokkien Chinese-Filipinos, whose ancestors sailed to Manila from that port. Commercial motives aside, there is something else here that is rather interesting, even touching, especially if we realize that there have been almost forty Chinese translations of Rizal's final poem, most of them the work of Hokkienese.

Yet probably the very first was done by none other than than Liang Ch'i-ch'ao, as early as 1901. It comes as a mild shock to realize that Liang was twelve years younger than Rizal, and only twenty-three when the Filipino was executed. Like Rizal a brilliant youngster, his wide-ranging critical articles on the state of China, revealed by its crushing defeat at the hands of the Japanese, led him to become one of the key figures in the famous "100 Days of Reform" in 1898. But when the Dowager Empress Tz'ü Hsi struck back, Liang, like many other liberals and progressives, had to flee for his life—to Japan. How he came to translate Rizal's poem is a question that cannot yet be answered conclusively. But a few things are certain. Liang was Cantonese, not Hokkienese, and moreover had lived in Peking since his late teens. It is very unlikely therefore that Amoy played any role in his writing. From the newspapers about which Rebecca Karl writes so informatively, he would have known about Rizal's death, but newspapers do not usually publish long poems, still less those in a language that very few readers understand.

---

138. One can have fun considering Rizal's brief diary of his trip across the United States in the late spring of 1888. After more than a week in quarantine in San Francisco Bay, he spent three days as a tourist in the city, then took the boat to the transcontinental railhead in Oakland. The next day, Monday May 7, he set off, passing through Sacramento and Mormon Salt Lake City, to Denver (May 9). The train reached Chicago on the early morning of the 11th, and left for New York that evening. Rizal's only comment on Chicago was that "every tobacco-shop has in front of it a statue of an *indio* [sic], each one different." He reached Manhattan on May 13, and boarded a ship for Europe on the 16th. He had nothing at all to say about the home of the Statue of Liberty. See his *Diarios y Memorias*, pp. 217–20.

The circumstantial evidence looks like this. Ponce was a close friend of Rizal, and deeply committed to his memory. On October 13, 1898, he wrote to Dr Eduard Soler (presumably bilingual in Spanish and German) in Berlin, thanking him for the German translation of Rizal's last poem and its publication in the bulletin of the Anthropologische Gesellschaft of which Rizal had been a member.[139] On February 28, 1899, Ponce wrote to Apacible about plans to reprint Rizal's works in Japan, mentioning that the cheapest printer was Shueisha, and noting that if the manuscripts were used rather than existing editions, it would involve extra work and cost more.[140] We also know that as early as November 1898, well before he met Sun Yat-sen, Ponce was in touch with Chinese "reformists." In a letter of November 19, 1898 he wrote to Apacible that the previous evening he had met "Lung Tai-kwang," self-described as the personal secretary of K'ang Yu-wei, leader of China's *partido reformista*, who arrived in Japan on May 25, and was planning a revolution to restore the "Kwan Han" (that is, Kuang Hsü) emperor to the throne.[141] "Lung Tai-kwang" must have been Hokkienese, since Ponce observed that the man knew Pawa personally. Finally, as evidence of Ponce's literary inclinations, on the whole rather rare among the *ilustrados* in Spain, there are three successively more irritated letters to Vergel de Dios, asking again and again for a copy of *Paris*, Zola's latest novel.[142] Furthermore, Ponce insisted on including the original Spanish text of Rizal's last poem in the Japanese version of his book on the Philippine Question. One curious feature of this version is that while the main text is written in the usual mixture of Chinese (*kanji*) and Japanese (*hiragana*) scripts, the introduction is composed in pure classical Chinese. In turn this suggests that, since one or both of the translators were fluent in classical Chinese, the pair were also responsible for the Chinese translation, which came out almost simultaneously. Should this conjecture prove correct, then Liang Ch'i-ch'ao's version was either cribbed directly from Miyamoto and Fujita, or, more likely, was a more elegant adaptation of their "Chinese" translation. The nagging partial problem is that though Liang and Ponce were certainly together in Japan, the latter seems totally unaware of this, and never mentions the former by name in his correspondence.

In November and December 1901, perhaps prodded by Liang but more

---

139. Ponce, *Cartas*, pp. 210–11. Ponce adds that he had heard about the translation from Blumentritt, who was surely behind the endeavor.

140. *Ibid.*, pp. 288–9. This may indicate that Ponce had the manuscripts in his possession or knew where he could lay hands on them. The books were to be in Spanish rather than Japanese.

141. *Ibid.*, pp. 223–5.

142. *Ibid.*, pp. 162–4; 232–5, 244–5.

likely by the newspapers, Ma Hsün-wu published a five-part series called "Fei-lu-pin Min-tang Ch'i-yi Chi" (The Uprising in the Philippines) in the *Hangch'ou Vernacular Newspaper*, following up in 1903 with a biography of Rizal in Liang Ch'i-ch'ao's influential magazine *Hsin-min Ts'ung-pao*, published in Japan. These articles may explain Lu Hsün's later references to *Mi último adiós* and *Noli me tangere*, his linking of Rizal with Sándor Petöfi and Adam Mickiewicz as great poet-patriots, and a new translation of Rizal's farewell poem by a student of Lu Hsün's, Li Chi-yeh, in the 1920s.[143] A generation later, during the 1940s, an avatar of Pawa, K'ai Chung-mei, fought in the Hua Ch'ih guerrilla units allied with the native Filipino left-wing Hukbalahap against the Japanese occupiers. In old age, returned to China, and using the *nom de plume* Tu Ai, he undertook a three-volume novelization of his wartime experiences. In the course of *Feng-yü T'ai-p'ing-yen* (Storm over the Pacific), Rizal's farewell poem is quoted in full or in substantial chunks at least four times, while references to the First Filipino and Josephine Bracken—as a woman warrior—litter the pages.[144] This all seems a little ironic in that Rizal, though partly of Hokkien descent, was not above—sometimes—a certain mild racism with regard to the Chinese. (But a long way from the virulence of Petöfi's venom against the ethnic minorities in "Hungary.")

Isabelo de los Reyes and Mariano Ponce: good men now mostly forgotten even in the Philippines, but crucial nodes in the infinitely complex intercontinental networks that characterize the Age of Early Globalization.

---

143. For these notes on Rizal's early reception in China, I would like to thank Wang Hui.

144. The first volume was published in Canton in 1983, and the second in Peking in 1991, the year before he died. A complete set of the three volumes, supervised by his widow, appeared only in 2002, in Chuhai. My thanks to Carol Hau for this plangent information.

Postscript

In January 2004, I was invited to give a preliminary lecture on some of the themes of this book by the famously radical-nationalist University of the Philippines, where the influence of (Ilocano) José María Sison's Maoist "new" Communist Party, founded at the end of 1968, remains quite strong. Arriving much too early, I filled in time at an open-air campus coffee-stall. A youngster came by to hand out leaflets to the customers, all of whom casually scrunched them up and threw them away once he had left. I was about to do the same when my eye caught the title of the one-page text. "Organize Without Leaders!" The content proved to be an attack on the hierarchies of the country—boss-ridden party-political, corporate capitalist, and also Maoist Communist—in the name of "horizontal" organized solidarity. The leaflet was unsigned, but a website was appended for further enquiries. This was a serendipity too good to keep to myself. I read it out loud to my audience, and was surprised that almost everyone seemed taken aback. But when I had finished speaking, many hurried up to ask for copies. I cannot be sure if Rizal would have been pleased by the theme park in Amoy, but I feel certain that Isabelo would have been enchanted by the leaflet and rushed to his laptop to explore the website *manila.indymedia.org*. He would have found that this website is linked to dozens of others of similar stripe around the world. Late Globalization?

Bibliography

Adam, Jad. "Striking a Blow for Freedom," *History Today*, 53:9 (September 2003), pp. 18–19

Agoncillo, Teodoro. *A Short History of the Philippines* (New York: Mentor, 1969)
—— *The Revolt of the Masses* (Quezon City: The University of the Philippines Press, 1956)

Akihisa, Matsuno. "Nihon no okeru Malay go no kaishi to tenkai." In Kondo Tatsuo, ed., *Wagakunini okeru gaikokugo kenkyu/kyoiku no shiteki kosatsu* (Osaka: Gaikokugo Gakko, 1990)

Anderson, Benedict R. O'G. "Forms of Consciousness in *Noli me tangere*," *Philippine Studies*, 51:4 (2000), pp. 505–29
—— *Imagined Communities* (London: Verso, 1991)
—— *The Spectre of Comparisons* (London: Verso, 1998)

Avrich, Paul. *An American Anarchist, The Life of Voltairine de Cleyre* (Princeton: Princeton University Press, 1978)

Balucan, Celerina G. "War Atrocities," *Kasaysayan*, 1:4 (December 2001), pp. 34–54.

Baudelaire, Charles. *Oeuvres complètes* (Paris: Louis Conard, 1933), vol. 7

Bécarud, Jean and Gilles Lapouge. *Anarchistes d'Espagne* (Paris: André Balland, 1970)

Bernheimer, Charles. *Figures of Ill Repute: Representing Prostitution in Nineteenth Century France* (Cambridge, MA: Harvard University Press, 1989)

Betances, Ramón Emeterio. "La autonomía en Manila." In Haroldo Dilla and Emilio Godínez, eds, *Ramón Emeterio Betances* (Habana: Casa de las Americas, 1983)
—— *Las Antillas para los antillanos*. Ed. Carlos M. Rama (San Juan Puerto Rico: Instituto del Cultura Puertorriqueña, 1975)

Blumentritt, Ferdinand. "Una visita," *La Solidaridad*, January 13 and 31, 1893

Bonoan, SJ, Raul K. *The Rizal–Pastells Correspondence* (Quezon City: Ateneo de Manila Press, 1994)

Bory, Jean-Louis. *Eugène Sue, le roi du roman populaire* (Paris: Hachette, 1962)

Bosch, Juan, *El Napoleón de las guerrillas* (Santo Domingo: Editorial Alfa y Omega, 1982)

Casanova, Pascale. *La République mondiale des lettres* (Paris: Éditions du Seuil, 1999).

Clark, T.J. *Farewell to an Idea* (New Haven: Yale University Press, 1999)

Coates, Austin. *Rizal – Philippine Nationalist and Patriot* (Manila: Solidaridad, 1992)

Comín Colomer, Eduardo. *Historia del anarquismo español* (Barcelona: Editorial AHR, 1956)

Cook, Bradford. Trans. *Mallarmé: Selected Prose Poems, Essays and Letters* (Baltimore: The Johns Hopkins University Press, 1956)

Corpuz, Onofre. *The Roots of the Filipino Nation* (Quezon City: The Aklahi Foundation, 1989), 2 vols.

Culler, Jonathan, and Pheng Cheah, eds, *Grounds of Comparison* (New York: Routledge, 2003)

Dallas, George. *At the Heart of a Tiger. Clémenceau and his World, 1841–1929* (New York: Carroll & Graf, 1993)

Daniel, Evan. "Leaves of Change: Cuban Tobacco Workers and the Struggle against Slavery and Spanish Imperial Rule, 1880s–1890s" (unpublished paper, 2003)

De la Costa, SJ, Horacio, ed. and trans. *The Trial of Rizal: W.E. Retana's Transcription of the Official Spanish Documents* (Quezon City: Ateneo de Manila Press, 1961)

De Ocampo, Esteban. *Rizal as a Bibliophile* (Manila: The Bibliographical Society of the Philippines, Occasional Papers, No. 2, 1960)

Dery, Luis C. "When the World Loved the Filipinos: Foreign Freedom Fighters in the Filipino Army during the Filipino-American War," *Kasaysayan*, 1:4 (December 2001), pp. 55–69

Epistola, Silvino V. *Hong Kong Junta* (Quezon City: University of the Philippines Press, 1996)

Esenwein, George Richard. *Anarchist Ideology and the Working Class Movement in Spain, 1868–1898* (Berkeley: University of California Press, 1989)

Estrade, Paul. "El Heraldo de la 'Independencia Absoluta.'" In Félix Ojeda Reyes and Paul Estrade, *Pasión por la Libertad* (San Juan, P.R.: Editorial de la Universidad de Puerto Rico, 2000)

—— *Solidaridad con Cuba Libre, 1895–1898. La impresionante labor del Dr Betances en París* (San Juan, P.R.: Editorial de la Universidad de Puerto Rico, 2001)

Farwell, Byron, ed. *Encyclopedia of Nineteenth Century Land Warfare* (New York: Norton, 2001)

Fernández, Frank. *La sangre de Santa Águeda* (Miami: Ediciones Universal, 1994)

Ferrer, Ada. *Insurgent Cuba: Race, Nation and Revolution, 1868–1898* (Chapel Hill: University of North Carolina Press, 1999)

Flaubert, Gustave. *La tentation de Saint-Antoine* (Paris: A. Quentin, 1885).

Footman, David. *Red Prelude* (London: Barrie & Rockleff, 1968)

Fowlie, Wallace. *Rimbaud: A Critical Study* (Chicago: University of Chicago Press, 1965)

Gonzáles Liquete, L. *Repertorio histórico, biográfico y bibliográfico* (Manila: Impr. Del Día Filipino, 1938)

Guerrero, León María. *The First Filipino, a Biography of José Rizal* (Manila: National Historical Institute, 1987)

Hall, D.G.E. *A History of South-East Asia* (London and New York: St. Martin's Press, 1968)

Halperin, Joan Ungersma. *Félix Fénéon, Aesthete and Anarchist in Fin-de-Siècle Paris* (New Haven: Yale University Press, 1988)

Hanson, Ellis. *Decadence and Catholicism* (Cambridge, MA: Harvard University Press, 1997)

Herbert, Eugenia. *The Artist and Social Reform: France and Belgium, 1885–1898* (New Haven: Yale University Press, 1961)

Huysmans, Joris-Karl. *À rebours* (Paris: Charpentier, 1884; Fasquelles: c. 1904). Translated into English as *Against the Grain* (New York: Lieber and Lewis, 1923), and *Against Nature* (London; Penguin Classics, 1959).

Ileto, Reynaldo Clemeña. *Pasyón and Revolution: Popular Movements in the Philippines, 1840–1910* (Quezon City: Ateneo de Manila Press, 1989)

James, C.L.R. *The Black Jacobins*, rev. ed. (New York: Vintage, 1989)

Joaquín, Nick. *A Question of Heroes* (Manila: Anvil, 2005)

Joll, James. *The Anarchists* (Cambridge, MA: Harvard University Press, 1980)

Karl, Rebecca. *Staging the World* (Durham, N.C.: Duke University Press, 2002)

Lanuza, Caesar Z. and Gregorio F. Zaide, *Rizal in Japan* (Tokyo: C.Z. Lanuza, 1961)

Laqueur, Walter. *A History of Terrorism*, rev. ed. (New Brunswick, N.J.: Transaction, 2000)

Lete, Eduardo de. "Redentores de Perro Chico," *La Solidaridad*, April 15, 1892

Llanes, José L. *The Life of Senator Isabelo de los Reyes* (monograph reprinted from the Weekly Magazine of the *Manila Chronicle*, 1949)

Maitron, Jean. *Le mouvement anarchiste en France* (Paris: Maspéro, 1975), 2 vols.

Majul, Cesar Adib. *Mabini and the Philippine Revolution* (Quezon City: University of the Philippines Press, 1996)

Martín Jiménez, Hilario. *Valeriano Weyler, de su Vida y personalidad, 1838–1930* (Santa Cruz de Tenerife: Ediciones del Umbral, 1998)

May, Glenn Anthony. *Battle for Batangas: A Philippine Province at War* (New Haven: Yale University Press, 1991)

Mojares, Resil B. *Brain of the Nation: Pedro Paterno, T.H. Pardo de Tavera, Isabelo de los Reyes and the Production of Modern Knowledge* (Quezon City: Ateneo de Manila University Press, 2006)

Moret, Segismundo. "El Japón y Las Islas Filipinas," *La España Moderna*, LXXIV (February 1895)

Naimark, Norman. *Terrorists and Social Democrats: The Russian Revolutionary Movement under Alexander III* (Cambridge, MA: Harvard University Press, 1983)

National Historical Institute. *Filipinos in History* (Manila: NHI, 1990–96), 5 vols.

Nitti, Francisoc. "Italian Anarchists," *North American Review*, 167:5 (November 1898), pp. 598–607

Nuñez Florencio, Rafael. *El terrorismo anarquista, 1888–1909* (Madrid: Siglo Veinteuno de España, SA, 1983)

Ocampo, Ambeth. *Rizal without the Overcoat* (Pasig City, Manila: Anvil, 2000)

—— *The Search for Rizal's Third Novel, Makamisa* (Pasig City, Manila: Anvil, 1993)

Offord, Derek. *The Russian Revolutionary Movement in the 1880s* (Cambridge: Cambridge University Press, 1986)

Ojeda Reyes, Félix. *El desterrado de París. Biografía del Doctor Ramón Emeterio Betances (1827–1898)* (San Juan: Ediciones Puerto Rico, 2001)

—— "Ramón Emeterio Betances, Patriarca de la Antillanía." In Félix Ojeda Reyes and Paul Estrade, eds. *Pasión por la Libertad* (San Juan, P.R.: Editorial la Universidad de Puerto Rico, 2000)

Ortiz Jr., David. *Paper Liberals. Press and Politics in Restoration Spain* (Westport, CT: Westwood Press, 2000)

Palma, Rafael. *Biografía de Rizal* (Manila: Bureau of Printing, 1949)

Pardo de Tavera, Trinidad. "Las Nihilistas" (typescript, n.d.)

Pernicone, Nunzio. *Italian Anarchism, 1864–1892* (Princeton: Princeton University Press, 1993)

Poe, Edgar Allan. *Tales* (Oneonta: Universal Library, 1930)

Ponce, Mariano. *Cartas sobre la Revolución, 1897–1900* (Manila: Bureau of Printing, 1932)

—— *Cuestion Filipina: una exposition historico-critica de hechos relativos á la guerra de la independencia*. Trans. H[eikuro] Miyamoto and Y.S. Foudzita (Tokyo: Tokyo Senmon Gakko, 1901)

Quinn, Patrick F. *The French Face of Edgar Poe* (Carbondale: Southern Illinois University Press, 1954)

Raynal, Guillaume-Thomas and Denis Diderot. *Histoire philosophique et politique des établissements & du commerce des Européens sans les deux Indes* (Geneva: Libraries Associás, 1775)

Retana, W.E. *Vida y escritos del Dr José Rizal* (Madrid: Victoriano Suárez, 1907), with "Epílogo" by Miguel de Unamuno

Reyes, Isabelo de los. *El Folk-Lore Filipino* (Manila: Tipo-Lithografía de Chofré y C., 1899)

—— *El folk-lore filipino*. English translation by Salud C. Dizon and Maria Elinora P. Imson (Quezon City: University of the Philippines Press, 1994)

—— *La sensacional memoria de Isabelo de los Reyes sobre la Revolución Filipina de 1896–1897* (Madrid: Tip. Lit. de J. Corrales, 1899)

Reyes y Sevilla, José. *Biografía del Senador Isabelo de los Reyes y Florentino* (Manila: Nueva Era, 1947)

Rizal, José. *Cartas á sus Padres y Hermanos* (Manila: Comisión del Centenario de José Rizal, 1961)

—— *Cartas entre Rizal y el Profesor Fernando Blumentritt, 1888–1890* (Manila: Comisión del Centenario de José Rizal, 1961)

—— *Cartas entre Rizal y los miembros de la familia, 1886–1887* (Manila: Comisión del Centenario de José Rizal, 1961)

—— *Cartas entre Rizal y sus colegas de la propaganda* (Manila: José Rizal Centennial Commission, 1961), 2 vols

—— *Diarios y Memorias* (Manila: Comisión del Centenario de José Rizal, 1961)

—— "Dimanche des Rameaux" (unpublished ms., 1887)

—— *Dr. José Rizal's Mi Último Adiós in Foreign and Local Translations* (Manila: National Historical Institute, 1989), 2 vols

—— *El Filibusterismo* (Manila: Instituto Nacional de Historia, 1990)

—— *El Filibusterismo* [facsimile edition] (Manila: Instituto Nacional de Historia, 1991)

—— *Epistolario Rizalino*, ed. Teodoro Kalaw (Manila: Bureau of Printing, 1931–35), 4 vols

—— "Essai sur Pierre Corneille" (unpublished ms., n.d.)

—— *Noli me tangere* (Manila: Instituto Nacional de Historia, 1978)

—— *Noli me tangere*, with introduction by Leopoldo Zea (Caracas: Biblioteca Ayacucho, 1976)

—— *N'y touchez pas!* Jovita Ventura Castro's translation of *Noli me tangere*, with introduction (Paris: Gallimard, 1980)

—— *One Hundred Letters of José Rizal* (Manila: National Historical Society, 1959)

—— *The Rizal–Blumentritt Correspondence, 1886–1896* (Manila: National Historical Institute, 1992), 2 vols

Robb, Graham. *Rimbaud* (London: Picador, 2000)

Rocker, Rudolf. *En la borrasca (Años de destierro)* (Puebla, Mexico: Edit. Cajica, 1967)

Rodrigues, Edgar, *Os Anarquistas, Trabalhadores italianos no Brasil* (Sao Paolo: Global editora e distribuidora, 1984).

Romero Maura, J. "Terrorism in Barcelona and its Impact on Spanish Politics, 1904–1909," *Past and Present*, 41 (December 1968)

Ross, Kristin. *The Emergence of Social Space: Rimbaud and the Paris Commune* (Minneapolis: University of Minnesota Press, 1988)

Roxas, Félix. *The World of Félix Roxas*. Trans. Ángel Estrada and Vicente del Carmen (Manila: Filipiniana Book Guild, 1970)

Saniel, Josefa M. *Japan and the Philippines, 1868–1898*, third edition (Manila: De la Salle University Press, 1998)

Sarkisyanz, Manuel. *Rizal and Republican Spain* (Manila: National Historical Institute, 1995)

Schumacher, SJ, John N. *The Propaganda Movement, 1880–1895*, rev. ed., (Quezon City: Ateneo de Manila Press, 1997)

Scott, William Henry. *The Unión Obrera Democrática: First Filipino Trade Union* (Quezon City: New Day, 1992)

See, Teresita Ang. "The Ethnic Chinese in the Filipino-American War and After," *Kasaysayan*, 1:4 (December 2001), pp. 83–92

Sempau, Ramón. *Los victimarios* (Barcelona: Manent, 1901)

Serrano, Carlos. *Final del imperio. España, 1895–1898* (Madrid: Siglo Veintiuno de España, SA, 1984)

Sichrovsky, Harry. *Ferdinand Blumentritt: An Austrian Life for the Philippines* (Manila: National Historical Institute, 1987). Translated from the German

Sue, Eugène. *The Wandering Jew* (London: Routledge and Sons, 1889)

Sweetman, David. *Explosive Acts. Toulouse-Lautrec, Oscar Wilde, Félix Fénéon and the Art and Anarchy of the Fin-de-Siècle* (London: Simon and Schuster, 1999)

Tamburini, Francesco. "Betances, los mambises italianos, y Michele Angiolillo." In Félix Ojeda Reyes and Paul Estrade, eds, *Pasión por la Libertad* (San Juan, P.R.: Editorial de la Universidad de Puerto Rico, 2000)

—— "Michele Angiolillo e l'assassinio dí Cánovas del Castillo," *Spagna contemporanea* [Allesandria, Piedmont] IV:9 (1996), pp. 101–30

Tarrida del Mármol, Fernando. "Aux inquisiteurs d'Espagne," *La Revue Blanche*, 12: 88 (February 1, 1897), pp. 117–20

—— "Un mois dans les prisons d'Espagne," *La Revue Blanche*, 11:81 (October 15, 1896), pp. 337–41

Thomas, Hugh. *Cuba: The Pursuit of Freedom* (New Brunswick, N.J.: Harper and Row, 1971)

Tortonese, Paolo. "La Morale e la favola: Lettura dei *Misteri di Parigi* como prototipo del *romain-feuilleton*" (unpublished ms., n.d.)

Urales, Federico (Joan Montseny). *Mi Vida* (Barcelona: Publicaciones de La Revista Blanca, 1930), 3 vols

Vincent, Paul. "Multatuli en Rizal Nader Bekeken," *Over Multatuli*, 5 (1980), pp. 58–67

Wionsek, Karl-Heinz, ed. *Germany, the Philippines, and the Spanish–American War.* Translated by Thomas Clark (Manila: National Historical Institute, 2000)

Wolff, Leon. *Little Brown Brother* (New York: Doubleday, 1961)

Index